The Human Rights State

THE
HUMAN RIGHTS
STATE

Justice Within and Beyond Sovereign Nations

Benjamin Gregg

PENN

UNIVERSITY OF PENNSYLVANIA PRESS

PHILADELPHIA

Published by
University of Pennsylvania Press
Philadelphia, Pennsylvania 19104-4112
www.upenn.edu/pennpress

Printed in the United States of America on acid-free paper
1 3 5 7 9 10 8 6 4 2

Library of Congress Cataloging-in-Publication Data

Gregg, Benjamin, 1954– author.
The human rights state : justice within and beyond sovereign
nations / Benjamin Gregg.
pages cm — (Pennsylvania studies in human rights)
Includes bibliographical references and index.
ISBN 978-0-8122-4805-0 (alk. paper)
1. Human rights. I. Title. II. Series: Pennsylvania studies in
human rights.
JC571.G7826 2016
323.01—dc23

2015032187

For my teachers

Seyla Benhabib, at Yale

Axel Honneth, at Berlin

Michael Walzer, at Princeton

Contents

A Project for the Free Embrace of Human Rights

The playwright Bertolt Brecht spent fourteen years in exile. He was officially stateless for twelve. He fled Germany in February 1933, one month after the Nazis took power. After shorter stays in various cities, including Prague, Vienna, Zürich, and Paris, he spent a longer period in Denmark and then in Sweden. When the Germans occupied Denmark and attacked Norway in 1940, and neutral Sweden allowed Germany transit routes for its Norwegian campaign, Brecht fled in April to Finland by ship. He remained in Finland until May 1941, when he left by train for Leningrad, then Moscow, then Vladivostok and, only nine days before the Nazis invaded the Soviet Union, by Swedish boat to Los Angeles, which he reached in July. He returned to Europe in 1947.

While he and his companions struggled to get visas to the United States, Brecht started a play in rural Marlebäck, four hours outside Helsinki, in 1940, and worked on it intermittently until 1944, in Los Angeles. He sets his *Flüchtlingsgespräche*, or *Conversations in Exile*, in a bar at the Helsinki Railway Station where two German refugees, Ziffel, a physicist, and Kalle, a laborer, while away their time sparring in a loosely connected series of meandering exchanges. "These encompass memories of childhood and school years as well as of exile, some of which . . . are recognizable as Brecht's own" (Parker 2014:421). At one point Ziffel says to Kalle, "The passport is the noblest part of a person. It isn't generated in the plain and simple way people are. A person can be begotten anywhere in the world, in the most frivolous of ways—but not a passport. That's why a passport, so long as it's a good one, is recognized—whereas a person can be ever so good yet still be denied recognition."[1] Brecht captures in this passage the topsy-turvy world of rights: what matters is not the human being but rather his or her legal status. Thus the person is reduced to an epiphenomenon of a formal document issued by a nation state. And a passport assumes some of the qualities usually attributed instead to human beings: nobility; grounds for social and legal recognition; the bearer of "goodness" and "badness."

This book offers a critique of this topsy-turvy logic. It then develops an alternative logic. This "inclusionary logic" is a vision not of rights in general but of human rights in particular. It has several core features. Consider each in turn.

Social Construction as Method

This book takes forward a project I began in *Human Rights as Social Construction*.[2] There I argue for human rights as worldly social constructions. Human rights in this context may take any number of overlapping forms, from the "human rights idea" to the "human rights project," from "human rights thinking" to "human rights communities," as well as human rights themselves.

To say that human rights are socially constructed is to regard them wholly as products of human imagination. It is to regard them as this-worldly products of human hand, as distinguished from otherworldly givens, whether theological or metaphysical.

This is a rather optimistic view. It is the conviction that we humans can pull ourselves up morally by our own normative bootstraps. It is the belief that communities can assume the stance of active producers of their fate rather than regarding themselves as passive "consumers" of otherworldly givens.

To say that human communities invent moralities is to say that moralities are cultural claims. In this sense I regard human rights as political phenomena, as a matter of political agency, toward social justice. Ideas of justice, behaviors that create and reinforce justice, and institutions that provide justice—for example, by treating all members of society as legal and moral equals—do not start out as universals. They start out as particular expressions of agency. They begin as historically and culturally particular. And they are always embedded in socially constructed structures: cultural traditions, philosophical schools, social mores, legal systems. This book seeks to show how, in the *longue durée*, human rights as political phenomena can aspire to eventual universal purchase. The idea of a human rights state is a means of advancing a realistic cosmopolitanism.[3]

As social constructions, human rights are contingent norms. That is, their validity depends on humans regarding them as valid. To construe the validity of human rights as relative to the humans who construct them is to view human rights in their element of moral relativism. It is to view them in their medium of historical and cultural perspectivalism. It is to view them as essentially "political" in nature. A specifically *political* social construction is a contingent, this-worldly idea. Its moral potential cannot be harvested unless it is always open to contestation, reinterpretation, and adaptation. Its moral potential needs a community open to negotiation and compromise in the effort to achieve agreement among participants on matters of human rights. The forging and reforging of agreement on human rights can still lead to a nonidiosyncratic perspective. In a postmetaphysical landscape, a nonidiosyncratic perspective replaces what religion and metaphysics regard as perspectives true or valid universally or a priori or eternally.

A nonidiosyncratic perspective is true or valid because it is held consensually, not because it is inherently neutral or acultural or transcendent. And if the validity of human rights is contingent, fallibilistic, and locally embedded, *truth* and *justice* at any given time refer to a temporary report from the field of experience and inquiry, a "snapshot" for current orientation, always revisable. Understood in this relativist sense, truth and justice are neither impossible nor drained of their capacity to motivate behavior. Rather, both truth and justice are driven not by some epistemological imperative for objectivity but by a pragmatic imperative for desired results. As social constructions, human rights are not some absolute or timeless cornerstone for moral theory. They are a "rhetorical vehicle" that can convey various meanings under different circumstances and serve multiple purposes in different contexts. Among these meanings and purposes are elements of justice, such as rights to life, safety, and personal liberty; to belief, expression, and conscience; to privacy and property.

On this approach, human rights are one more example of what human culture can imagine. While their historical achievement would be an extraordinary event in human history, human rights are not themselves something special or extraordinary. They are not the work of extraordinary individuals or groups, and the most common people in the most ordinary of circumstances can imagine and create them. They do not require any special way of thinking. They work with readily understandable intuitions, such as the moral usefulness of putting oneself in the other's shoes. They work with well-known ideas such as "prudential reciprocity," which moti-vates behavior along the lines of mutual benefit. Such mundane characteris-tics mark potential for beginning to develop a human rights consciousness in almost any community in which people can be motivated to practice reciprocity and are capable of putting themselves in the other's shoes.[4]

Yet social construction is not just one more comprehensive view. It can coexist with a wide range of competing comprehensive doctrines. For example, it can cooperate with persons of faith who share the goal of advancing human rights. Regardless of its empirical, secular orientation within the social sciences, my proposal in no way seeks to dissuade the faithful from their faith. Even as I reject "theological and metaphysical foundations of human rights as counterproductive," I dismiss neither inso-far as either offers an "important way for some people in some communi-ties to access human rights language" (Wolfsteller 2014:496).

To dismiss any particular motivation to an embrace of human rights would defeat my pragmatic orientation. That orientation emphasizes the search for resources for advancing human rights. Resources might be found in some elements of local culture and experience. Further, human rights are best implemented from within the local community. And the local com-munity best implements them. They are best implemented in terms that resonate as much as possible with that community—even as human rights also challenge the community to reimagine beliefs and practices in ways more human rights friendly.

Non-social-constructionist presuppositions, such as religious faith, can work in tandem with the social constructionism they reject and that I advo-cate as more practicable and generalizable. They can work in tandem toward the same goal: to encourage a free embrace of human rights. Social construc-tion does not require addressees of the human rights project to adopt a social-constructionist standpoint. (By *human rights project* I mean the project of advancing human rights globally, through persuasion. As for *addressees*, I focus on the citizens of nation states, as I explain below.) Social construction can reach individuals and communities without having to abandon, whole-sale, their thick normative commitments. After all, most persons invested in supernatural revelation also accept claims of a very different sort—for exam-ple, those that lead to standard medical diagnosis and treatment.

One might argue that if transcendental norms can only be the product of imagination, then I am no less dogmatic than my adversaries, for exam-ple, the legal philosopher Michael Perry (2007). One might argue to the same conclusion if, as I assert, the moral self-ennoblement of human beings is precisely that of humankind giving itself norms of social and political behavior. Perry asserts that human rights are only coherent given a belief in God and in the "sacredness" of human beings.[5] I counter that social constructions are not necessarily exclusive whereas every religion is. Even as it is hardly acultural, or presuppositionless, or unembedded in history and culture, social construction is never as particular as any argument grounded in revelation. It can work with rival approaches to human rights.

A Wholly Naturalistic Conception of Human Beings

I approach the *human* in the phrase *human rights* in terms of a wholly naturalistic conception of humanity. That conception takes human nature as biologically understood. It eschews supernatural explanations, whether theological or metaphysical. To be sure, human nature biologically understood guarantees nothing in a political way or otherwise in a value-driven sense. It entails nothing normative. Human rights, for example, cannot be derived from natural facts. That the genome of any one human individual can represent the genome of the species entails no moral norms, and the similarity of one person's DNA to another's entails no moral or legal obligations of one to the other.

A naturalistic approach to the human of human rights proceeds along several dimensions. Consider two. Consider the fact that all humans share the same genome. No one should be surprised if someone were inspired to give this fact a cultural overlay, perhaps in ways suggestive for the social construction of norms. For example, most human rights abusers identify their victims in terms of their membership in particular groups (religion, race, or caste, among others). In this context, the human rights idea could be advanced if at least some abusers came to realize that such memberships are in fact constructions. By contrast, the species-wide genetic identity of all individuals is not. To be sure, this biological "is" generates no normative "ought." But it opens up a human rights–friendly vantage point that will resonate with some people.

Second, cultural agreements on human rights can draw on natural emotional dispositions as a resource. That is, "natural" altruism can be fostered and institutionalized by cultural means, in various forms of socialization. Elsewhere I draw on research in neurobiology to suggest that mutualism and altruism are biological dispositions. They can be harnessed by various kinds of socialization. In this way they encourage sympathy and understanding for the idea of human rights. One kind of socialization, supported by a kind of "sentimental education" found in European intellectual history, encourages solidarity. It could buttress rationally motivated practices of solidarity based on human rights.

To be sure, some emotional dispositions are incompatible with human rights thinking. And most dispositions are complex enough to go in more than one direction. For example, sympathy for one's own tribe hardly entails barbarism toward other tribes—but it could serve such a basis. Where dispositions are compatible or even supportive of human rights thinking, they provide a standpoint—an internal standpoint, not imposed from outside—from which to identify human rights abuses. They provide a standpoint for identifying these abuses as they occur in behavior allowed or even encouraged in other areas of the same religion, culture, or tradition.

Such dispositions will never do the work that human rights advocates might hope for. Nor will another possible resource for advancing human rights thinking that I mentioned earlier: prudential reciprocity. But the fact that a particular resource cannot guarantee success, or that it might be deployed contrary to human rights, is a fact about the limitations of resources. To abandon resources if they cannot guarantee success, or guarantee against misuse, would be self-defeating.

Human Rights Advanced Through Persuasion, Not Coercion

Because human rights, like all moral norms, are social constructions, they can only be valid for their addressees if those addressees freely, self-reflexively come to embrace them. A free embrace is truly free only if it occurs not only at a communal level but at the level of individual members as well. Embracing human rights in this way requires institutionalized socialization. If these norms become entrenched in a community's social institutions—such as the legal order and public education—they in turn reinforce the development of individual *human rights personalities*. They do so by socializing people into a solidarity based on mutual expectation: local participants grant themselves human rights and they mutually recognize each other's self-grants. Some cultural and psychological processes of cultural socialization offer resources here. For example, *socialization into assertive selfhood* is a cultural and historical process that endows addressees with the psychological wherewithal and self-confidence to claim human rights for themselves.

Socialization into assertive selfhood does not entail homogeneity. It does not lead to homogeneity as a homogeneous identity shared by all members of a political community. It generates no homogenizing, universally shared belief in some particular cultural construction of "human nature." It requires no world state unifying the plethora of competing cultures any world state would encompass. (I evaluate the idea of a world state, and alternatives to it, in the Coda.) On the contrary, members of a highly individuated society are integrated through "difference" rather than "identity." Georg Simmel showed as much more than a century ago. Social integration in complex modern societies involves individuals constantly weaving themselves into multiple "webs of affiliation" through interaction with members of a range of different social groups. Webs raise awareness for the interests and feelings of others *as* "others" and, despite all their differences, both group-based differences and differences among individuals. Simmel shows that webs of affiliation increase difference among persons rather than decreasing it. The individual increasingly differentiates him- or herself as the number of affiliations increases.

Someone socialized into assertive selfhood acquires the capacity to author his or her own human rights. To claim rights is the first step toward eventually gaining them, and assertive selfhood both reflects and motivates this moral autonomy. The human rights project facilitates the development of a personality structure of assertive selfhood. That project is one of collective political action. As such, it is one more resource for helping individuals develop *assertive selfhood* and a *human rights personality*. In part, the individual develops by recognizing others in their self-granting activity. And he or she develops by collectively challenging nation state-authorities to recognize and respect the self-granted human rights. This book is an extended argument for developing these kinds of activities, collectively, in a *human rights state*.

A human rights state would remedy the topsy-turvy world of rights that Brecht captures so well in *Flüchtlingsgespräche*. One element is the participant with his or her human rights personality able (in concert with others) to authorize and grant him- or herself human rights independently of a nation state's legal and political institutions. Such a personality is not necessarily "based on inner consistency, rational insight into the primacy of moral norms as well as a high level of self-reflexivity" (Wolfsteller 2014:496). A pragmatist approach can work with the cognitive and moral inconsistencies of real human beings. A localist approach is sensitive to the "historical specificity of political events and institutions" (ibid., 496). It is attuned to the power that inflects social institutions and relations.

Brecht makes the point that humans do not possess rights independently of nation states. He makes the point that nation states not individuals determine who is worthy of legal status, deserving of rights. He employs the Marxian trope of people reduced to behaving like things and things elevated to behaving like people:[6] the person is reduced to an epiphenomenon of a formal document issued by a nation state. The passport, not the passport bearer, has status and influence on the border between two states.

But the point is not that laws are bad as such but that good law is law that serves human beings by empowering them rather than abusing human beings by excluding them from legal status. The notion of the human rights state is a way to solve the problem that Brecht captures in the case of the exile, the refugee, and the stateless person. And the device of the human rights state solves the problem for citizens of nation states that do not recognize human rights as well. For the idea of a human rights state is the idea of transforming nation states that do not recognize human rights into ones that do. Transformation proceeds through the political advocacy of common people who together would form a particular human rights state. The ultimate goal of political advocacy is a type of juridification just the opposite of Brecht's topsy-turvy world.[7]

The ultimate goal is for these self-granted human rights to find recognition by nation states. They need state recognition to realize their aspiration to stable, consistent, and permanent validity that is effective in practical ways. The goal of juridifying human rights within a nation state (a topic I return to in the Coda) is the opposite of fetishizing law to the detriment of humans. Juridified, human rights will do the most to help people at the bottom of social hierarchies and oppressed minorities and socially marginalized groups to find or create protection from mistreatment. Activists who deploy human rights as a moral language to win for themselves the human rights they want is a primary step along this path. The ultimate step, to be reached in the distant future and only after much hard work and not inconsiderable good fortune, is to win, in part through the role played by the human rights state advocated in this book, human rights *within* a nation state.

Toward a Universal Embrace of Human Rights as a Contingent, Historical Achievement

To locate the validity of human rights in their addressees rather than in some global institution (if not in some otherworldly source) might seem to forfeit the aspiration of human rights to *universal* validity. But I argue that universal validity so construed does not forfeit that aspiration. I argue that it circumvents the metaphysical limbo of intractable debates over nature, source, contents, and entailments of human rights. That limbo generates puzzlements, not answers. It offers no techniques for application in the field of advancing human rights across national borders and across the globe. In fact, it works *against* the human rights project by leading to positions that *exclude* some groups of people from human rights.

Approaches across a wide spectrum of understandings of social justice all deploy exclusion as one means of identifying those who qualify for social justice or fuller forms of social justice. Consider five examples.[8] The sociological theorist Niklas Luhmann (1998:1023) asserts that two people who are cognitively unequal—because one can reason better than the other—are, as a consequence, morally unequal as well. He who reasons better is, by virtue of superior reasoning, better able to guide his life by the normative principles of human rights. For the most prominent theorist of political liberalism in the late twentieth century, John Rawls (1993:41, 70–73), "outlaw regimes" exclude themselves from the rule of "reasonable and just law" and are justly vulnerable to intervention by liberal peoples. Jean-François Lyotard (1993:135, 141–142), who defines postmodernism as a "fatigue with grand narratives," regards freedom of expression as the single most fundamental human right. Man excludes himself from this right until he frees himself from "his animal nature" by subjecting himself to the civilizing formation of culture. Amitai Etzioni (2010), a prominent advocate of communitarianism, identifies people within liberal democratic communities who exclude themselves from human rights, indeed from all normative insight, because they are mentally ill or incline to the ideological distortions of popular culture or fermented liquors or other chemical substances.

By contrast with these various approaches, my social-constructionist method follows a *logic of inclusion*. It renders human rights more accessible than anything offered by these alternatives. Social construction can do so because it allows local participants, by their own best lights, to develop human rights, and to do so locally. One chronic barrier to advancing human rights—abiding differences within and among communities, traditions, economies, political regimes, and ways of thinking—falls away for a method that begins locally and expands outward toward partial overlaps with other locally originating projects for human rights.

For what could be more inclusive than recognizing the human rights project as one in which, in principle, any person, anywhere, at any time, can participate? A project of potentially universal participation is a project of (socially constructed) universal content, a project of (socially constructed) universal validity—universal at least in potential. But this universal project is not universal because it is in some sense otherworldly. On the contrary, it advances human rights in ways entirely this-worldly. This-worldly are social constructions that can be undertaken by the participants themselves. Participants first need to be persuaded that they are capable of authoring their own human rights. Then they need to mutually recognize, within the group, their self-granted rights. At that point participants seek to expand those rights into the corresponding nation state. Self-authorship and expansion outward proceed through persuasion, not coercion. Persuasion takes many forms. This book emphasizes socialization, especially different types of education.

Participants Need Not Agree on All Aspects of Human Rights

Persuasion to freely embrace human rights does not require participants to overcome all their differences in belief and perspective. Complete agreement is empirically unlikely anyway, given the sheer complexity of the human rights idea. It is doubtful given the deep interpretability of so many of its terms and presuppositions. More important, persuasion need not place hurdles in the way of adherents of very different traditions who nonetheless might be persuaded to embrace one or the other idea of human rights.[9] I agree with the spirit captured in a well-known characterization of the various members of the committee that drafted the United Nations' Universal Declaration of Human Rights: "we agree about the rights but on condition no one asks us why" (Glendon 2001:77).[10] Agreement on some rights, in some applications, is enough to make progress; agreement on possible foundations is not necessary.

My project is not motivated by some prior commitment to human rights. It begins with the bare idea of human rights, at first quite indeterminate in meaning. Nor does it start with some agreed-on basis for human rights. It couldn't because the idea of human rights, as long as it is indeterminate in meaning, cannot involve bases. My project is guided by a pragmatic imperative for desired results. The pragmatist goal is not for everyone to agree on a foundation for human rights; the goal is for participants to be able to freely embrace and practice human rights on whatever basis, directed by whatever theory, given whatever presuppositions. This approach *generates* commitment rather than presupposing it.

Drawing on the spirit of a social scientific account of human rights, I do not believe that a commitment to human rights must be grounded in anything further than an intuition about justice, an interest in justice, a motivation to do justice. I do not believe that ultimate justification for people's normative convictions need lie outside and beyond human imagination and agency. Entirely unnecessary is divine intervention or metaphysical landscape, in either case waiting to be discovered by special minds. I seek a view compatible with social science, one that views human rights as something made not found. Social construction is such a standpoint. It investigates the ways that humans invent their normative grounds and have always invented their normative grounds. It assumes that any normative grounds whatsoever can only be invented by particular groups in particular cultures and contexts over time, usually modified and remodified and reinterpreted by successive groups as long as those norms have current purchase and have not become relegated to no more than an entry in history books. From a social scientific perspective, when it comes to practical guidelines for moral behavior—including human rights–oriented behavior—humans can rely on nothing but their own collective constructions.

All addressees of any human rights whatsoever can and should participate in the articulation, interpretation, and deployment of human rights. Doing so involves constructing, discussing, interpreting, and vernacularizing the human rights idea. It is the work of ordinary people, in democratic communities as well as in nondemocratic communities, influencing public culture. As I have already emphasized, participants are unlikely to agree on all points. They are more likely to generate a range of variation in their understandings, definitions, interpretations, and ideas about deployment. But consensus is not necessary for participants to form a group that is coherent in its self-understanding and adequately motivated. These very differences, generated by the participants themselves, are signal aspects of a self-determining political community that recognizes as legitimate both the process and the nonconsensual outcome. A process involving free expression and free association is, of course, much easier to realize in democratic communities. But sometimes it can also be possible in some nondemocratic communities. It does not require that all political communities be the same. It does not presuppose a world community. It does not undermine the current world system of nation states. But it certainly challenges all nation states from a human rights perspective.

Disharmony and disagreement can, in some cases, be useful and productive. The human rights project, like any nondogmatic normative project, must be fallibilistic, hence an open-ended quest, anticipating a more just world to come even as it can never completely or quickly realize that which it anticipates.[11] For reassurance and guidance as to what *rights* are and *justice* is (rather than to anything not socially constructed), this project can only refer to humans themselves, not to gods or transcendental principles.

To be sure, it always matters a great deal if participants disagree about how best to identify, define, and apply human rights and about how to reconcile competing rights. (Thus Chapter 8 argues against construing democracy as a human right but is open to working alongside other human rights advocates who insist that democracy must be a human right.) The human rights project makes progress wherever participants can forge overlaps among competing belief systems. It achieves progress with each enlargement, however limited, of overlapping beliefs and commitments to human rights. Andrew Koppelman (2014:380) well grasps this point:

> People with different metaphysical assumptions can and sometimes do converge on the same principles of human rights, but each of them gets there by reference to her own comprehensive view. This is what John Rawls had in mind when he argued for an "overlapping consensus" on the principles of political cooperation. In an overlapping consensus, [participants] may disagree about the ultimate foundations of the political principles that govern them, but they agree upon the principles, those principles are moral ones, and they are affirmed on moral grounds.[12]

The Human Rights State

Human Rights as Social Construction ends with a proposal for a "human rights state." It seeks to replace the nation state with a human rights state.

By contrast, *The Human Rights State* does not propose an alternative to the nation state but rather its modification, namely the diminution of its territorial sovereignty to an extent necessary to make human rights possible as a domestically anchored institution, indeed as an aspect internal to its national constitution. This shift has two motivations. First, replacing the nation state with an alternative is exceedingly unlikely empirically. Correspondingly, doing away with nationalism (as *Human Rights as Social Construction* proposes) would be more difficult that modifying nationalism into a human rights-nationalism (which *The Human Rights State* attempts). To be sure, only some nation states might be capable of this modification, and such a development would represent a great advance in the human rights project even if that development were hardly universal. Second, the nation state need not intrinsically preclude human rights if it can be modified in the extent of its sovereignty. So *The Human Rights State* views the nation state, and several of its core features, as *resources* for advancing the human rights project, if those features might be modified in various ways, many of which I detail throughout the book.

In this book, by *human rights state* I mean a metaphorical polity constituted by interested, self-selected members of a corresponding nation state. Members constitute themselves as a human rights state by authoring their own human rights and mutually recognizing that authorship among themselves. A human rights state seeks to advance a free embrace of human rights in the corresponding nation state. It seeks to advance human rights as an internal feature of the nation state, in short, to encourage local political and legal systems to generate *domestic* legal obligations to abide by human rights.[13] By way of introduction to this notion, I first distinguish a metaphorical human rights state from the state and the nation state. Then I sketch the tense relationship between a human rights state and the corresponding nation state. Finally, I characterize the human rights state in terms of practical strategies toward justice without borders.

A Metaphorical Human Rights State as Distinguished from the State and Nation State

By *metaphor* I mean a polity of the imagination, a polity without territorial component because it exists in the minds and behaviors of the participants. They practice their self-granted human rights among themselves as a model and example for the corresponding nation state. While one cannot be a member of a metaphor, one can be a member of a political initiative or social movement, one guided by principles. I do not advocate a metaphorical understanding of human rights; I advocate metaphor as a device for practical effect. I propose a metaphorical understanding to be realized in the world, in relation to a state.

Neither political institution nor legal system, a human rights state constitutes a critical moral standard. As a critical moral standard, the human rights state is more than an idea; it is political initiative. Its makeup is unusual: activists united in promoting human rights within the corresponding nation state, activists who mutually recognize each other's human rights, activists who practice human rights among themselves and in their relations with others. It is a social, indeed political, organization that displays patterned behavior and is guided by certain rules.

By *state*, as distinguished from a nation state in particular, I mean an apparatus primarily bureaucratic-administrative: the legally defined organization of divided powers and formal procedures for deciding everything from political representation to public policy to tax collection. By contrast, a *nation state* embraces the pre-political solidarity generators of blood and ethnicity, or language and religion, or beliefs about a shared fate, or some combination, perhaps with other generators as well. The correspondence between a territorialized state and a population geographically bounded defines membership in a nation state. That correspondence constitutes a "nation." Many members belong to a particular nation on the basis of their territorial nationality. *To belong* means not only to identify with that territory, individually and together with others, but also, in some cases, to derive specific rights and duties from it. Inclusion in a nation always entails the exclusion of nonmembers.

A *human rights state* aspires to global institutions that leave a great deal of administrative and other matters to sovereign states while internationalizing the recognition and defense of human rights even against offending sovereign states. A community of human rights states (which I sketch in the Coda) could one day culminate in the creation of global institutions that would leave a great deal of administrative and other matters to sovereign states but that would internationalize the recognition and defense of human rights.

The Tense Relationship Between a Human Rights State
and the Corresponding Nation State

Ideally there would be one human rights state corresponding to each nation state in the world (or corresponding to other forms of governance where the nation state is not the primary locus of power, such as tribes or corporations). But the possibility of even one human rights state does not require that every last state embrace human rights.

A state that already observes human rights is not itself a human rights state. Such a state does not need a human rights state precisely because it already observes rights. The human rights state is a means to encourage a nation state to adopt these rights.

I imagine many different human rights states. Each would have its particular membership. Each, its distinct range of understandings of human rights. Each, embedded in its local cultural contexts. Each, a critical moral standard by which to measure the corresponding nation state with respect to human rights recognition and adherence. Thus the members of any particular human rights state do not include all of humanity. But if all nation states embraced the human rights advocacy of the corresponding human rights states, all of humanity would be members of a human rights community.[14]

A human rights state stands in tense relation to a nation state. Tensions persist between a nation state and a human rights state as long as the nation state resists the human rights state's efforts to get the nation state to adopt cosmopolitan human rights as one of its regular, internal, domestic features.

A given human rights state is formed primarily of citizens of a corresponding nation state, and a given human rights state stands in the greatest tension with a corresponding nation state that rejects human rights altogether.[15] Citizenship in the corresponding nation state is no requirement for membership in the human rights state. But for practical reasons most members of the human rights state likely will be citizens of the corresponding nation state.

The Human Rights State in Terms of Practical Strategies
Toward Justice Without Borders

I support my proposal for human rights states with an array of practical strategies of solidary groups within a nation state seeking to diminish nation state sovereignty to the extent necessary for human rights to become valid across and despite national boundaries. I sketch these strategies in the chapter-by-chapter overview below.

To be sure, a human rights state cannot deliver anyone, or any nation state, directly from the myriad, often intractable problems of modern political community. It cannot create conflict-free political communities or untroubled trans-state relations. It cannot end the constant need for social, political, and legal struggles, or for negotiations and compromises at all levels of political community. But it can contribute to making human rights more widely available in a world of nation states. It can do so even as it implies no single modality of membership in political community, nor a uniform one. It contributes to an abiding aspiration of a realistic utopia of universal human rights.

That utopian vision begins with the hunch that human rights can be a mundane, everyday political movement of ordinary persons in many places (if not everywhere equally, and not at all times). To be sure, some political environments make human rights advocacy very dangerous; others suggest its utter futility. This book works this hunch into an insight by reimagining state sovereignty as compatible with sovereignty-defying human rights. It decouples the having of rights from the territory that today is generally the condition of having rights. It displaces to the individual the bordering functions of the nation state. The ultimate goal of what could eventually become an international movement of human rights states is *justice without borders*, an aspect of universal justice. This book adumbrates elements of one path to that goal. But *justice without borders* is not a world without borders. It is a world of borders modified to permit human rights within nation states.

Chapter-by-Chapter Overview

The three chapters that make up Part I develop key features of a human rights state. Chapter 1 urges an idea of human rights that members of a group would grant to themselves within or alongside a particular nation state. Chapter 2 frames human rights as *deterritorialized* in a way historically unprecedented: they would obtain in the person of a human being rather than, as now, because he or she happens to stand on a particular territory that happens to embrace human rights. Chapter 3 renders human rights, now reconceived, as a protective boundary displaced from the nation state to the human body.

Consider now each of these chapters in detail. Chapter 1 develops the notion of a human rights state along six dimensions: first, as a metaphor; second, as plural in number, with different human rights states overlapping with each other; third, each human rights state is capable of constructing human rights as "status functions" with "deontic power"; fourth, these functions and powers effectively deterritorialize human rights; fifth, each human rights state exists alongside a corresponding nation state and alongside international organizations; finally, different human rights states together form an international political community, not a world state but a kind of Kantian federation.[16]

Chapter 2 unfolds one of the ways in which the members of a human rights state constitute it. It displaces the locus of rights from national territory to individual participants. This chapter transfers the basis of human rights from national, territorial belonging to human action and political performance. Then it explains how individuals would be motivated to participate in a human rights state. Third, it explicates participation in part as the donning of a "human rights backpack." It ends by analyzing citizenship in a human rights state as the nonformalized power of its participants, a power not tied to the nation state.

Chapter 3 examines the failure of territorialized citizenship to protect against enslavement and the nonterritorial alternative. Then it considers the single most important route to diminishing slavery—namely, reducing poverty—and considers various difficulties involved in poverty reduction. To facilitate progress in the face of these difficulties, it develops a procedure parallel to the backpack of Chapter 2. It proposes construing the human body (and the bodies of slaves, in particular) as analogous to political territory and it proposes displacing boundaries from the nation state to the body of the human rights bearer. It proposes construing the body as its own bordering capacity. It deploys this model by criticizing nation state territory that cannot or does not prevent slavery. It criticizes nation state territory on the basis of a different kind of territory: the moral territory of the self. It then works out three respects in which the body as symbol challenges nonprotective citizenship. And it shows how this model can internationalize domestic opposition to slavery.

Three chapters compose Part II. They deploy the metaphor of a human rights state as a politics of persuasion, not coercion. They deploy this metaphor in three widely divergent venues: Chapter 4, in a university curriculum; Chapter 5, in post-authoritarian Eastern Europe; Chapter 6, in rapidly developing digital technology. In greater detail: Chapter 4 explores ways in which Western youth at university can develop and deploy thinking about human rights as a cognitive style. A cognitive style oriented on human rights rests on two presuppositions: that human rights are social constructions and hence that they are morally relativist and perspectival. The chapter shows how human rights, in terms of a cognitive style, might approach the practice of child labor in general and child-labor-encouraging aspects of poor agrarian communities in particular. Then it specifies normative bases of a human rights style, bases that emerge from its analysis.

Chapter 5 turns to informal, political education in the newly democratizing countries of Eastern Europe. Emphasizing the importance of path dependency for the possible success of a civic education driven by a human rights cognitive style, it analyzes the role of several institutions in developing potential for a human rights culture. First it develops an approach to human rights advocacy by building on the notion of cognitive style introduced in the previous chapter. Then it situates that notion in the context of civic education. Third, it considers forms of civic education toward encouraging active civic participation. Finally, it sketches three models that deploy this approach in diverse educational settings in liberalizing communities today.

Chapter 6 extends the concern with how the human rights project can be advanced by examining the human rights potential of uncoupling, in cyberspace, the individual's social and political identity from his or her social and political voice. First it identifies the Internet's general potential to advance human rights, as well as some of the problems that discourage that potential. In particular, the Internet can advance the cause of human rights by changing civil society by means of digital abstraction from human bodies and national borders. It can advance human rights also by facilitating critical public opinion. The chapter then limns the parameters of possible Internet contributions to the human rights state. The last section examines the intersection of culture and nature in digital technology.

Part III, made up of the last three chapters, addresses several of the challenges faced by the human rights state. Chapter 7 asks: How can someone swear allegiance to both a national identity and the cosmopolitan identity of human rights? Chapter 8 asks: If democratic communities are distinctly friendlier toward the human rights idea than are nondemocratic communities, is democracy itself a condition for the possibility of human rights—in a world much of which is decidedly nondemocratic? And Chapter 9: Can human rights ever be advanced through humanitarian military interventions, even in cases of grave human rights abuses?

Consider each in greater detail. Chapter 7 rejects arguments that regard human rights and patriotism as somehow naturally or internally compatible. It combines the conviction that human rights require a political, territorial space with the conviction that motivation in political community is unlikely absent emotional affect. It combines these convictions by making the human rights point of view integral to a citizen's point of view *as a citizen*. It does so first by developing human rights patriotism as a politics of metaphor that, second, leads to a transnational patriotism that, third, is a constitutionally supported attachment both national and cosmopolitan.

Chapter 8 shows how the rule of law advances human rights globally more effectively than democracy. It shows that, however ambitious it is in some nation states, it is less ambitious than the development of democracy. To determine what might best be constructed locally as a human right, it proposes the capacity of the candidate norm to be freely embraced by its addressees. It then argues that the rule of law is the better alternative to constructing democracy as a human right. Third, it examines the noncosmopolitan quality of democracy, as well as the rule of law and the possibility of self-determination even in the absence of democracy. Finally, toward advancing the human rights project, it proposes the legalism not of democracy but of the rule of law.

Chapter 9 asks: From a human rights standpoint, what conditions of brutality and oppression justify coercive intervention in a sovereign nation state? To answer this question, it addresses the goal of humanitarian intervention as well as the paradoxical status of state sovereignty. Then it argues that sovereignty is necessary for human rights and suggests a realistic understanding of state sovereignty in the context of humanitarian intervention. It then advocates a human rights minimalism, one neither value neutral nor nonpartisan: the minimalist goal of intervention is to stop the killing, nothing more. For intervention cannot do the work that only domestic politics can do, including the work of a human rights state. The chapter argues for unilateralism rather than multilateralism in most cases. It finds no universal a priori responsibility to protect.

A brief coda sketches one urgent area for future work: the problems and prospects of a community of nation states, each member having constitutionalized human rights domestically. An association of members sharing a domestic commitment to human rights revises contemporary notions of both national sovereignty and political territoriality. And, not least, it reworks the normative grammar of statehood in terms of domestic cosmopolitanism.

PART I

The Human Rights State: Politics by Metaphor

Human Rights as Metaphor

From the standpoint of social construction, rights are contingent, historically specific social constructions. Often rights are constructed in reaction to developments in the relevant social context. (Contexts are many and varied, from social movements to technological innovations, from demographic changes, to economic crises, to health disasters.) Rights, so understood, are achieved not given. Hannah Arendt (1968:301) makes just this point: "We are not born equal; we become equal as members of a group on the strength of our decision to guarantee ourselves mutually equal rights." Arendt describes a specifically political context: the formation of social groups—with features of membership and decision making, guided by principles of equality, and recognizing rights—is political in the sense of ideas, beliefs, and behavior related to governance of one form or another.

This book pursues politics in a sense more narrow. It pursues arguments for and efforts toward institutionalizing human rights in a nation state. Here the word *politics* refers to an effort ambitious and unlikely but not impossible. Jacques Rancière's (2010:68) description is useful here: "Political predicates are open predicates: they open up a dispute about what they entail, whom they concern and in which cases." I imagine politics as robust openness to possibilities never before realized, possibilities bordering on utopian—at least on first view. I imagine "opening up a dispute"— beginning with the readers of this book—about the idea of transforming the contemporary nation state in profound ways. I propose nothing less than persuading nation states to incorporate human rights as an internal feature.

By persuasion I mean a contest of ideas, with persuasion by the peculiarly forceless force of the better argument.[1] Politics is always the stuff of ideas, from norms to laws, from rights to duties, from group identities to personal convictions. By means of shared ideas, politics attempts to construct, organize, regulate, perpetuate, and interpret social life. Changes in social life involve changing ideas widely shared among members of that community.

One way to change widely shared ideas is to argue *metaphorically*. As a figure of speech, a metaphor conveys an idea through the power of suggestion. One refers to X by means of word or phrase that literally denotes Y. In this way one suggests similarities or analogies between X and Y.

Immanuel Kant practiced metaphorical thinking in this sense. He gives *Zum ewigen Frieden* (1795) the form of an international treaty. But in content, as well, it is a metaphor for an international peace treaty and a federation of like-minded republics. It must have astounded his contemporaries with its vision of a global balance among peoples. Prussia, which Kant left not once in his lifetime, in 1795 signed a peace treaty with the revolutionary French republic established in 1789. Not so the other German states. Not so England or Austria or Portugal or the Italian states. To this day, Kant's Enlightenment vision of human progress presupposes a world peace that remains counterfactual. My proposal for metaphorical thinking is Kantian in just this sense: a utopian idea that aspires to be a concrete carrier of hope because it is oriented on possible, if difficult and counterintuitive, political practice.[2]

I use metaphor to advocate something never before realized, something bordering on the utopian. Advocacy takes the form of imagining an existing nation state that does not embrace human rights. A human rights state is a metaphorical community directed at a corresponding nation state. A human rights state advocates human rights as a constituent element of that nation state.

The book is divided into three parts. The first articulates the idea of a human rights state along several dimensions. This first chapter imagines human rights as something that members of a political community might themselves author and grant to themselves. They would do so within or alongside a particular nation state, targeting it for transformation into a state that embraces human rights as part of its internal constitution. Chapter 2 shows how human rights, so imagined, would be "deterritorialized." That is, human rights would then be bound to the person of a human being. When it comes to human rights, being a person would trump membership in a particular territorial nation. Chapter 3 takes this vision one step further. It shows that human rights, so understood, would form a protective boundary displaced from the nation state to the human body.

The book focuses on membership in one type of political community in particular: the nation state. As citizenship, membership excludes noncitizens: a political community's inclusion of some persons via citizenship necessarily excludes others. Exclusion from membership entails exclusion from various kinds of rights. The idea of human rights is an aspiration to humankind's universal inclusion in a community of a particular kind of right. The United Nations' 1948 Universal Declaration of Human Rights expresses this aspiration. But in one passage it does so confusedly, in a way that undermines the human rights idea. It states: "Everyone has the right to a nationality." A nationality that is not sovereign offers no rights to its members; and only those of the world's nations attached to states confer legal rights with domestic purchase and have an international status as sovereign. Hence a *right to a nationality* makes sense only as a *right to citizenship* in some nation state or another.

No one has such a right. No one can have such a right given the current configuration of the nation state as a community of closed borders. The nation state is a community always particular, never universal. The nation state is logically prior to its citizen: any given person can be a citizen of a state but only if some particular state allows it. (Most states today allow membership via *jus soli*, *jus sanguinis*, or naturalization.) Allowances are prerogatives of a sovereign state. A nation state forced by outsiders to accept, as citizens, persons it otherwise rejects, is violated in its sovereignty. Sovereignty so conceived operates along a "logic of exclusion": each sovereign entity excludes every other.[3] A nation state inhabits a more or less homogeneous legal space and exercises potentially unlimited legal authority within it.

In such a world, how are human rights possible? Precisely by dint of sovereignty, a nation state excludes human rights as well. No citizen enjoys human rights if the host nation state declines to offer them. Even states that currently recognize one or the other human right likely align relevant human rights policies across "trade, development, and foreign affairs that sometimes work at 'cross purposes' with human rights obligations" (Seppala 2009:412).

Human rights under constrained circumstances are better than none. Better still would be human rights that cannot be trumped by trade, development, or foreign affairs. And better still would be human rights that cannot be trumped by the individual's membership in a sovereign nation state. In fact, most victims of human rights violations are citizens residing in their own country. In many cases, the state or government or some other authority is itself the violator.

So if any nation state ever recognizes human rights, then it does not do so because its status as a state depends on such recognition. Its status as a state *in no way* depends on such recognition. Rather, state recognition of human rights is an act of gratuitous generosity. Gratuity by definition is uncertain, unpredictable, without guarantee—all the more for those who need it most: the weak and the marginalized, the refugee and the stateless person, no less than citizens who are members of oppressed or despised groups. The idea of human rights, in its strongest form, challenges the idea of rights as a merely gratuitous grant. I propose human rights states as a means toward realizing that idea.

My proposal is practical. In 1789, revolutionary France's Déclaration des droits de l'homme et du citoyen captured the state's exclusionary logic. The declaration sought to make all members of the *état civil* legally equal to each other.[4] Many inhabitants were not members of the *état civil* and had no means of becoming members—unless the state made them members. The documents of 1789 and 1948, in advancing human rights, fail to realize these rights' logic of inclusion: inclusion regardless of a person's citizenship status, despite a person's territorial location, and notwithstanding a world organized into state sovereignties. My proposal develops this logic of inclusion through the idea of some citizens of a particular nation state "practicing" a corresponding human rights state. Practice does not become possible by repudiating the claims of the revolutionary French state's declaration. It does not become possible by dismissing the claims of the United Nations' declaration sixteen decades later. It becomes possible by realizing those claims, and doing so by overcoming aspects of a nation state's exclusionary logic in the form of citizenship. A realistic utopia, a practical cosmopolitanism, requires reconceptualizing human rights in ways that facilitate their advance by heightening their practicability.

I develop the notion of a human rights state along several dimensions: (1) as a metaphor; (2) as plural in number, with different human rights states overlapping with each other, (3) each capable of constructing human rights as "status functions" with "deontic power" toward (4) deterritorializing human rights. (5) I show how each human rights state exists alongside a corresponding nation state, and alongside international organizations, and (6) how different human rights states form a community.

The Human Rights State as Metaphor

The goal of the metaphorical human rights state is freedom from the fundamental dilemma confronting the project of advancing the free embrace of human rights around the world: state sovereignty. A human rights state frees itself *as a metaphor*: it is not an actual state but a device or mechanism of advocacy. It advocates a future nation state that embraces human rights as a necessary feature internal to itself, not as something external and expendable.

As a means of advocacy, a human rights state is an act of political imagination. It is imagination with the concrete utopian goal of encouraging a nation state to make human rights an element internal to its domestic constitution. So a human rights state is advocacy by metaphor. Here we have the imaginative, utopian element in metaphorical thinking. A human rights state reimagines the actual nation state counterfactually with the human rights commitment it advocates. It does so as a way to advocate within or alongside the corresponding nation state.

The metaphor does not mimic or mirror a nation state as such but rather models what a nation state would include in its political self-understanding if it were to adopt human rights as part of its self-understanding. It is a placeholder for the corresponding nation state as if that nation state embraced human rights, or embraced them more strongly. The metaphor stands in for conditions in which the civil rights of the sovereign state coexist with human rights not limited by state sovereignty.

This particular metaphor is involved in the business of representation. First of all, it represents a counterfactual. This is a counterfactual to which activists in a human rights state aspire. It represents a counterfactual no less to other citizens of the corresponding nation state, persons who may or may not agree with the activists. Further, it represents a social network of human rights bearers within a nation state. These are persons who have granted themselves human rights and who collectively recognize that grant among themselves. By doing so, they seek to provoke discussion in the corresponding nation state. The goal of that discussion is persuasion. A human rights state would persuade more and more people not only of the human rights idea as such; it would persuade people of this idea as something possible in a nation state, as an integral element of the state.

A human rights state represents its members in another sense as well: human rights bearers as the self-reflective, self-legitimizing authors of their own human rights. For there is no human rights constituency prior to the process by which individuals, in concert with other individuals, collectively authorize and mutually recognize their own human rights. By mutually recognizing among themselves the self-authored human rights not available in the corresponding nation state, "constituted by others as a being worthy of equal moral respect" (Benhabib 2013b: 43), the participants practice among themselves what they advocate for all other citizens in a nation state. They advocate the coexistence of the nation state and human rights. They promote the conjunction of civil rights and human rights.

As representation, a human rights state does not practice identity as the *politics of presence*. It creates and unifies a community of human rights advocates who challenge forces hostile to human rights. These forces include any given nation state in a particular respect. Hostile to human rights is territorial sovereignty configured in ways that preclude human rights as a constitutive *internal feature* of the nation state rather than a cancerous foreign body.

A human rights state practices a politics of *deferred presence*:[5] it is the deferred presence of a future form of a current nation state. In this future form, it embraces human rights. A politics of deferred presence is advocacy; like all advocacy, it may well fail, at least in some cases, at least some of the time. If it fails in all cases, all of the time, its value may still be hortatory but certainly not practical.

Human Rights States: Plural in Number and Distinct in Kind

I propose one human rights state each for each nation state in the world.[6] Each human rights state can be distinguished from every other one—even as each shares a great deal with every other. All human rights states advocate the embrace of human rights in the corresponding nation state. In this one respect, different human rights states are identical. They pursue the same general goal—even as each is dedicated to a particular nation state, and even as the unique conditions of each nation state preclude a "one-size-fits-all" human rights state.[7]

Differences among nation states generate some differences among corresponding human rights states. For example, the human rights plausible in a liberal democratic community differ from those possible, it at all, in an authoritarian state. The individual freedoms of the former allow for many human rights of the individual discouraged or blocked in the authoritarian state. More generally, communities differentiated along all the expectable dimensions of division—history, economy, culture, geography, language, faith, and so forth—will hardly generate exactly the same conceptions and lists of human rights. But diversity among conceptions and lists of human rights does not undermine the project of advancing human rights.[8] That differing lists from various human rights states would overlap only partially, and partially disagree with each other, hardly undermines a cosmopolitan project. Cosmopolitanism is advanced wherever there is agreement, however limited. Consensus would advance a universalistic project maximally but is not necessary for the project's very possibility. And consensus is unlikely in any case.

Put differently: a world state is singular; human rights states are always plural. The plurality of human rights states follows from design: one human rights state for each nation state (and each would be somewhat peculiar, corresponding to the peculiarity of each nation state). But pluralism also in the sense of difference and contingency allows a certain degree of inclusiveness, in distinction from the exclusivity of the traditional sovereign state with its narrow definitions of citizenship and its patrolled and monitored borders. Moreover, a human rights state's logic of inclusion means that different human rights states *include each other* as human rights–embracing groups. They include each other because they are fundamentally the same: each includes all others in its vision of human rights as transnational in their validity. They do so without collectively constituting one or the other form of a world state.

Human Rights as Status Functions with Deontic Power

A human rights state takes the individual's species membership as the criterion of potential membership in a human rights state. By *species membership* I do not mean the simple fact of being human, biologically understood, for biology carries no status function; no fact of the natural universe does. I understand the circumstance of being human politically. These are environments of social and political institutions. These are socially constructed conditions.

One social construction is core to any conception of behavior-guiding norms on this approach: "status functions" with "deontic powers." I draw on John Searle's work to conceive of human rights as deontic powers deriving from assigned status. A *status function* is a work of collective intentionality: members of a community generate, recognize, and perpetuate it collectively. According to Searle, humans can "impose functions on objects and people where the objects and the people cannot perform the functions solely in virtue of their physical structure." The "performance of the function requires that there be a collectively recognized status that the person or object has, and it is only in virtue of that status that the person or object can perform the function in question" (Searle 2010:7).[9] Status, associations, and rules are social constructions. They can generate "institutional facts" in the sense of someone's possessing rights or legal membership.

No tension develops between advocating the metaphorical, imaginative possibilities of a human rights state, on the one hand, and recognizing institutional facts that exercise deontic powers, on the other. It is not that a human rights state imagines possibility whereas institutional facts can only legitimize accepted reality. Rather, institutional facts, including deontic powers, are the products of imagination, as is a human rights state. Its metaphorical, imaginative possibilities are precisely the imaginative possibilities of creating human rights as deontic powers within the nation state, transforming its exclusionary logic into an inclusionary logic.

Institutional facts obtain only within the institution: someone who has rights has them because they are attached, institutionally, to one's position or status within that institution. For example, a person has attained one kind of status function who, through a legitimate process of selection, gains the legal authority to legislate for a legal community, having been assigned the status function of a legislator. Communities grant status functions to codified practices as well—for example, in the form of legally recognized private property or domicile rights. Further, communities grant status functions to legitimizing rituals, such as swearing a legally binding oath to uphold a public office or to tell the truth in courts of law. Performed within recognized spaces under specified circumstances, these special actions are invested with a legally binding power they do not otherwise possess. Finally, status functions take the form of any number of ordinary, everyday institutions, such as legal tender; in the position of prime minister or police officer; in marriage; and in other institutions that unite individuals into a recognized group, from university faculties to fire departments to diplomatic corps to taxing authorities.

A status function is possible only if embedded within a system of social recognition. When someone recognizes a status function, he or she grants it deontic power; the individual recognizes that he or she is obligated by that function. One is obligated to recognize the Supreme Court's interpretation of the constitution even if one disagrees with it, for example. One does not recognize the members of the majority as private individuals but rather in their institutionalized function as justices. My interpretation of the constitution has no deontic force because I lack the necessary status function.

Status functions carry deontic powers in that "they carry rights, duties, obligations, requirements, permissions, authorizations, entitlements, and so on" (Searle 2010:8–9). They are "positive" as rights and "negative" as obligations. They are essential to social life; once recognized, deontic powers "provide us with reasons for acting that are independent of our inclinations and desires" (ibid., 9). Every person born into a particular community is born into any number of already existing social institutions with status functions that carry deontic powers.

Status functions with deontic powers are vital to social stability. Stability would be impossible if, for example, members of a liberal constitutional democracy did not regard themselves as bound even by those judicial decisions they regard as wrongly decided. These decisions are binding not because of anything inherent in the decisions themselves but because of the deontic power of the court's formal legal status, as defined by the constitution, and by its status as elaborated over time by historical practice (such as the never constitutionalized custom of judicial review in the United States). In other words, decisions are binding as a matter of communal self-understanding. Status functions and deontic powers are phenomena shared by members of a political community. They are not objective but intersubjective.

Human Rights Deterritorialized

The capacity of a human rights state to exceed territory is its capacity to exceed a nation state's exclusionary logic. The idea of exceeding a nation state is not new; a variety of social systems already challenge the state's logic of exclusion. Prominent examples come from the sphere of technology. Here we find community formation (as well as social movements) through digital technology such as the Internet. We engage in location-independent communication. We observe transportation technologies that facilitate the flow of information, goods, services, and people across borders. The cultural sphere also provides examples. Here I would point to transnational communication flows, lifestyles, as well as consumption patterns. I would point as well to certain global risks—environmental crises and sometimes solutions—as well as types of crime that flow from abroad. The political sphere offers further examples, such as the general trend, with ever-greater migration, toward legal provisions for legal residence and naturalization.

Other striking examples come from the economic sphere. Here we see the mobility of capital, commodities, services, and technologies. We observe multinational corporations not tied to territorial sovereignty. We note international free trade agreements. We witness labor migration and market penetration. The economic sphere also provides compelling examples of how some postnational trends diminish some of the lives they influence. The integration of poorer countries into the global market, and their regulation by supranational entities, involve structural adjustments to the national economy. These adjustments often include reducing state expenditures, social services, and welfare for the poor. Postnational, multilateral institutions such as the International Monetary Fund (IMF), the World Bank, and the World Trade Organization (WTO) often curtail the national sovereignty of weaker members in economic domains.

For its part, a human rights state, which diminishes a country's national sovereignty to the extent entailed by domestic recognition of human rights, does not require a nation state to transfer responsibilities for managing economic and social relations to parastatal, nongovernmental, private or commercial actors, or to exercise public functions in partnership with them. Instead, a human rights state transforms domestic law. It transforms sovereignty-reinforcing domestic law as currently configured. As currently configured, it neither offers nor protects human rights. In some cases it provides civil rights, but those are tied to territorially bounded citizenship (and in some cases to membership in preferred groups, such as ethnic, religious, or socioeconomic groups).

Again, the capacity of a human rights state to exceed territory is its capacity to exceed a nation state's exclusionary logic. The idea of exceeding a nation state is already familiar in some forms. I propose a new form: the human rights state. A human rights state deterritorializes human rights. That is, it deterritorializes the practice of recognizing human rights.

Members, as human rights advocates, mutually recognize themselves as possessing human rights despite the corresponding nation state's rejection of human rights.

Self-recognition contributes to a platform for advocacy that reinforces itself with group solidarity. Advocacy takes the form of a counterfactual claim: *despite what a nation state claims, we claim human rights for ourselves*, today within the human rights state, eventually within the nation state.

Note that the deterritorialization of human rights through a human rights state does not lead to some kind of postnational citizenship. The physical nation state and the metaphorical human rights state coexist side by side, as the individual is a member of both. Two analogies illuminate this feature of coexistence.[10]

Médecins Sans Frontières (MSF) offers one parallel. It is a transnational nongovernmental organization (NGO) that deterritorializes a nation state in ways that could allow it to recognize and protect human rights (but not to adjudicate disputes—I address adjudication as a feature of my second example, below).[11] Transnational organizations such as MSF intervene across nation state borders. They establish pockets within a nation state in which the NGO recognizes, for its own purposes, at least some individuals as bearing human rights. These humanitarian zones have the capacity to form a kind of human rights state. Even as they are temporary, fragile, insecure, and without central authority, they constitute a venue for human rights practice even if only on a narrow basis, and even if only for a limited time.

As a nongovernmental medical and humanitarian organization, MSF recognizes its addressees as human rights bearers—unlike the host nation state. It transcends national boundaries not only by sending physicians across them. It surpasses state borders by asserting a universal right of assistance. It exceeds international frontiers by establishing, if only temporarily, loosely protected humanitarian sanctuaries.

Such measures challenge the host state's territorial authority with respect to human rights whenever recognition trumps a nation state's rejection of human rights. These measures challenge the host state's territorial authority by providing a humanitarian service themselves.

MSF defines the addressees of its work in a human rights–friendly way: any person without regard to political allegiance, religious faith, racial or ethnic characteristics, cultural membership, socioeconomic status, sex, and so forth. It defines itself over against the host state as "neutral," "independent," and "impartial." It resists the particular identifiers that otherwise classify individuals as members of this or that particular community with these specific domestic rights.

In the absence of any effective global law enforcement of human rights, the MSF example provides answers to several questions: Who or what bears obligations to recognize the self-granted rights of participants in a human rights state? Who or what enforces human rights and adjudicates relevant disputes?

Like MSF, a human rights state operates *within* a nation state yet *independently* of it. More precisely, it challenges a nation state without allowing itself to be reduced to a nation state. And like MSF, a human rights state sometimes finds support outside a nation state. It finds support when "identities previously unseen by international law" became "recognized through their attachment to non-state players. For instance, membership of a non-governmental organization or a religious body could be recognized in international law as granting standing" (Rubenstein and Adler 2000:547).

But a human rights state is different from those NGOs that facilitate the neoliberal withdrawal of a nation state from cosmopolitan normative commitments and responsibilities. A human rights state pursues a nation state's eventual embrace of human rights. The human rights project aims to change state behavior and the behavior of groups within the political community; it counters efforts and trends that leave the state out of that project.

This analogy between a human rights state and MSF highlights a potential weakness of any particular human rights state. NGOs may lack "policy making experience" (ICISS [International Commission on Intervention and State Sovereignty] 2001:73). They may be "unhelpfully divided over which precise policy course is optimal" (ibid.) They may be "reluctant publicly (as distinct from privately) to endorse coercive measures which may be necessary, but which are not easy for governments or intergovernmental institutions to deliver without overt support" (ibid.). A human rights state could be equally plagued by any of these problems. The composition of its members derives from the commitment of participants to human rights and not, say, from technical expertise or political savvy. This is a problem for any social movement by definition: not professional organizations but grassroots activism by ordinary people.

I find a second analogy in the legal sphere. It helps us imagine a human rights state as it might be developed alongside a nation state through the interpretative incorporation of human rights treaties into domestic law.[12] Interpretation of this sort is possible if domestic courts view their roles as "dualist." On the one hand, participating courts are deeply rooted in the domestic legal regime, with their legitimacy deriving from domestic constitutional texts and with final allegiance owed to domestic legal sources (rather than to international human rights treaties). On the other hand, courts could explore, on a case-by-case basis, the extent to which they might legitimately reach out to specific international sources for assistance. Through nuanced interpretive incorporation techniques, in their work domestic courts might utilize human rights treaties (and perhaps human rights scholarship and jurisprudence) and draw on the experience of domestic courts in other countries that also pursue incorporation techniques in this sense.[13]

By *jurisprudential techniques* I mean an evaluative framework that mediates between the domestic legal system and international legal regimes.[14] The court would ask itself: What is the domestic value of any given human rights document? That is, to what extent is the treaty an authoritative expression of the views of the domestic polity? The higher the domestic value—the greater the entrenchment of the treaty in a country's political and legal culture—the more leeway courts might give themselves to further incorporate relevant provisions into domestic law. To be sure, treaties may enjoy high value in one domestic legal system and low value in another. While such differences among various systems generate problems, such a situation would still be preferable to the status quo.

A court might also determine a human rights treaty's domestic value by examining legislative and executive intent of a nation state regarding that treaty: Has it been ratified? Did the executive branch attach reservations, understandings, or declarations modifying the treaty commitments with respect to particular treaty provisions? Beyond the lack of implementing legislation, have policy makers taken additional measures that indicate support for the treaty? Assessment of "domestic value" need not be limited to the views of the federal government. Assessment might consider expressions of strong commitment to the treaty by state governments or municipalities, if not popular expressions of commitment.

National and International Organizations Alongside the State

A human rights state operates alongside a corresponding nation state, various international organizations, and aspects of some international human rights law.

Human Rights State Operating Alongside
the Corresponding Nation State

A human rights state does not spell the demise of the corresponding nation state. It weakens a nation state's territorial sovereignty along one dimension. It weakens nation state sovereignty with respect to its capacity to deny or violate human rights. In some cases, other aspects of a particular nation state are very much human rights friendly. Such aspects would only be enhanced, never diminished, by a corresponding human rights state. These aspects include the provision of civil rights, the citizen's entitlement to diplomatic protection, and the sovereign right of a nation state to decline to extradite its own nationals to foreign authorities.[15]

Coexistence alongside a human rights state provides a platform for motivated persons[16] to advocate human rights as an internal feature of the corresponding nation state. Participants mutually recognizing each other's self-granted human rights constitute a human rights state. A human rights state seeks to make that recognition and self-granting acceptable within the terms of a modified nation state sovereignty.[17] Sovereignty would be weakened to the extent necessary to make domestic human rights possible.

A human rights state is not necessarily, immediately, or always a useful, let alone powerful platform for advocating against a human rights–hostile nation state. In some cases it can be no more than a puny, powerless opponent against immense odds. But a human rights state need not be everywhere significant to be significant in some cases. And the project to advance human rights is not defeated if it proceeds effectively in some cases but not in others.

With the advent of a human rights state, the corresponding nation state retains most of its current functions. For example,

> markets, NGOs, media companies, commercial organizations and interests, and all the other institutions that propel globalization need a secure environment to prosper. They look to the state to protect them from criminal or terrorist attack; to ensure law and order and the stabilization and enforcement of property rights; to develop communications infrastructure; to prepare the labor supply through education and training; and, more generally, to provide economic support through congenial tax regimes, subsidies, or other forms of state intervention. (Axtmann 2004:271)

Nation states continue to provide the most plausible, basic unit for international political structures and organizations that allow for the participation of nonstates as well, such as multinational corporations and NGOs.

Further, with the advent of a corresponding human rights state, a nation state retains its role in securing social integration, communal solidarity, and welfare in the face of so many threatening forces, including socioeconomic inequalities, ethnic or religious conflicts, regionalism, as well as the locally disruptive and dislocating consequences of globalization.[18] In this context, some states sometimes act as critics of international organizations. And some states occasionally reinforce the work of international organizations through domestic law and local powers.[19]

Finally, in the presence of a human rights state, nation states continue to mediate between structures larger than the state (such as the global economy) and structures below the level of the state (such as local economic systems). Just as substate organizations are regulated, so too organizations beyond the state are regulated (as they are today, above all in the economic sphere, by the International Monetary Fund, the World Trade Organization, the World Bank, and meetings of the G7).

Human Rights State Operating Alongside Various International Organizations

A human rights state does not advocate the coercive imposition of human rights from outside. Its goal is persuasion within a nation state, addressed to the nation state.[20] The goal of persuasion is the addressee's free embrace of human rights. If it succeeds, success would hardly rob the United Nations or other human rights bodies of their raison d'être. While these bodies cannot guarantee human rights, they can contribute in various ways toward promoting and facilitating cooperation in international law, security, economic development, and conflict resolution. Such cooperation would be an achievement in itself. But it would also improve various environments for the human rights project.

Human Rights State Operating Alongside Aspects of Some International Human Rights Law

International human rights law includes forms of protection of stateless persons as well as the legal practice of national, and especially international, courts (notably the European Court of Human Rights). The problem is not that protections do not exist. The problem is that they are usually weak and scarcely accessible and that they are undermined by nation states. Consider, for example, the United Nations and the United Nations Charter. They establish a system of international human rights law. But they do not do so by analogy to domestic laws with a system of bureaucracies, police, and judiciaries that guarantee and enforce laws and punish infractions. The United Nations creates a growing series of linked conventions, treaties, organizations, and political bodies.

To be sure, international human rights law is not law in any straightforward sense. Any work it actually does is often distinct from the claims it makes. Consider the preamble to the United Nations Charter. It states that members "reaffirm faith in fundamental human rights, in the dignity and worth of the human person, in the equal rights of men and women." But such "faith" is hardly binding, such that many members systematically discriminate against women.[21] Or consider Article 56 of the United Nations Charter. It declares that "All Members pledge themselves to take joint and separate action in co-operation with the Organization for the achievement of the purposes set forth in Article 55," which in turn states that the United Nations shall promote "universal respect for, and observance of, human rights." Yet many members do not observe human rights and hardly promote them locally, let alone universally.[22] One might think that all members of the United Nations are legally obligated to observe these provisions. Yet more than a few UN members violate human rights constantly and severely, such that a state's status as a signatory to these conventions predicts nothing about its actual behavior.[23] And the UN Charter's references to human rights are general and vague. It specifies no specific legal rights and mandates no enforcement procedures.

By contrast, the participants themselves, not third parties, construct a human rights state. It is constructed locally and not by distant elites. It is performed by ordinary people, not by local elites. Participants in a human rights state are motivated to observe human rights, for they are themselves the authors of those rights. By contrast, formal instruments of the United Nations are appeals directed at passive recipients.

A Community of Human Rights States

A human rights state instantiates the self-granted human rights of its members. Its first goal is to meld with a nation state such that a nation state adopts this already-existing human rights regime. Neither step would end the Westphalian system of nation states except with respect to the ways it currently blocks or precludes human rights. Participants authorize human rights as legitimate, formalized power that does not rely on outside institutions such as the United Nations General Assembly or Security Council. The identification of human rights with a nation state gives human rights the power of a nation state that supports them. States that escape the power of human rights remain nonparticipating states. And many nation states can be expected to resist the corresponding human rights state.

The second and ultimate goal of a human rights state is for nation states, each having adopted its own human rights regime, to undertake a form not of communal global governance, nor some kind of benevolent hegemony,[24] but global coverage.[25] By *global coverage* I mean a normative vision for nonhegemonic global politics in an age in which nation states have a reduced steering capacity. In a world "constituted almost exclusively by territorial political communities enjoying sovereign rights" or "controlled by either single or multiple hegemonic centers of territorial power of global and regional scope or by market-based global business and banking elites," global coverage by human rights–embracing nation states would seek to diminish the high levels of violence, militarism, corruption, injustice, and exploitation so characteristic of international affairs (Falk 2009:15).

Global coverage exceeds transnational relations centered on one sphere of authority—nation states—to reflect a multipolar world order with a wide range of authoring. Authors might include "nongovernmental organizations, transnational corporations," and "supranational actors, such as the European Commission" (Dingwerth and Pattbert 2006:191). They could embrace "judicial actors, such as the Dispute Settlement Body of the World Trade Organization (WTO) or the International Criminal Court (ICC); intergovernmental organizations, such as the World Bank" (ibid.). They could include "hybrid and private organizations, such as the World Conservation Union or Forest Stewardship Council (FSC)" (ibid.).

Nation states that come to embrace human rights as elements internal to their organization then aspire, through global coverage, to the concrete utopia of dramatically reduced levels of poverty and other material inequalities in the present world order. They seek a realignment of massive power imbalances among states, regions, and economies. They promote the rule of law at a global level.[26] They recommend a canon of shared norms that support the rule of law and institutions for dealing with various problems. And they seek integrative networking between state, substate, and suprastate levels of governance.

It bears noting that the cosmopolitanism of global coverage is distinct from that of the United Nations, including its human rights treaties, its Commission on Human Rights, or its Security Council. Here cosmopolitanism is dissimilar to human rights systems within the European Union or as instantiated by nongovernmental organizations. It diverges from international criminal tribunals. It is different from the "formal institutions and organizations through which the management of international affairs is or is not sustained. The United Nations system and national governments are surely central to the conduct of global governance, but they are only part of the full picture" (Rosenau 1995:13).

A human rights state and a *system* of human rights states take pluralist theory to the level of international affairs in response to issues that exceed the steering capacity of individual nation states. Pluralist theory corresponds to a broad diversity of forms of social organization and political decision making, some of them quite independent of the state.

For the foreseeable future a nation state will remain the basic unit of international relations, where *international relations* are understood as "politics among nations" (Morgenthau 1948). But the nation state will not constitute the basic unit of international relations in a future age of global coverage. With its focus on nonstate actors, and its multiactor perspective on world politics, a community of human rights state incrementally contributes to the emergence of this future.[27]

A community of human rights states need not be defeated by the copresence of non–human rights states, even as differences between the two types of community sometimes will spawn conflict. Conflict is likely because global justice in the context of a community of human rights states includes the project of encouraging nation states to recognize and respect the human rights of its national citizens and other residents and of persons neither its citizens nor its residents. A community of human rights states may sometimes succeed in discouraging national sovereignty from preventing the extension of human rights across national borders. Likely it will often fail.

A community of human rights states confronts a wide variety of steering mechanisms and spheres of influence: "global social movements; civil society; the activities of international organizations; the changing regulative capacity of states; private organizations; public-private networks; transnational rule making; and forms of private authority" (Dingwerth and Pattbert 2006:189). It confronts a world of international organizations that are more than fora for cooperation among states: organizations with legal personality under international law and their own governing power.

A community of human rights states can work with any number of current organizations. It can work with the Inter-American Human Rights System and the African Charter on Human and Peoples' Rights, with the UN Human Rights Commission and the UN High Commissioner for Human Rights, with UN Criminal Tribunals for Rwanda (1994) and Yugoslavia (1993), with NGOs such as Amnesty International, Human Rights Watch, the International Commission of Jurists, Médecins Sans Frontières, Oxfam, and CARE. But it cannot work, or cannot work well, with the UN Security Council, which all too often struggles with the national interests of individual members. Indeed, a human rights state entails reform of the UN system toward eliminating the special privileges of the five victors of the Second World War.

In Chapter 8 I show that a community of human rights states fosters the rule of law. A community could contribute to the creation of an independent judiciary that treated nation states equally, especially those that have embraced human rights through a human rights state. A network of human rights states might build, for example, on the International Criminal Court, "which proposes a capacity to hold leaders of sovereign states accountable for certain enumerated crimes" (Falk 2009:23). An increasingly global rule of law, responsive to a community of human rights states, or to a community of human rights–respecting nation states, offers a means to an increasingly global form of justice. Only global justice can address the gaping disparity and gross inequality among nation states in different regions of the world. It can do so in part by restraining the excesses of the global market economy.

A community of human rights states is a community in which each member displaces the locus of rights from national territory to individual participants. Human rights, so imagined, are deterritorialized: human rights now bound to the person of a human being and no longer to national territories. As I show in Chapter 2, these persons can be thought of as wearing a "human rights backpack."

Chapter 2

———

Human Rights in a Backpack

In Chapter 1 I depicted a human rights state as a collective political act of persons who grant themselves human rights. They do so to craft a vantage from which to advocate for adoption of human rights by the corresponding nation state. As addressees of human rights, they recognize themselves as self-determining normative agents.[1] Self-grantors are normatively active, not passive. They themselves warrant and secure the human rights they bear. But the human rights state is not an end in itself. It is a means to pursuing ever-wider recognition of these self-authored human rights, ultimately in the corresponding nation state.

This chapter develops two aspects of a human rights state. The rights it offers are "deterritorialized." And they are "worn" by participants in a kind of "backpack." So understood, human rights are resolutely political. Their content and validity are socially constructed. Their universality is an aspiration to be achieved through social movements. Human rights so understood are not pre-political, ahistorical, theological, or metaphysical "essences" incarnated in each member of the species. They are social constructions and their goal is the political one of advancing human rights belief, commitment, and practice.

Human rights immediately confront an obstacle in the territorial sovereignty of a nation state. Sovereign territory is physical geography but it is more. Territory is *political* geography whenever it determines a person's status with regard to rights on the basis of a person's legally defined geographical identity.[2] It establishes the difference between a legal insider and an outsider. It establishes what insider status entails: Habeas corpus? Due process? Access to lawyers? Political geography governs whether someone has an Arendtian (1968) "right to have rights" as a "right to belong to a political community" (Arendt 1949:37) or a right to "live under constitutional, limited government" (Arendt 1990:149).[3]

Geography—political and physical—is a matter of limits and borders, of power and authority, of a capacity for coercion and violence. National law codifies spatial margins—for example, where governmental reach ends at national boundaries and where citizens' civil rights[4] end there as well. Noncitizens living beyond those borders have no claim to any form of legal status within those borders. To be sure, international law or humanitarian intervention[5] might temporarily protect, or even empower, a domestic victim of local or governmental depredation. But if so, then only on a temporary basis that does not solve the underlying problems and causes of rightlessness. Political geography trumps claims to human rights understood as rights not limited by national borders.[6] Two notable exceptions concern the European Union and the European Convention on Human Rights. While notable, these exceptions are so unique that they could not possibly be generalized to any other part of the world. Europe's wealth, traditions of the rule of law and the welfare state, and peaceful internal relations cannot be matched anywhere on the planet.

In Guantánamo, political geography trumps human rights in a different sense. Following the 11 September 2001 terrorist attacks on the United States—spawning American-led wars, first in Afghanistan, then in Iraq— the Bush administration established a detention center at Cuba's Bahía de Guantánamo. The Department of Justice declared the center beyond American legal jurisdiction. The first twenty prisoners arrived in January 2002; today it still incarcerates about 120.[7] The Bush administration argued that the Geneva Conventions do not protect these prisoners. Yet the United States Supreme Court ruled in 2006 that prisoners are entitled to the minimal protections provided by Common Article 3 (a ruling the Defense Department subsequently embraced).[8] Those protections include a prohibition of torture. Yet in 2009 a former Bush administration official conceded that Mohammed al-Qahtani had been tortured at Guantánamo. Here we have an example of how national politics can extend across borders and trump international law.

The idea of rights independent of a nation state remain aspirational in many parts of the world. Yet that aspiration runs up against a paradox: human rights *require* the very boundaries they would transgress (hence my abiding concern throughout this book with the nation state).

The United Nations' 1948 Universal Declaration of Human Rights instantiates this paradox. It speaks the language of universally valid propositions when it proclaims human rights as if they were always already universally valid. But where it specifies venues for human rights practice, it presupposes a nation state. It construes legal validity as state-based and state-generated and delimited by state borders. If one believes human rights to be valid, one likely believes them to be legally valid in one or the other sense of legality. According to the declaration—the world's most widely referenced statement of human rights—rights to life, liberty, and personal security require the *state* as enforcer. Further, other rights imply a particular kind of state-based *legal system*, one that recognizes a person in his or her legal equality, such as a right to remedy by competent tribunal, a right to a fair and public hearing, or a right to be considered innocent until proven guilty. According to the declaration, other rights are actionable only through state-based *institutions of political participation*, allowing for peaceful assembly and association, free elections, and participation in government. And still other rights require various kinds of state-based *economic institutions*: a right to own property, to social security, to desirable work and trade-union membership, to an adequate standard of living, to rest and leisure.

To be sure, a state apparatus, a legal system, institutions of political participation, and economic institutions do not of themselves constitute a nation state—but all nation states have administrative, legal, political, and economic institutions. They may generate forms of political belonging but not necessarily a specifically *national* belonging. For example, a right to social security certainly presupposes some kinds of state-based institutions but not necessarily a nation state. The functional need for political institutions is not a need for a nation state in particular.

Still, the nation state remains the single most relevant political institution for the human rights project. And the Universal Declaration of Human Rights is best read with reference to the state. If the declaration's twenty-nine fundamental rights do not presuppose a nation state in particular as the irreplaceable venue for human rights practice, they do presuppose a state, for only a state can provide the various institutions such as social security. But because the national state is the default form of the contemporary state, the functional need for a state today usually issues into the nation state.

In one respect, the declaration presupposes the nation state explicitly, where it speaks of a person's right to a nationality. While a nationality without a state is possible, only a state, not a nationality, can provide the various institutions integral to modern political community, including ones legal, economic, and political. And outside a state one can hardly enjoy the social institutions identified in the declaration.

If human rights are understood in the sense of the declaration, someone without a state has no human rights—and someone with a state does not necessarily enjoy them. (And because the nation state is the only state form with global purchase today, I will speak of a nation state.) The paradox, then: to possess human rights presupposes membership in a nation state— yet the sovereign nation state, *in its very design*, rejects the domestic validity of any rights not legislated domestically (or assented to by treaty).

For the foreseeable future, then, the territorial nation state will continue to be central to the human rights project. This central status is a problem, but it is more than a problem: it can be a resource, as I will show. I propose a human rights–facilitative way forward by analogy to a classical Greek topos: the spear that alone can heal the wound it caused.[9] In other words, human rights require the very boundaries they would transgress. A human rights state, as a form of political behavior, seeks to change the nation state from one that does not recognize and defend human rights into one that does. A human rights state thus negates the usual consequence of political geography: one has rights (*if* one has rights at all) because one happens to stand on a particular, bounded geographic area (a nation state that recognizes the individual as a citizen or as a noncitizen with rights). A human rights state transforms the corresponding nation state into a state that recognizes its citizens as persons with rights that exceed the nation's own boundaries. That is, a nation state ceases to be a problem for human rights and becomes their most promising prospect—but only if some of a nation state's citizens can construct, within it and alongside it, a metaphorical human rights state. The utopian imagination that deploys metaphor needs always and everywhere to keep sight of mundane reality. The human rights state does this through performance, through an agonistic politics I describe below.

I develop my argument in four steps: (1) I transfer the basis of human rights from national, territorial belonging to human action and political performance; (2) I explain how individuals could be motivated to participate in a human rights state; (3) I explicate participation in part as the donning of a "human rights backpack"; and (4) I explicate citizenship in a human rights state as the nonformalized power of its participants, a power not tied to the nation state.

Transferring the Basis of Human Rights from National, Territorial Belonging to Human Action and Political Performance

I propose political *behavior* as an alternative to political *geography*. That is, I displace national geography with individual behavior. I do so by transferring the basis of human rights away from a person's legal status, a status tied to some particular physical territory. I transfer it to the person's human rights advocacy with like-minded political confrères, in concert, within a group.

The individual, in concert with other individuals, makes claims to human rights and does so "performatively." The group "performs" a kind of citizenship in a human rights state. Performing citizenship in a metaphorical human rights state uncouples human rights from national territory; citizenship in a metaphor is nonterritorial. Citizenship in a metaphor is more than magical thinking only if it has real-world effects. Effects follow from political advocacy toward moving the corresponding nation state to adopt human rights as an internal aspect of its legal self-understanding. Political advocacy here takes the form of political performance. This is what *citizenship in a metaphor* means: advocacy and persuasion as political performance. Citizenship in a human rights state is a kind of "proto-citizenship" in the targeted nation state. It anticipates the development of a nation state citizenship that embraces human rights: a citizenship not yet realized, a conception that orients political advocacy targeting a nation state that has yet to embrace human rights.[10] A realistic utopia, a practical cosmopolitanism, given wings by metaphorical thinking.

Transforming self-declared rights into rights recognized by the corresponding nation state begins with the realization that human rights have little prospect if they cannot be realized within nation states. The path to that goal will not leave the nation state unchanged; it will diminish state sovereignty along the way, as human rights gain increasing purchase within a nation state. A nation state diminished in its sovereignty no longer determines if human rights obtain on its otherwise sovereign territory. The nation state will resist such diminution and a human rights state must proceed agonistically. *Human rights state agonistes* is political performance, performance as citizenship, citizenship in a human rights state. Citizenship in a metaphor challenges a nation state to forfeit a measure of its sovereignty by offering rights beyond citizenship rights: human rights.

Agonistic politics is not politics as usual; citizenship *performed* is distinct from citizenship *legislated*. To perform human rights agonistically, as a critique of a nation state, is to sign one's own emancipation proclamation with the pen of a human rights state.[11] Performance is directed at a nation state from which it seeks human rights. It is also directed at participants, generating a solidarity that motivates and sustains participation. One kind of performance is authorship: to perform is to author, in this case when participants declare their own human rights to themselves and to their group—a human rights state.

Here I distinguish between claims as such and the right to makes claims (or the right to be a participant in the enterprise of claiming rights). Let me explain. A human rights state provides participants the opportunity to generate human rights *even before* those rights find recognition by their institutional environment, by their nation state. To be sure, a nation state may never recognize the claim makers' self-asserted right to make claims. It may never recognize the substantive claims themselves. One cannot change the world simply by making declarations about it; one cannot change the world with magical thinking; one cannot simply declare one's rights and thereby acquire them.

How, then, can self-declared rights come to be recognized by others and ultimately by a nation state? Jacques Rancière offers one cue:

There is no man of the Rights of Man, but there is no need for such a man. The strength of those rights lies in the back-and-forth movement between the first inscription of the right and the dissensual stage on which it is put to state. This is why the subjects of the Soviet constitution could make reference to the Rights of Man against the laws that denied their effectivity. This is also why citizens of states ruled by religious law or by the mere arbitrariness of their governments, even the clandestine immigrants in the zones of transit of our countries of the populations in the camps of refugees, can invoke them. These rights are theirs when they can do something with them to construct a dissensus against the denial of the rights they suffer. (Rancière 2004:305–306)

Sometimes groups and individuals can provoke a political system by making claims about it, specifically by opposing one's oppression within it and not only (as in the case of the former Soviet Union) where the state has pledged in its own laws, or in international instruments, to observe laws it violates. *Performance* then means giving critical voice to the fact of being denied what the law, at least on paper, promises. A person claims toward others—performs for others—a right to have rights first of all as a right to oppose one's exclusion in practice from the law on paper.[12]

Rancière emphasizes the capacity of people to "construct a dissensus against the denial of the rights they suffer." It requires that participants' claims to a right to oppose exclusion from the law as written *transcend* the circumstances of its origins. This capacity is effective only if it can free itself from a nation state's monopoly on the right to grant rights. Transcending nation state limitations on human rights is precisely what a human rights state seeks. That is, the nonterritorial space of a human rights state—space neither determined nor recognized by a nation state and by international law—seeks to empower participants. It does so by framing the human rights idea as a capacity for public authority *even without* nation state recognition. The human rights state demands recognition by creating a "space" for reconciling cosmopolitan human rights and particularistic national citizenship rights. It seeks reconciliation in a nation state of diminished sovereignty. At the point of reconciliation, the citizen's human rights are no longer excluded by national boundaries.

Motivation to Participate in a Human Rights State

Membership in a human rights state bestows rights, and it confers the protection that comes from being part of a group that recognizes those rights. In cases where the nation state or other forces do not penetrate all social spheres, real protection will be possible within the limits of that sphere. In cases of authoritarian and especially totalitarian states, protection within a human rights state is unlikely. Membership in a human rights belief system empowers the participants to advocacy in some cases but not all. But it gives hope in all.

So what might motivate a citizen of a nation state to participate in the corresponding human rights state? Solidarity, reinforcing group work, shared advocacy, political commitment: these are aspects, each with emotional and cognitive features that might guide cosmopolitan interest in pursuing the human rights project. To provide an example of how motivating interest might be formed and sustained, I sketch a scenario embodied in reciprocal expectations of a group. In this case, the group would unify around a political metaphor that transcends the territorial nation state by decoupling human rights from political geography. Drawing on the work of Randall Collins, one could imagine attachment along several dimensions: as patterns of social interaction that are both motivated and motivating via emotional energy stored in particular symbols. Participation in a human rights state generates solidarity grounded in feelings of morality. Such feelings take the form of "emotional entrainment" or "collective effervescence." I turn to each of these dimensions.

Attachments as Patterns of Social Interaction

Sustained, shared motivation within a community can flow from patterns of social interaction. Flow is more likely if participants can regard their interaction as morally invested and as prescriptive for their social behavior. Morally motivating interactional patterns are likely to have some kind of emotional component inasmuch as they involve particular stands on divisive or controversial issues, the sort of issues likely to excite passions: Do my human rights entail obligations to persons outside my political community? Should democratic communities be subject to outside rules not determined by the *demos*? Do human rights trump local ways of life and cultural preference incompatible with human rights?

Emotional energy is a resource particularly in a context in which participants are equally endowed with the same resource. Participants may be motivated collectively when their respective resources mesh. These terms describe the shared experience of moral solidarity or trust (Collins 2004:xiv). A human rights state provides that kind of experience to participants. Participants in face-to-face circuits of interaction are more likely to entertain human rights because of personal contact with other participants. Without close ties, participation dissolves, commitment fades, shared motivation wanes. To be sure, less personal circuits of interaction must be possible as well if solidarity is to be sustained among thousands or millions of persons who are the citizens of a nation state and the potential members of a human rights state alongside it.

Attachment to Patterns of Social Interaction Motivated and Motivating by Emotional Energy

A human rights state is an "imagined community" but not along the lines of Benedict Anderson's (1983) well-known description of the nation state.

Anderson describes a community often in a passive voice: membership imagined and not, as in the case of a human rights state, performed. A human rights state lives from the immediate performative, interactional, emotion-bound advocacy for human rights vis-à-vis the corresponding nation state. The passively imagined community of the nation state may be like a human rights state in that both require solidarity with other members. Both require trust among members.

By contrast, in a human rights state, solidarity and trust provide participants with "emotional payoffs" that motivate participants in their advocacy of human rights (Collins 2004:xv). Note that the imagined community of the nation state is not an advocacy group. It does not face a human rights state's abiding problem that such moments of emotional payoffs can be all too ephemeral. One solution is to transform short-term emotions into long-term emotions by "storing" emotions in symbols that have the power to reinvoke those emotions (ibid., 81). A central task of the human rights project is to constantly revivify emotions of normatively directed energy so that a human rights state is more than a "volatile and episodic experience that comes out just at moments of high ritual intensity" (ibid., 83).[13]

Emotional Energy Stored in Particular Symbols

The human rights idea might itself serve as a symbol to invoke the group solidarity needed to motivate participation in a human rights state. The idea of the individual as human rights bearing is abstract. It becomes concrete, and perhaps more motivating, as soon as particular groups are envisaged as rights bearing (child brides, for example, a group I address in Chapter 3).

Consider a different example: the human body, in all its vulnerability, can be thought of in the abstract but is for us always also concrete, above all as our own bodies. The notion of the body motivates participation in a human rights state especially when particular bodies or the bodies of particular groups (women, for example) are envisaged. Laden with emotional meaning, a symbol such as the human rights idea, or the human body, can "store" the emotional energy that sometimes may lend participants courage and confidence. Emotional energy "stored" by human rights symbols might take the form of "morally suffused energy" that "makes the individual feel not only good, but exalted, with the sense of doing what is most important and most valuable" (Collins 2004:39).

Participation in a Human Rights State Generates Solidarity
Grounded in Feelings of Morality

Participation in a human rights state offers shared membership and solidarity grounded in "feelings of morality: the sense of rightness in adhering to the group, respecting its symbols, and defending both against transgressors" (ibid., 49). Participation of this emotional quality may lead to a "sense of moral evil or impropriety in violating the group's solidarity and its symbolic representations" (ibid.).

A human rights–reinforcing context has functional requirements that ritual symbols meet in part. Effective symbols are effective because they valorize human rights. They do so by valorizing the individual as rights bearer or by ennobling the human body as meriting protection from abuse by others.

These elements motivate participation in a human rights state if they can affirm an acceptable status quo (or if they can contribute to the critique of an unacceptable one). Human rights–relevant ritual encourages human rights–relevant rules of conduct. It encourages members of a human rights state to observe those rules. The phrases *human rights reinforcing* and *human rights relevant* refer to the humanistic "sacralization" of the individual—of his or her body, say—as human rights bearing. When participants regard themselves and fellow participants as "sacred objects," they link themselves through this morally exalted symbol of group membership. *Sacred* in this context is not theological but normative in the sense of being inviolable, with a right to its integrity.

Feelings of Morality in the Form of Emotional Entrainment
or Collective Effervescence

Participation helps bind individuals to human rights consciousness and commitment, as do symbols and rituals. As a political metaphor, a human rights state is embodied in reciprocal expectations of the group by means of what Collins, building on Émile Durkheim (1965:250–252), calls "interaction ritual chains." Ritual in this sense is a pattern with two dimensions: participants are mutually focused on human rights, and they share an emotional experience. In their regard for themselves and others as human rights bearing, participants collectively experience an "entrainment" that builds up over time. Commitment in a human rights state constitutes a kind of heightened intersubjectivity, what Durkheim describes as a "collective effervescence" or "collective consciousness." Collins (2004:81) redescribes this heightened intersubjectivity as "high levels of emotional entrainment." Emotional entrainment operates in terms of vivid symbols or markers of group identity. Carried by rituals, these symbols can be internalized by participants without in any way homogenizing them.

Human Rights in a Backpack

When citizens of a nation state become motivated to participate in a corresponding human rights state, what do they become? What do they become as "citizens" of a metaphor? They become human rights advocates toward their nation state.

Advocacy takes many forms. One form is clearly performative: to perform, in a human rights state, the human rights that participants do not have in the corresponding nation state. They perform human rights in this sense by enjoying human rights, in concert, in this metaphor. They perform by decoupling human rights from geographic coordinates. For the human rights state offers human rights without geographic coordinates. A metaphor is nowhere.

A human rights state thus replaces geographic national borders with nongeographic boundaries. Nongeographic boundaries, the boundaries of the human rights state, are "incarnated into" the individual (regardless of his or her citizenship status in a nation state). That is, the individual metaphorically "wears" human rights. He or she wears them by analogy to wearing a backpack. By displacing, to the individual, the primary bordering authority of the world today—national territorial jurisdiction—a human rights backpack establishes the bearer's political agency in a cosmopolitan sense, at least aspirationally. It does so by challenging a nation state's sovereignty with respect to human rights, as participants mutually recognize each other's status as fellow human rights bearers. Backpackers do not wait for recognition by the corresponding nation state to practice recognition among themselves. This is what it means to be a member or "citizen" of a metaphorical human rights state.[14] Its nongeographic boundaries do not exclude outsiders; they indicate where human rights begin—namely, with the person of the bearer, wherever he or she stands.

Bordering by the human rights backpack diminishes the territorial nation state's legal capacity, at least in the human rights state. Once the nation state has embraced human rights, all of its residents bear the backpack. The nation state no longer marks off rights bearers from non–rights bearers *with respect to human rights*.[15]

The metaphorical backpack performs a human rights state when its members grant themselves human rights and recognize that grant among themselves. That grant is what I mean when I say that participants *don* a human rights backpack. The performance is the donning of the backpack, of displaying the backpack, of carrying human rights in the backpack, or sharing the backpack's human rights with others. The backpack's performativity is the performativity of political advocacy,[16] including the efforts at persuasion in arguments against any nation state that precludes human rights.

Three aspects of the human rights backpack bear special attention. It is not as unfamiliar as one might think *a prima vista*; and it is an imperfect metaphor. It confers on the individual the agency currently held by the nation state and its borders. And even as the backpack endogenizes (in a human rights state) some functions currently attributed to nation state borders, it does not destroy a nation state but modifies it by limiting its sovereignty. I examine each aspect in turn.

Human Rights Backpack: Not Entirely Unfamiliar and an Imperfect Metaphor

The backpack metaphor is familiar in some domestic contexts: in states that offer citizens a backpack containing domestic rights.[17] Members enjoy the same domestic rights regardless of where, on national territory, they are located physically. This backpack counts among the greatest merits of those states that in fact offer one. Entitlement to a backpack ranks high on the list of things people mean when they speak of the possible benefits of citizenship. Persons who enjoy domestic rights enjoy rights that are available usually only *within* a nation state's territorially bounded realm. Anyone persuaded that domestic rights should obtain without regard to the geographical location of the rights bearer will regard human rights attractive for the same reason.

Like most metaphors, *backpack* is imperfect. An actual backpack can be taken off, whereas the metaphorical backpack I image is more politically compelling if, once slipped on, cannot be alienated. Further, a physical backpack can be stolen. A metaphorical one could certainly be denied but never stolen.

Human Rights Backpack Confers on the Individual the Agency Currently Held by the Nation State

This approach to human rights advocacy enhances individual agency. And it diminishes state sovereignty. It does so inasmuch as the backpack's contents are indifferent to the wearer's political-geographic location. What matters is what the backpack "contains" or "carries," not the backpacker's political-territorial location.

The backpack metaphor encapsulates a central argument of this book: that historical practice has always gotten the relationship between legal rights and physical geography exactly backward. In our era of the sovereign nation state, in almost all cases national territory determines if a particular member of our species has legal rights *of any sort*, quite aside from the very different form of rights instantiated in human rights. Thus one is more likely to enjoy human rights in Costa Rica or Japan, say, than in Sudan, Indonesia, or Belarus.[18] Having human rights depends on the individual's citizenship status at that location: in India, Dalits are less likely to enjoy human rights than high-caste citizens, and even in Norway noncitizens, at least some noncitizens, are much more vulnerable than citizens.

I argue in the aspirational spirit of universal inclusion in the right to have human rights. Such a right competes against a nation state's principle of almost universal exclusion (most humans are excluded from the citizenry of any state, even the most populous). I aspire to a world of nation states in which one's status as a human being, not the territory one inhabits, determines whether one bears human rights.

The backpack defines participants in ways roughly analogous to the passports that have come to define the international traveler since the First World War. Passports have standardized the criteria for recognizing someone as legally entitled to enter and depart sovereign territories. Just as a passport marks the legal terms by which nation states classify the international traveler with respect to right of entry,[19] in a human rights state, the individual's metaphorical backpack marks the presence of a human rights bearer.[20]

Hence wherever the backpack "goes," there, too, "go" human rights.[21] But in the current context of any particular campaign for human rights within a particular nation state, the current, preliminary goal is human rights recognition within a nation state. The ultimate goal is to realize what the human rights backpack currently promises only in principle. The individual carries them in the nation state even as it does not recognize them. The human rights state seeks that recognition.

Human Rights Backpack Endogenizes Some Functions Currently Attributed to Nation State Borders Without Destroying a Nation State

Chapter 1 proposes self-authored human rights as status functions with deontic powers. The backpack proposed in the current chapter can hardly replace a nation state's territorial exclusivity with a nonnational, nonterritorial, deontic power. But it can provocatively *complement* a nation state with human rights as a nonnational, nonterritorial, deontic power. The goal, within a nation state, is for that power to trigger an emerging dynamic that culminates in eliding a nation state's territorial exclusivity to the extent necessary to realize human rights within and among nation states. This effort begins by creating the conditions for eventual replacement as follows. The human rights backpack provides a protective border "around" the individual. It is effective within a human rights state because all members recognize those rights. But it seeks to become protective in a nation state as well, through the state's eventual adoption of human rights as an internal feature.

As a mobile carrier of human rights, the backpack endogenizes (in a human rights state) some functions currently attributed to nation state borders. Note that national borders are themselves status functions with deontic powers. They are exogenous to the persons they affect. The goal of the backpack is to render them endogenous to the backpacker *in the nation state.*

Endogenization of the human rights backpack in the nation state proceeds along intersubjective lines. Assigned status functions with deontic powers are intersubjective acts. They are behaviors of individuals, more or less in concert, at least some of the time. A status function operates within the community that assigns it, which is to say, it operates only where it is socially recognized. Status assignation is status recognition. The human rights project—the project of advancing human rights in as many ways as possible—here takes the form of persuading nation states to recognize the human rights that members of a human rights state have assigned themselves, in public fora such as the political sphere, but also in private fora such as the family. The project does not undermine a nation state but rather qualifies its sovereignty with respect to human rights.

To conceive of human rights as status functions with deontic powers is to render them works of collective intentionality, works of shared understandings and practices.[22] To so conceive of human rights is to provide a particular social and legal status to the assignee. *Status* means how one may expect to be treated by others on the basis of regularly redeemed expectations, but also how one expects to treat others on the basis of that assignation.[23] Expectations of this kind encourage recognition of the status function. Recognition is an achievement of political community. It entails the embrace of human rights as a public code of behavior but also as a personal code. Participants possess human rights if they collectively grant themselves human rights but only if they do so within a social field that recognizes that grant.[24] Participants constitute their own field of recognition as the metaphorical human rights state. It challenges a nation state toward recognizing a human rights state already in its midst, to adopt, as integral to its self-understanding, the human rights that members of a human rights state already claim.

These three actions—self-assignation, mutual recognition, and challenging a nation state—do not destroy a nation state; they modify it by limiting its sovereignty. To take the edge off the charge that this vision is wholly unrealistic—or the charge that the backpack metaphor is no more than a rhetorical way of simply claiming that rights really should, somehow, transcend the nation state—Chapter 1 notes social constructions, albeit of a very different kind, that readily cross national borders. The most striking examples are economic: cross-border flows of capital, services, and labor. If capital can cross borders so readily, why not rights? If the market economy can be globalized, why not human rights?[25]

Human Rights State Citizenship: Nonformalized Power
Not Tied to the Nation State

With its model of citizenship—a citizenship nonterritorial and nonnational —a human rights state challenges the targeted nation state in multiple ways.

Over against the nation state it constitutes a new form of power: nonformalized power or power only partly formalized, and it constitutes a power not tied to the sovereign nation state. But a human rights state does not replace the nation state. Indeed, the cosmopolitanism of a human rights state does not envision world government, world citizenship, or even a worldwide federation of nation states. Consider each of these aspects in turn.

Human Rights State Constitutes Nonformalized Power or Power Only Partly Formalized

Citizenship in a human rights state follows from human rights as nonterritorially bound status functions with deontic powers. It circumvents the territorial sovereignty of the traditional nation state. It rejects a nation state's hierarchy of legitimate power and allegiance. It refuses a hierarchy that places the territorial state, rather than the human individual, at the top. And in this way a human rights state introduces into a nation state a new form of power: nonformalized power or power only partly formalized. By *nonformalized power* I mean "being an actor even though lacking power" (Sassen 2002:23). *Nonformalized* does not mean lacking all means of political agency. It means possessing a currently powerless political agency even if only in opposition to the status quo. Here we have the initial status of someone within a nation state with human rights citizenship.[26]

Human Rights State Constitutes a Power Not Tied to the Sovereign Nation State

In a world of nation states, citizenship can only be national. Hence a state's national aspect shifts if the institution of citizenship shifts. Citizenship configured as *jus soli*, or right of the soil, or birthright citizenship, deriving from a child's having been born in the territory of the related state, is very different from citizenship configured as *jus sanguinis*, right of blood, deriving from the child's parents' citizenship.

A nation state's national aspect shifts when challenged by the advent of a national citizen's simultaneous citizenship in a human rights state. A human rights state challenges the corresponding nation state to render human rights integral to itself, in this way to collapse citizenship rights with human rights. In this respect my approach accords with Arendt's idea of a "right to have rights" interpreted as a *statist* account of human rights.[27]

But statism need not mean that a nation state is the be-all and end-all of human rights. The phrase *a right to have rights* may be read as statist: as a cosmopolitan right to national particularism. In other words, a cosmopolitan right to membership in this or that particular political community. In that case, the individual bearer of human rights has a parochial status, not a cosmopolitan one. A parochial status is a matter of the person's political membership: Does membership in this particular nation state provide human rights? If so, how are human rights defined? What does the list of human rights include?

By contrast to a parochial status I propose a cosmopolitan status, the status of a human rights state. The idea of that state is the idea of cosmopolitan rights, as rights that exceed a nation state's boundaries without abandoning the nation state. Here I take my cue from Claude Lefort's image of power not tied to the sovereign nation state: "These rights of man mark a disentangling of right and power. Right and power are no longer condensed around the same pole. If it is to be legitimate, power must henceforth conform to right, but it does not control the principle of right" (Lefort 1988:31). Lefort observes the disaggregation of right and power at work in the 1789 Déclaration des droits de l'homme et du citoyen: the "paradox was that rights are named by human beings—and that this in itself indicates their ability to name themselves, to designate themselves in their humanity, in their existence as individuals, and to designate their humanity in the mode of coexistence, in the manner of their living together in the 'city'— and that right is not reducible to human artifice" (Lefort 1988:39). I do not read the phrase *not reducible to human artifice* as referring to otherworldly sources of human rights. I read it as the social constructionist idea of *self-authored* human rights. I refer to *addressees* of human rights who are simultaneously the *authors* of those rights. (*Authorship* here accords with what, in earlier pages, I describe as political performance.) In other words, even people without political power in a nation state can author their own human rights. Even people without power can be agents. One who assigns oneself human rights is an agent, at least within a community that recognizes that self-assignation: a human rights state. In doing so, the performers exceed a nation state at those points where the state threatens, denies, or violates human rights.

Human Rights State Does Not Replace the Nation State

The cosmopolitanism of a human rights state does not entail world government, world citizenship, or even a worldwide federation of nation states. Nor does a collection of human rights states collectively constitute some kind of global sovereign. Rather, each human rights state encourages the corresponding nation state to adopt the human rights already specified, adopted, and recognized within the corresponding human rights state. A human rights state integrates a cosmopolitan conception of politics with the particularistic quality of individuals' actual political lives and the contingencies and specificities of social circumstances.

Here Marx's (2000) critique of Bruno Bauer offers guidance on how to imagine this configuration of particular and cosmopolitan elements. According to Bauer, emancipation in nineteenth-century Europe requires that all individuals abandon their particularistic identities. It requires that people replace particularistic identities with cosmopolitan commitments, preferences, and interests of a worldly republican community. Marx rejects this vision because it (unintentionally) depoliticizes and privatizes the public sphere of civil society.[28] To privatize the political sphere is to surrender it to the demesne of capital where popular struggles cannot achieve social and political recognition. But what Marx does not offer in his critique, a human rights state does: it integrates the cosmopolitan and the parochial. It unites cosmopolitan rights of republican citizenship with the particularistic circumstances of any given individual. It does so when it achieves its goal of persuading the corresponding nation state to constitutionalize human rights domestically.

To be sure, while rights are effective in a practical sense only if they become institutionalized, some forms of institutionalization can also undermine rights. Integrating the cosmopolitan and the particular means institutionalizing human rights such that they also exceed that institutionalization. Rights that exceed their institutionalization are rights that need not depend on the institution for their exercise (including rights to criticize the institution itself). Institutionalization of this sort allows people to resist and oppose it whenever it violates human rights.

If human rights are located only in civil society, they are particular, not cosmopolitan; they affirm the status of the citizen but not the status of a human being as such. The citizen of a human rights state, by contrast, is a "proto-citizen" of a nation state. In a human rights state, the participants' human rights constitute cosmopolitan demands addressed to a particularistic nation state. Cosmopolitan emancipation through a human rights state is not merely emancipation unto the particularistic, parochial interests of the private property owner. A right to have rights is the right to be a member of a particular political community in which human rights are now provided.[29]

This chapter shows how participants in a human rights state, by granting themselves human rights independently of nation state recognition, thereby don a human rights backpack. Chapter 3 outlines a parallel procedure. It shows how participants displace the boundaries of human rights protection from the nation state to the individual's body.

To heighten the means of integrating a human rights state into the corresponding nation state, I offer two procedures toward the same goal rather than just one. Integration comes about through politics carried by citizens of the nation state, now transformed through their participation in a human rights state.

Chapter 3

The Body as Human Rights Boundary

Chapter 2 outfitted the participants in a human rights state with backpacks that metaphorically carry the human rights denied, rejected, or even violated by the corresponding nation state. This chapter crafts an additional, complementary means to challenge the human rights–denying nation state. It focuses on ways of culturally construing the body to advance the human rights project: human rights advocacy as a kind of biopolitics. It argues for a kind of boundary displacement, from nation state to the body of the advocate. It situates this proposal in the context of slavery as one possible field for deploying a biopolitics of this sort.

Slavery[1] is recorded in most of the world's ancient civilizations and in some of history's oldest records. The Code of Hammurabi circa 1760 B.C.E. treats it as a fully normalized practice. At the beginning of the nineteenth century an "estimated three-quarters of all people alive were trapped in bondage against their will either in some form of slavery or serfdom" (Forsythe 2009:399). Slavery is not legal anywhere in the world today. Where it exists, it no longer takes the form of the legalized, race-based slavery that allowed victims to be owned, bought, and sold as private property during the Atlantic slave trade of the sixteenth to the nineteenth centuries that victimized more than 12 million Africans.[2]

Estimates for worldwide slavery today range between 27 and 31 million persons.[3] It reaches across all borders. It is found on every continent. Its products flow into global supply chains and local shops.[4] Contemporary slavery takes many forms, including servitude, coerced marriage, forced labor, bonded labor, debt bondage, human trafficking,[5] and, in the case of children, their sale, exploitation, or placement in military service as porters and cooks, but also as combatants.[6]

Some victims are captured or kidnapped. Others are lured with false promises of work or education. Still others, particularly in West Africa and

South Asia, are born into hereditary slavery.[7] Some are sold into unpaid domestic work or unpaid work on, say, fishing boats.[8] Others are held for exploitation, others for "marriage." Slavers control the enslaved—economically, socially, sexually—through coercion, deception, violence or its threat. Some slavers rationalize enslavement in terms of discrimination of differences in nationality, race, ethnicity, religion, sex, caste, tribal system, customs, or mores. In all its forms, slavery deprives the individual of liberty in choice, behavior, and movement.

Unlike murder or theft, slavery is not always readily apparent to the outsider. It can be ambiguous along various of its dimensions: hidden within homes, worksites, and whole communities and apparent only if one understands something about the participants and their relationships to each other. For example, Japanese are unlikely to be enslaved in Japan, unlike a poor Filipino or Thai resident, especially given poverty in the country of origin. Slavery is greatest in poor countries; wealthier countries are more likely to function as transit points. The risk of enslavement varies widely. The "measurement of risk must be understood within the webs and networks that tie together the origin, transit, and destination countries" (Walk Free Foundation 2013:12). Approximately 76 percent of all enslaved persons live in one of twenty countries: Mauritania, Haiti, Pakistan, India, Nepal, Moldova, Benin, Côte d'Ivoire, the Gambia, Gabon, India, China, Pakistan, Nigeria, Ethiopia, Russia, Thailand, Democratic Republic of the Congo, Myanmar, Bangladesh (ibid).

Most slaves are citizens of the country of enslavement. No country has more slaves than India, with between 13.3 and 14.7 million, many in debt bondage or bonded labor (ibid., 43–49). China, with 2.8 to 3.1 million enslaved persons, is second in absolute numbers. Principle forms are coerced labor of men, women, and children (including domestic servitude and forced begging), as well as the sexual exploitation of women and children, in addition to forced marriage (ibid., 7). Slavery in Pakistan ranges between 2 and 2.2 million and draws on a large population of displaced persons under circumstances of a weak rule of law (ibid., 39–42). In Mauritania, a West African nation with deeply entrenched hereditary slavery, between 140,000 and 160,000 people are enslaved out of a population of 3.8 million. Slavery here takes the additional forms of child marriage and human trafficking (ibid., 32–35). Slavery in Haiti, a Caribbean nation plagued by disasters both natural and political, still maintains old practices of child slavery (the *restavek* system)[9] as well as child marriage and human trafficking. Slaves number between 200,000 and 220,000 out of a population of 10.2 million (ibid., 36–38).

Almost every country in the world has laws criminalizing various forms of modern slavery (ibid., 30); many have ratified international covenants to the same end.[10] While most forms of slavery are illegal wherever practiced, in the developing world relevant laws are hardly enforced. In highly developed countries, relevant legislation is not enforced effectively. For example, the U.S. State Department's 2013 *Trafficking in Persons Report* identified almost 47,000 victims globally in 2012 yet reports only 7,700 prosecutions and only 4,750 convictions.[11]

In this chapter I (1) examine the failure of territorialized citizenship to protect against enslavement and the nonterritorial alternative. (2) I then consider the single most important route to diminishing slavery, namely, by reducing poverty, and note the difficulties involved in poverty reduction. (3) To facilitate progress in the face of these difficulties, I offer a procedure parallel to the backpack of Chapter 2. I propose construing the human body (and the bodies of slaves, in particular) as analogous to political territory, toward a kind of boundary displacement, from nation state to the body of the human rights bearer. I argue for framing the body as its own bordering capacity. I then deploy this model (4) by opposing nation state territory that cannot or does not prevent slavery with the moral territory of the self; (5) by working out three respects in which the body as symbol challenges nonprotective citizenship; and (6) by showing how this model can internationalize domestic opposition to slavery.

Failure of Territorialized Citizenship to Protect Against Enslavement and the Nonterritorial Alternative

The state in some cases offers itself as the first line of defense against slavery.[12] Many states are in a position to allocate national budgets to fund law enforcement, to legislate and enforce criminal laws, and to provide victim support services. Some are in a position to provide help to vulnerable sectors, such as migrant laborers and workers in the informal economy. States find support in international instruments that prohibit slavery, including the Universal Declaration of Human Rights, article 4, which reads: "No one shall be held in slavery or servitude; slavery and the slave trade shall be prohibited in all their forms." And the International Court of Justice has ruled that protection from slavery (and from piracy, genocide, torture, and racial discrimination) is an obligation of the state toward the "international community" and, as such, is an obligation of all states.[13]

But experience shows that nation state citizenship in many cases fails to protect against enslavement, particularly in economically weak states, in politically unstable areas, and wherever women are subject to widespread, systematic discrimination.[14] And the nation state often fails to prevent the scourge of trafficking in wealthier regions in which many of the enslaved are not citizens. The nation state has been largely unsuccessful in combating slavery on its own territory—for example, in Mauritania, Haiti, Pakistan, India, Nepal, Moldova, Benin, Cote d'Ivoire, the Gambia, and Gabon. In five of these countries, the enslavement of citizens is facilitated by culturally sanctioned practices such as caste and debt bondage (in Pakistan and India) or chattel slavery (of the Haratins in Mauritania). The customary practice of *vidomegon* (giving up children to traffickers) in Benin,[15] like that of *restavek* in Haiti, fuels child slavery in particular (Walk Free Foundation 2013:30). Poverty (perhaps accompanied by various forms of discrimination) facilitates slavery often institutionalized in culturally tolerated forms. In India, Nepal, Gabon, and Moldova, heavy cross-border migration renders migrants vulnerable to exploitation.

Given the failure of the territorially based political personhood of citizenship to protect many persons from enslavement, I propose an alternative: human rights as deterritorialized personhood. This approach does not *replace* citizenship in a nation state but aspires to *change* it.

Diminish Slavery by Reducing Poverty

Where the status of being a citizen cannot protect the citizen from enslavement, the "belonging" that describes citizenship is a fugitive form of belonging. That is, if "belonging" is a matter of inclusion in a community of rights and mutual recognition, then the citizenship status of the enslaved person is in fact an exclusion from rights and recognition.

Inclusion in a community of rights and mutual recognition gives the borders of the community a positive valence: the boundaries of the community mark the presence of rights and recognition that likely are absent beyond those borders. But for the enslaved citizen, the borders are either meaningless—one is as vulnerable to exploitation on one side of the border as on the other—or they are invidious in the sense of sovereign boundaries that render behavior and conditions within those boundaries "hands-off" to outside critics (and perhaps inside critics as well).

Slavery is a system of power relations reinforced by social structures. The single most powerful structural cause of slavery is the poverty of the enslaved and of those vulnerable to being enslaved.[16] Poverty, in the context of a highly uneven distribution of resources within a community and across communities, is one root cause. Economic inequality and poverty easily undermine good governance and accountability, and in this way, too, they hinder the human rights project. In many cases perhaps the single most effective means to diminishing slavery is economic. Economic means include social and economic development on the one hand and, on the other, a fair distribution of resources or wealth redistribution. Both approaches are immediately controversial; both are difficult to realize.

Still, one can imagine various possibilities, beginning with a world state. It could pursue global distributive justice in the manner of the modern welfare state. The welfare state is a system in which the state takes key responsibility for failures of the market economy to provide adequate resources to all citizens to protect the health and the economic and social well-being of all citizens, and particularly those in financial or social need, who receive benefits. The equitable distribution of wealth serves equality of opportunity and public responsibility for members unable to secure the minimal provisions for what that society regards as adequate.

A world state, if it were just and efficient and not corrupt, might contribute powerfully to the reduction of poverty worldwide. It could offer global distributive justice through strong support of local communities. It could support local initiatives to advance development, good governance, the rule of law, even human rights.[17] A global state with a monist constitutional order would have the means to distributive (or redistributive) socioeconomic justice, including public policy and law. It might offer the benefits of administration that is centralized and uniform. It could seek consensus, or it could use coercion to just ends to a degree far greater than can a nation state. It might secure a just redistribution.

But even if it were democratic, and even if it respected rights as it pursued distributive justice and freedom for all persons, it might constitute something of a coercive apparatus with its own interests, given the risks inherent to a large apparatus; it might lean toward tyranny, imperialism, and militarism. Other coercive risks might be economic, "including threats of trade and financial sanctions; withdrawal of investment; threats to withdraw IMF or World Bank support and the curtailment of aid and other assistance" (ICISS 2001:24).[18] A world state might provide some benefits but only at the cost of the freedom of individuals, groups, regions, and at the expense of diversity and societal plurality. Assistance even from a global state may fail to prevent or alleviate conflicts or problems and may even exacerbate them.

A federation of states offers a second possibility. On the one hand, a federation is much less likely than a world state to be tyrannical. On the other hand, it would lack the coercive capacity of a world state to impose law and public policy from the center. Further, federal unions cannot easily levy the same set of policies on diverse members, whereas a centralized global state could, at least more easily, and is more likely to be willing to do so. Consequently federations are much less likely to achieve economic justice through egalitarian wealth redistribution than a centralized state.

In light of the difficulties involved with either a world state or a federation of states, I propose an alternative: deterritorialized personhood, or "body as boundary."

The Body, in Analogy to Political Territory, with Its Own Bordering Capacity

The danger of enslavement is one of many ways in which the body is vulnerable. In its natural vulnerability to disease, aging, and death, aspects of any one body mirror the physical vulnerability of all bodies.[19] A person's embodiment allows him or her to understand vulnerability in any other human being; it makes possible an intuitive correspondence with every other person's embodiedness.[20] The body is not only a physical phenomenon, of course; it is a cultural one as well.

In its vulnerability to enslavement, the body raises questions about the bordering function of a nation state. In the anthropologist Mary Douglas we find one answer to these questions; we find it in the analogy she draws. She allows the body to stand for any bounded system. The body's boundaries (physical, legal, and moral) can represent vulnerable political borders.[21] In this sense, the human body, as vulnerable to slavery, corresponds to a nation state as incapable of preventing the enslavement of some of its citizens. Sovereign boundaries endanger human bodies by not extending to *all* resident bodies the national rights available to *some*.[22]

Given the implausibility of either a world state or a federation of states, the problem of enslavement might be countered—at least sometimes, at least in some of its aspects—by a new and different way of regarding the body. I propose such a way. It analogizes the body to political territory and challenge slavers, slaves, and potential victims of enslavement in terms of political territory. It does so in ways that advance the project for human rights. For it views slavery as a type of social control within exploitative systems of labor; it sees national borders as protecting market niches.[23] Like all plausible solutions, it is only partial at best. It focuses less on rescuing the currently enslaved than on preventing slavery in the first place. It displaces a basically defensive stance with a more offensive one, toward generating an empowering self-regard in persons who are otherwise powerless.

To the extent that a state's physical borders do not aid the enslaved— most slaves are citizens of the country in which they are enslaved—and because borders do not offer a means for the autonomy of the enslaved, I advocate a different kind of border. The usual kind is national; most nation states exercise bordering functions, at least in ordinary circumstances (extraordinary circumstances include war or occupation). As an alternative, I propose replacing "external" jurisdiction with "internal" jurisdiction. I propose *endogenizing the bordering function* by transferring it from the nation state to the individual members of a human rights state. Then border jurisdiction ceases to be a matter of *where* an individual resides and becomes a matter of *what* an individual has been assigned. Or the border becomes a matter of what the individual (as a member of a human rights state) *assigns him- or herself*. This step realizes the human rights backpack I outline in Chapter 2. The backpack modifies national boundaries in their traditional function of geographic bordering. It replaces legal jurisdiction tied to geographic space.[24]

This proposal would change the status quo in which the bordering function of national boundaries bars entry to the nation state by outsiders, unless and until they individually receive permission to enter (and to remain only as long as the nation state allows). The proposal leads to a situation in which the individual body (of a human rights state participant) acquires its own bordering capacity. The proposal asserts the presence of human rights that the nation state rejects. Then human rights would be present in the individual person. It would be present not as some natural or theological feature but as a political achievement of a human rights state that aspires to transform the corresponding nation state.

But I do not argue that just as states have boundaries, so, too, do bodies—and therefore that slavery is a human rights violation. It is not my contention that, simply by analogy to political communities with bordering functions, bodies should have them as well. In proposing that individual bodies endogenize, within themselves, the traditional bordering function of a nation state, I do not declare all bodies to have a universal human right to be free from enslavement. Rather, I encourage local bodies, as participants in a human rights state, to "author" their own human rights (and to seek recognition of those rights ultimately from a nation state). A bordering capacity embedded in the person is human rights jurisdiction "internalized." Where human rights are self-authored, the author acquires his or her own bordering capacity. That is, human rights are "located" in the person who carries a human rights boundary "within" him- or herself. The individual metaphorically "embodies" that boundary. Here the defining feature is a bordering authority, detached from national territorial jurisdiction and displaced onto the individual. The individual "carries" this border around with him- or herself on the basis of a status recognized by the metaphorical human rights state. A human rights state recognizes the human rights of its members by recognizing their agency as individuals capable of assigning themselves human rights.

Using the Moral Territory of the Self to Oppose Nation State Territory That Cannot or Does Not Prevent Slavery

This approach offers a new and innovative argument regarding the politics of self-ownership and the politics of personhood. By envisioning human rights as bounded in their validity not by nation states but by resident individuals, it rejects the widespread notion that only strong international institutions can oppose repressive or barbaric behavior by states toward their populace. (And, as I argue here and again in the Coda, international institutions have not proven particularly effective.) By rejecting the belief that state power determines the possibility of human rights in any given nation state, the proposal opens up a perspective on the peculiar force of nonstate-based rights within the state, in the bodies of citizens, as a force within the state to challenge the state toward advancing human rights.

The body, now understood as a human rights boundary—with rights "located" in the person who carries a human rights boundary "within" him-or herself—renders human rights–protective borders mobile. Borders are "carried" by the person as he or she moves within a territory or from one territory to the next. Borders have multiple locations: each individual, or each body, potentially constitutes one more human rights border. Borders so conceived constitute what Saskia Sassen (in a very different context and not with respect to human rights) discusses as "long transnational chains of locations" located "deep inside national territorial and institutional domains" (Sassen 2006:416). Each location marks the presence of a human rights bearer. There are as many "locations" for the border as there are persons. Each participant is a participant in a human rights state; each constitutes one more "human rights border."

Now human rights are no longer anchored in national collectivities. They are no longer dependent on a nation state and no longer embedded in national geography. Deterritorialized, human rights now correlate with the *moral* territory of the human self. Moral territory endogenizes the nonnational agenda of human rights. Moral territory challenges national territory as the legitimate authority, exclusive and final, as a barrier to cosmopolitan rights.

By *moral territory* I mean something Durkheimian: that the individual "depends upon [others] to the very extent he is distinguished from them" in relationships inherently moral (Durkheim 1984:172). For human rights are phenomena neither objective nor subjective but rather intersubjective. They are norms possible only through other human beings, in *interactional territories*. Although spatial, these territories need not be drawn on a geopolitical map; they can be mapped onto human selves. I call such territories *territories of the self*. Territory of this sort is a social space of individual self-determination. The individual authors his or her own human rights as an act of self-determination in moral space.

The moral territory of the human self challenges conventional understandings of the geographic territory of a nation state.[25] It grasps a person's enslavement as a kind of "illegal occupation" or as a "colonization" of this moral territory. Slavery then appears analogous to an "invasion," "occupation," or "colonization" of the body. Throughout history, to this day, wars have been fought over territory (and presumably will continue to be in the future). Soldiers are citizens willing to fight, to kill, and to die for national territory. The moral territory of the self enjoins not wars but political movements to combat, resist, and end the annexation and subjugation of the enslaved person's life. The human rights project formulates a human right to be free from slavery in terms of resisting and stopping the invasion, ending the occupation and regaining control over the formerly occupied, and turning back colonization. The approach thematizes the enslaved person as a territorialized body. The goal is to free the body from this enslaving territorialization, or from a territorialization that cannot protect the body from enslavement. The goal is to deterritorialize the body.

Deterritorialization means political personhood uncoupled from a nation state. In the standard form of citizenship,[26] "political personhood" depends on a legally articulated connection between *this* particular body and *that* particular territory. It links a physical, political presence within a geographic field of official, state-based recognition. Recognition is twofold. In the public sphere, a person can be recognized legally as entitled to vote or to run for office. In the private sphere, a person can be recognized with a right to decide whether to bear children and how best to raise them. In both spheres, the individual can be recognized with a right, say, not to be monitored or controlled by the state in certain of his or her preferences, from political viewpoint to religious confession to private correspondence.

Deterritorializing political personhood does not entail the person's disembodiment (by contrast with the digital technology I discuss in Chapter 6 as a resource for the human rights project). On the contrary, it allows for any number of embodied expressions. States, bureaucracies, and legal systems regard the body as the seat of the individual's power and capacity for cooperation with others—but also as the seat of resistance to others. Citizenship—as a status shared within a group but also, for some persons, as a highly individual political identity—is also tied to the individual's physical body. Think of the embodied political agency expressed in the formal principle of political equality. As a member of the community of the enfranchised, no less than as someone voting his or her particular preferences, the formula "one person, one vote" captures the individual in somatic terms: literally, one body equals one vote.[27]

To be sure, political personhood distinguishes as well between physical body and moral self. When I speak of *physical body*, I refer to *having* a body; when I speak of *moral self*, I mean *being* a body. These distinct but complementary aspects of a human being come together in the human rights bearer. To have a body "embedded" with human rights is not simply to *have* a body; it is to *be* a body as well.[28] To say that one *has* a body is to invoke a physical dimension, a natural phenomenon. To say that one *is* a body is to invoke a cognitive and moral dimension; it refers to this or that cultural understanding, collectively developed over time. Here we have the basis for the individual's capacity to identify with his or her physical embodiment. Humans have no less a capacity to identify morally with the embodiment of others. The upshot of embodied expressions of political personhood: to identify with others is to recognize others' capacity to bear human rights.[29] *Political personhood* then means the body as embedded with human rights.

Some victims are highly motivated to resist enslavement. More important is to motivate those victims or potential victims who currently cannot imagine resistance. This model motivates by educating in the politics of self-ownership and moral personhood. It raises the consciousness of persons who otherwise do not regard themselves as worthy of a right to have rights, let alone worthy of creating their own human rights. Again, the means of raising this consciousness, toward a politics of moral personhood, is a human rights attitude toward the body. Namely, the human body is at once *particular*—everyone has his or her own, distinct body—and *universal*—from the standpoint of the species, all bodies are equally members in the sense that the genome of any given human being can equally well represent the genome of the human species. Because slavery constitutes the same condition of oppression for any human being, the moral territory of the human self offers itself as a universal symbol of humanity, a symbol of the species understood not biologically but morally, in the sense that slavery violates human rights (as distinct from violating, say, economic logic or traditional cultural practice). It offers itself because humans share an immediate and intuitive understanding of embodiedness,[30] including the fragility of the body physically, socially (in terms of socially consequential perceptions; for example, of skin pigmentation), and in terms of freedom of movement.

Three Respects in Which the Body as Symbol Challenges Nonprotective Citizenship

I propose displacing this veneration of the particular nation state[31] to the body by analogy to the ritual veneration of territory in the form of a nation state, as I explain below. As a universal symbol of humanity, the body could become an object of veneration in a sense not religious or metaphysical but rather political. As a venerated symbol, the body then refers not only to the vulnerable physicality of embodiedness but equally to the socially constructed capacity to bear rights. If that capacity depends on the particular territory in which the individual finds him- or herself, geographic territory may be regarded as a source of human rights—one that too often fails.

This symbol possesses the emotional power to unify human rights advocates into a metaphorical human rights state. As a form of shared commitment, a human rights state exists in the minds of advocates alongside the territorial nation state of which many, if not most, of these persons are citizens. It challenges the nation state with respect to human rights claims against slavery. It broadens, beyond governments and international organizations, the field on which human rights are pursued. It expands the arena of participants beyond elites to ordinary men and women who make their own claims to rights-based empowerment—as distinguished from human rights as a top-down gratuitous grant from the powerful. In these ways it rejects the conventional state-centric orientation largely blind to possibilities for *local* spheres for human rights advocacy. Further, it does not depend on either of two common substitutes for state-centrism. It does not depend on the idea of a global civil society.[32] It does not depend on great events in history as catalyst or motor (the Magna Carta, the French and American Revolutions, the Holocaust, the formation of the United Nations, the collapse of the Soviet Union, religious fundamentalism and terrorism on a global scale). With Amnesty International and Human Rights Watch, my proposal shares a commitment to mobilizing transnational groups of citizens and noncitizens. It mobilizes them as actors in the international system conventionally reduced to the power and politics of states and powerful international organizations. But unlike Amnesty International or Human Rights Watch, the proposal does not depend on international rights regimes in the mold of foreign interventions. It is, instead, initially *localist*: ordinary people engaged on-site, constructing a human rights state in the ways outlined above. This educative model enables persons now enslaved, or persons vulnerable to enslavement, to become participants in the human rights project. It teaches them to insist, against a nation state, that their bodies mark a universally valid right to be free of enslavement and to reject a citizenship that does not protect them from enslavement.

Reconceiving the body as a human rights boundary (like the backpack metaphor) makes individuals responsible, to a degree, for their own human rights participation. It shifts the burden for articulating, defending, and protecting human rights from states and international institutions to inter-subjective exchanges. What I earlier referred to as the *moral territory of the self* emphasizes the authorship of rights more than the recognition or protection of rights. Human rights are what one claims, not simply what one has. Therefore I emphasize human rights advocacy and education more than human rights military intervention.[33] Educating individuals in the politics of self-ownership and moral personhood encourages positive change, however gradual. In the case of slavery, which often stems from ingrained practices and prejudices, reconceiving the body encourages participants to reject traditional or socially sanctioned patterns of enslavement, challenging compliance with hostile environments. This is a long-term solution to the long-term problem of slavery.[34]

Now consider this model in some of the most pressing contexts of slavery today. Of the estimated 29.8 million persons enslaved in the world today, about 72 percent live in Asia. Much slavery in India derives from the traditional practices of hereditary debt bondage.[35] Some derives from human trafficking among Indian states (Walk Free Foundation 2013:23). In Africa, the high risk of enslavement (in countries such as the Democratic Republic of the Congo and Mauritania) reflects "centuries-old patterns of enslavement, often based on colonial conflicts and injustice exacerbated by contemporary armed conflict. Ongoing conflicts, extremes of poverty, high levels of corruption, and the impact of resource exploitation to feed global markets all increase the risk of enslavement in many African countries [where another 17 percent of the world's enslaved population lives]. Child and forced marriages are still tolerated in the context of informal or 'traditional' legal systems in many countries" (ibid., 25).

What does my educative model offer? First, it does not reduce human rights to a matter of a nation state as a sovereign entity. It views hereditary debt bondage as something that state legislation cannot affect—for example, through prohibition—but rather as an issue best addressed through a local cultural reevaluation of the status quo understanding of legal inheritance, that children cannot be obligated by the responsibilities of their parents. Territory is not at issue here.

Second, by replacing territorial inclusiveness with inclusion on the basis of one's body, an educative model approaches child and forced marriages by attacking the informal or traditional legal systems unaffected by formal systems.

Third, by advancing human rights through nonstate-based rights within the state, in the bodies of citizens, locally, an educative model focuses on encouraging possible victims to reject, as natural or unavoidable, their disadvantages that result from corruption, poverty, or armed conflict. (Indeed, as phenomena, corruption, armed conflict, and especially poverty are much larger than slavery and cannot be eradicated by eradicating slavery by itself.) If the state is unable to protect the individual from these scourges, it cannot claim to be legitimate.

Fourth, an educative model encourages nonstate actors in new forms of activism animated by new ways of conceiving human rights bearers and carried by ordinary, nonprivileged, vulnerable people, and supported by nongovernmental organizations as far as possible. It encourages them to regard their very bodies as marking a universally valid right to be free of local resource exploitation to feed global markets.

Fifth, by opposing the quietist idea of rights universally valid because they are otherworldly—that is, by casting human rights as an open-ended, down-to-earth political project—an educative model encourages participants to reject centuries-old patterns of enslavement, based often on colonial conflicts and injustice. The past need not condemn the future, and tradition as such provides no reason for compliance.

To be sure, an educative model is limited above all with respect to issues of generating participation by enslaved persons, by persons vulnerable to enslavement, and by slavers themselves. The model's promise depends on participation, indeed on the continual spread of participation among ever more persons. Participation is transterritorial and counternationalist: because they are mobile, human rights endogenized in the individual's body are transterritorial; and endogenization is counternationalist.[36] Participation follows from human bodies conceived as symbols of a human right to be free of enslavement: bodies so conceived become a kind of cross-border moral flow. The idea of cross-border flows is familiar from other contexts, such as movements of goods, information, and ideas, but also of laborers, migrants, and refugees. By analogy, an educative model envisages moral flow as the investment of individuals with human rights irrespective of their geographic location and national membership status.

Here an educative model runs up against its limits. Moral territories of the human self are participatory spaces, and participatory spaces can be political spaces.[37] The politics of bodily presence is a human rights politics.[38] The individual's body "acquire[s] presence in a broader political process that escapes the boundaries of the formal polity" if that "broadly political process" is the process of the participants (Sassen 2002:23).

But not all persons will regard themselves as human rights worthy. Some will decline to participate in a human rights state. A human rights state is a community of interest rather than one of territory. But persons who, for whatever reason, do not share that interest then do not occupy that human rights–protected space. So while human rights are possible only if they exceed state-based territorialization, they are not possible if they exceed the interest, commitment, or participation of the individual address-ees of human rights. In other words, the individual trumps territorial sover-eignty only if he or she recognizes in him- or herself human rights with a presence beyond a nation state. Social spaces of sharedness, as territories of the self, can offer what geographic territories preclude, but only for partici-pants. Note that the term *participants* refers not only to the enslaved but potentially to the national community that, if not motivated by human rights, might still be motivated for economic reasons. After all, the "cost of ending slavery is just a fraction of the amount that freed slaves will pump into the global economy" (Bales and Choi-Fitzpatrick 2012:196).[39]

But even against this discouraging background, the educative model continues to offer innovative arguments for a politics of self-ownership and personhood. First, the notion of the moral territory of the human self is carried by participants' deep emotions. These emotions are connected to "symbols that represent the group"—what Émile Durkheim calls "sacred objects." *Group* refers to human rights advocates in any particular venue. Any given venue displays site-specific inheritances (child marriage, for example) and site-specific concerns (above all, local forms of poverty). Par-ticipants treat the symbol with human rights–inspired respect first by treat-ing their own body with respect and, by extension, by treating other bodies with respect. They are motivated to find reasons to defend bodies against the "disrespect" of slavers who, as fellow citizens, are not outsiders but rather "renegade insiders" (Collins 2004:49).

Second, this notion is sustained by a kind of ritual—not a single, iso-lated ritual but rather a chain of rituals in the form of a humanistic cult of the human body. A human rights state valorizes the individual with the practical intent of achieving the goals of the human rights project. It con-ceptualizes the individual in terms of the body. It regards the body, a uni-versal feature of the species, as symbolizing the human rights of all members of the species. A ritual chain draws on aspects of the local cultural environment that are human rights friendly, whether religious or legal, political or economic. By *human rights friendly* I mean cultural resources that offer support to individuals in granting themselves human rights. Such addressees-cum-authors of human rights must include the weakest, poorest, and most vulnerable members of society. The ritual chain encourages solidarity through group cohesion. It encourages solidarity through shared recognition of meanings and values relevant to human rights and moral outrage at violations of this cult of the human rights–bearing body.[40]

Third, participants can be motivated through symbols by cultivating human rights–relevant emotions within the group. Participants can be motivated by encouraging a set of beliefs and practices supported by sentiments of the body as sacrosanct. Sustained in these ways, a human rights state depends on a steady thickening and lengthening of a transnational chain of body-centered human rights locations. The chain is built up, person by person, as the number of participants in a human rights state increases. As links in transnational chains, individual human rights carriers constitute a metaphorical human rights citizenship alongside national citizenship. To be sure, metaphorical human rights citizenship will always stand in tension with the nation state that does not recognize human rights.[41] Tension emerges, for example, wherever this deterritorialized understanding of human rights challenges those aspects of the territorial nation state violative of human rights. This understanding teaches citizens to reject a citizenship that does not protect them against enslavement. It teaches them to advocate for a political membership that disallows their enslavement.

Internationalizing Domestic Opposition to Slavery

An educative model of citizenship replaces the traditional "external" jurisdiction tied to geographic space and national membership with "internal" jurisdiction. It endogenizes the bordering function. It transfers the bordering function from the nation state to the individual members of a human rights state. The body becomes its own bordering capability.[42] And it becomes itself an agenda for a human right not to be enslaved. As a moral territory, the body endogenizes the nonnational agenda of human rights. *Endogenization* means that each human link in a transnational chain of human rights locations functions as a human rights border. The links constitute a human rights state, with the human body as human rights boundary. The endogenization of nonnational agendas is quite advanced in the economic sphere, in the form of corporate firms and financial markets, and especially in the new concentrations of power and "legitimacy" that attach to global firms and markets. In other words, this approach connects local opposition to slavery with international opposition; it connects local movements with movements beyond national borders.

To treat the body as a universal symbol of human rights fits with the idea of the addressees of human rights as equally the authors of those rights. People can self-assign human rights only within some kind of field of recognition, but that field could, initially, be no larger than the victims (or potential victims) themselves. Participants in a human rights state then seek to extend that field, potentially internationally. Recognition generates inclusive forms of political community, with norms collectively binding on its members. A human rights state seeks to bind ever more people and institutions to recognition of the body as a symbol of a human right to be free of enslavement, against all factors used to justify enslavement today (including a person's poverty, ethnicity, culture, language, religion, or status of parents as indebted). Recognition of the participants' claims begins with the participants themselves and immediately extends to all other human rights states.

Consider an analogy. For rights that have no territorial basis, consider the right within a community of faith to read that community's most sacred normative text. Take the historical example of the Bible in Europe. Once only ordained clerics had that right, but it was transposed first to confirmed members of the church and second to all who professed appropriate beliefs (to be sure, a transposition that was fought all the way). And along the way, the availability of translations into the vernacular developed as well as the doctrine of the priesthood of all believers. Note that these participants embodied the rights and the limits of those rights.[43] And the right belongs to anyone who belongs to the set of believers. It belongs to the individual by means of his or her claiming, for example: "I take my stand on a right upheld by fellow believers."

A nation state that adopts this perspective, through the pressure of a human rights state, might then regard any domestic antislavery legislation as universal in extent. For example, the Thirteenth Amendment to the United States Constitution, adopted in 1865, reads: "Neither slavery nor involuntary servitude, except as a punishment for crime whereof the party shall have been duly convicted, shall exist within the United States, or any place subject to their jurisdiction." Read from the standpoint of a human rights state, the text means not only that no U.S. citizens can own a slave; its means that no citizen can own another person regardless of that person's location, including outside national territory. It not only means that any economic activity that supports slavery is illegal; it means that American enterprise, including those abroad, cannot engage in any commerce that in any way supports slavery anywhere in the world. It not only forbids any form of enslaved labor; it forbids subcontracting persons or entities associated with coerced labor, and it forbids the purchase of commodities or components produced by enslaved labor. No American company, wherever it is located, may legally profit from slavery. Read in this expansive way, the Thirteenth Amendment binds all American companies. One could identify parallels in other countries that have laws against slavery. But a human rights state goes further than domestic legislation.[44] It regards prohibitions following from the Thirteenth Amendment as prohibitions following from individuals and communities that give themselves their own human rights to be free of enslavement.

As for states that embrace human rights to some extent, and countries with the smallest number of slaves (Iceland, Ireland, United Kingdom, New Zealand, Switzerland, Sweden, Norway, Luxembourg, Finland, and Denmark), slavery mostly takes the form of exploiting vulnerable migrants, "domestic workers in diplomatic households or irregular migrants working in the informal economy" (Walk Free Foundation 2013:30). To target trafficking, a human rights state can draw on a number of national resources. Some are legal. These include the strong rule of law and low levels of corruption; means of identifying and supporting victims; specialized law enforcement units with funds, training, and equipment. Other national resources are organizational. Examples include strong child protection systems; national rapporteurs who heighten accountability; and nongovernmental organizations allowed to operate freely. Some resources are economic, such as significant national budget allocations.

This chapter completes the first of this book's three parts. It introduced the human rights state as a form of political advocacy by means of metaphor. The human rights state is a metaphor for the corresponding nation state, *as if* the nation state embraced human rights as an internal feature (Chapter 1). It imagines human rights as borne by the individual, not by the national territory on which the individual stands (Chapter 2). And it transfers human rights–protective boundaries from nation states to individual bodies (this chapter). Part II changes gears. It examines how a human rights state might be deployed, as a means of persuasion, in contexts quite beyond those examined in Part I.

PART II

The Human Rights State Through Persuasion,
Not Coercion

Chapter 4

———

Teaching Human Rights as a Cognitive Style

Part I developed the metaphor of a human rights state as a means to advancing the project for the free embrace of human rights worldwide. Part II now explores the human rights state as a politics of persuasion not coercion. It surveys three widely divergent venues for advancing the free embrace of human rights by educative, communicative means: in the university curriculum (Chapter 4), in postcommunist Eastern Europe (Chapter 5), and in digital technology (Chapter 6).

This chapter investigates persuasion in the formal setting of higher education. It pursues persuasion as a "cognitive style" that orients norm-guided behavior. Every social order produces norms. Every political community depends on the widespread, dependable observance of norms over time. The various ways in which the individual binds him- or herself to these norms are pervasive aspects of social life. An individual need not be motivated by some conscious, reflected conviction about the value of highly organized social life. Rarely does an individual consciously decide to embrace life in a particular society. He or she need not consciously decide, at least not where the social order is functionally necessary for its members in immediate ways. The social order is functionally necessary for securing an ordered existence, say, and for steady employment, for health care, and for economic life.

Norms need to be generalized throughout a community to bind it. For example, communication requires generalized symbols, languages, vocabularies, and understandings for its very possibility. An increase in symbolic generalizations increases the range of possible communication. Inasmuch as the "situations of ego and alter are never completely identical," the wider the range of generalizations, the greater the possibility of bridging the differences between the respective situations of two or more individuals (Luhmann 1995:327). Bridging some of the differences between two or more people is, of course, one way to describe persuasion by discursive means.

The idea of human rights is a normative idea; it seeks social justice. This chapter examines discursive means to advance human rights thinking. It shows how people may come to bind themselves to the human rights norm. And it focuses on one particular group, college students. The question is how, in the university classroom, students might bind themselves to this norm. I propose one means in particular: by acquiring a "human rights consciousness."

To render this nebulous term concrete and useful in the politics of advancing human rights, I approach "human rights consciousness" as a particular cognitive style. By *cognitive styles* I mean ways of attending to the world. Each style is specialized for one purpose or another. Each has its own criteria for functionality and dysfunction. Consider, for example, the distinct cognitive style of natural science. It approaches the natural world in ways helpful to formulating empirically testable hypotheses about the natural world. Its approach must allow for hypotheses always open to challenge. This approach expects its hypotheses to be revised or discarded with new information or theoretical frameworks.

By contrast, the cognitive style of modern legal systems approaches the social world in terms of changeable, positive laws that remain legal until formally changed. Just how different this cognitive style is from that of natural science is reflected in the fact that many laws, such as constitutional provisions for federalism or the franchise, do not change often (through amendments or judicial interpretation) or easily (constitutions are difficult to amend and judges emphasize continuity with past understandings over breaking with the past through new understandings).

Consider now human rights as a particular cognitive style that can be taught to college students.[1] Teaching contributes to human rights–relevant forms of social justice to the extent that some of these students eventually participate in the human rights project.

One way to approach a human rights cognitive style is to consider a very different kind of style as a foil. For example, compared with a religious style, a human rights style is distinctly more political.[2] By *political* I refer to a range of readily identifiable features. Politics may include prudential considerations of reciprocity among specific participants—as distinguished from the disinterested, generalized love advocated by many religions. Politics is often an instrumental means to ends, such as removing obstacles in the world to some public policy—by contrast to religious faith that regards itself as an end in itself and in part with such intrinsic ends as finding inner peace. Some kinds of politics require the realistic expectation of permanent competition, such that politics more liberal or democratic expects to have its authority challenged on a permanent basis (although authoritarian politics certainly expects no such challenge), whereas most religions in many respects understand their authority to be unchallengeable and doctrinal faith to be forever unassailable. Politics may be orientated on probabilistic and contingent claims about the good life (and allowance that more than one outlook may be plausible or desirable), toward achieving agreement, whereas many a religion aspires to a consensual embrace of a single set of truths revealed not achieved. Some kinds of politics recognize the permanent requirement of a good deal of rational justification (such as prudential reasoning toward a contingent acceptance of authority, or claims about public utility) to create and maintain loyalty—by contrast to religious communities based on devotion to principles such as love and care, acceptance and charity, that are grounded in faith not reason (in the sense of obedience to divine commandment, say). Politics may regard permanent dissensus not just as a permanent feature of the (more liberal, democratic) political landscape but, within limits, as a positive feature, whereas a religion can be more unequivocal, absolute, and final insofar as it expects, at least as an ultimate goal, unanimity in truth, opinion, and purpose. Religions may expect the individual to obey their version of moral law for its own sake, while perhaps no rule in secular politics is so regarded.

To be sure, all cognitive styles exert some pressure in the direction of conformity. Each style tends to bind a person socialized within it. With conviction go emotions, and robust convictions elicit strong emotions. Conviction and emotion alike generate feelings of obligation in the carrier. A political style, like a theological one, often forms part of a larger symbolic system in which the carrier participates to some extent, such as an institutionalized religion or a political party. If a cognitive style is confronted or damaged or challenged, it usually attempts to reestablish itself through reformation or a revised identity or new elites, for example.

To be sure, no style generates a complete consensus among all members. No style produces a one-to-one correspondence between a particular style and a particular moral outlook.[3] Further, in their behavior at any given moment, individuals likely apply several cognitive styles simultaneously. Thus a natural scientist may contemplate the nonscientific, moral, political, or economic upshots of his or her work.[4] To be sure, sometimes a given cognitive style is "chiefly relevant and provides a first answer to the question 'What is it that's going on here?' The answer: an event or deed," an event or deed *described in terms of a particular cognitive style* (Goffman 1974:25).[5] More often, however, styles are multiply present, for example, where different styles, in the same context, do different work: "We waited till the rain stopped"—here we have a naturalistic style—"and then started the game again"—here we have a self-consciously artificial style (ibid.).

My proposal for a human rights style in the context of higher education immediately raises two questions: What is a human rights–relevant cognitive style? And how might a college-level curriculum, interested in social justice, develop such a style among interested students?[6]

What Is a Human Rights–Relevant Cognitive Style?

A cognitive style oriented on human rights seeks, across the most varied social, economic, and cultural conditions, to recognize the individual as someone worthy of human rights. It assumes that, without such generalized recognition within a community and across different communities, human rights are not possible. It shares with a religious style the conviction that the "person as a whole is always intended—in contrast to the estimation of individual merits, capacities, or competence in a profession, in sports, in love" (Luhmann 1995:235). But whereas many moral systems, and certainly systems of faith, automatically attribute value to the person, a human rights style regards attribution as something to be achieved through political action. *To be achieved* means that the universal norm to which human rights aspire is neither natural nor transcendental (in the sense of theology or metaphysics) but rather political.

Further, a human rights style is directed at institutions, such as nation states. It is also directed at cultural beliefs and practices—for example, socially constructed inequalities between men and women with regard to access to education, political participation, or employment. Within institutions and practices, human rights regularly run up against boundaries. The claim to validity made by human rights extends, in actual experience, no further than the limits demarcated by particular institutions and practices, organizations and traditions. Yet precisely as a cognitive style, human rights can affect institutions and beliefs. The political project of advancing the free embrace of human rights requires that the individual's community estimate the individual not worse or lower than the individual estimates him- or herself.

How Might a College-Level Curriculum, Interested in Social Justice, Develop Such a Style Among Interested Students?

As a social institution, what is specific to the college classroom? More than legislatures or citizen action groups, more than agricultural enterprises or corporate boardrooms, more than quality media or popular entertainment, the college classroom is peculiarly dedicated to careful thought, probing analysis, but also to daring imagination. And it is relieved from the politician's heavy obligation to *act*. The college classroom is well situated to provide students with a basis for imagining a better politics for the future— but only if it pursues the major social and political problems and controversies of today.

University instruction is well suited to the fact that human rights are themselves controversial. The very idea of human rights is inherently controversial, certainly from the standpoint of rights conceived as positive law that require institutions of enforcement. Intellectual controversy, at its best, stimulates critical thinking and alternative approaches. And advocates of human rights do well to engage skeptics, such as groups or regimes that dismiss the idea of human rights as such, or their practicability in many parts of the world. Such skeptics can point out that human rights thinking has yet to transform the national sovereignty of any state. They can note that noncompliance with international human rights laws rarely incurs a loss of legitimacy for the offending regime. They can say that neither individuals nor ethnic minorities have strengthened their legal status under the aegis of any human rights declaration. They can show that neither the high adoption rate of human rights treaties, nor a dramatic rise in domestic war crime trials in the past two decades, has challenged the sanctity of nation state sovereignty. They can emphasize that nowhere in the world today is any conception of legitimate national interest articulated in terms of human rights. And they can highlight the chronic lack of agreement across the globe about the very idea of human rights itself, as well as its definition, interpretation, and application, even its history.

Such challenges to the human rights project hardly defeat it. But they certainly provide welcome opportunities for innovation in college-level curricula. Challenges can be taught in ways that directly address their strengths and weaknesses. I propose addressing such challenges by grasping human rights as a particular cognitive style. How? Students begin with the following thought: if a given cognitive style is deeply intertwined with this or that particular way of life, it is more likely to influence its carriers than a cognitive style more or less external to its carriers' way of life. Then students consider the following idea: that which, in liberal polities, appears to many citizens as something universally good may appear in illiberal polities to repress local interests, cultural identities, ways of life, perhaps even local economic interests of weakly situated populations. Students ask themselves: Is the work of human rights the work of making others more like us (we who advocate human rights as a global vision)? Or is the goal of advancing human rights to inculcate habitual behaviors, perhaps encouraged by parents or other significant models, toward habits of caring that ideally "became molded into an altruistic personality" (Monroe 2003:408)?

The cognitive style oriented on human rights that I propose can answer such questions. In working out its features, I presuppose two things: (1) that human rights are social constructions and (2) that they are morally relativist and perspectival. Next I show how human rights, in terms of a cognitive style, might approach (3) the practice of child labor in general and (4) child labor–encouraging aspects of poor agrarian communities in particular.[7] (5) I then specify normative bases of a human rights style. These bases emerge from the following analysis.[8]

First Presupposition: Human Rights Are Social Constructions

I develop my notion of a cognitive style by drawing on Alfred Schutz and Erving Goffman. Schutz distinguishes the "ontological structure of the objects" from the "meaning of our experience" (Schutz 1962:230). The "meaning of our experience" refers to what members of a community share intersubjectively, and in particular what they treat as social reality (ibid.).

Cognitive styles purvey social meanings; they invest observations and experiences with common significance. Viewed as a cognitive style, human rights do not appear as something acultural or as some kind of ontological given. They appear as an artifact of the human mind, as a particular cultural preference. The "humans" of "human rights" appear as evolved animals who invest their experience with the meanings they create in generating the "world of everyday life, the common-sense world" (Schutz 1962:294). That world—the only one in which notions of moral behavior and just communities has any practical consequence—has a "paramount position among the various provinces of reality, since only within it does communication with our fellowmen become possible. But, from the outset, the common-sense world is a sociocultural world. The many questions" about the "intersubjectivity of the symbolic relations originate within it, are determined by it, and find their solution within it" (ibid.).

From a commonsense standpoint, human rights are plausibly deployed in one field and one field only: in the wholly natural world of human beings. As communities, humans socially construct norms for themselves; the human rights project pursues the local social construction of human rights. On this approach, human rights are this-worldly social constructions rather than otherworldly theological or metaphysical absolutes. From a constructionist standpoint, human rights, like all normative claims, can only be something particular, a moral localism—at least initially.

By *moral localism* I mean that human rights claims are valid at first only for the community that embraces them. If in time those claims come to be embraced globally, their validity becomes universal.[9] Moral universality is then a contingent, historical achievement and not in any sense a priori. Human rights cannot be immediately valid for all persons at all times in all places. For social construction, no moral vision can. Claims such as *"All persons* have a right not to be tortured" are no more immediately defensible than propositions like *"All persons* are ends in themselves" or "Jesus died for the sins of *all persons"* or "Capital punishment is cruel for *all persons."*

But moral localism *can* achieve an ever-wider embrace, precisely as a social construction, and in particular as a political project, one that engages local cognitive styles in terms of the human rights project. By *political* in this context I mean not the imposition of a human rights culture on this or that community but rather making the very idea of human rights plausible and compelling to local addressees. The addressees of human rights themselves construe, locally, which social and political arrangements best offer justice to members and outsiders, in public life and in private life.

Political in this context also means interpreting features of the target community, as well as human rights themselves, in the sense of making the human rights idea plausible across differences in cultures, traditions, and economies. Cognitive styles have practical application only through interpretation. Questions of who is authorized to interpret with authority for the group, how best to adjudicate among competing interpretations, and which interpretations to prefer are political. They are political as the authoritative distribution of socially binding meanings and behavior-guiding rules. Consider for example a range of highly patterned behaviors, each guided by a particular cognitive style—each "political" in its own way. Consider behaviors from playing the violin according to a sheet of music or a tradition of technique ("How does one best bow this Bach solo partita?"), to driving a car in accordance with traffic rules some of which are interpretable ("If driving two miles per hour above the posted speed limit is not pursued as a violation, what about ten miles above?"), to practicing a religion ("Why is wine consumed in the Eucharist different from wine consumed in a restaurant?"), to pursuing research in molecular biology ("Does the local scientific community expect a confidence level of 90 percent or 95 percent?"). In reaching an answer in each case, these various styles allow for ranges of interpretations of relevant factors. And each allows for different levels of style-appropriate competence.

Interpretation is also a means of persuasion, for example by advocating aspects of one cognitive style over another. Interpretation that reduces alternatives to the interpreter's standpoint may render its addressees narrow. But interpretation of a different sort broadens the mind. The intellectual broadening at the core of a college education—of a liberal arts education in particular—includes the understanding that a local way of life is not the only possible space for moral intersubjectivity. A student expands his or her intellectual horizons by grasping that the sharing of behavior-guiding norms is possible beyond the parameters of any particular way of life and despite abiding differences among the sharers. The student enlarges his or her world by understanding that persons of different political, cultural, religious, or moral convictions can still interact and sometimes even pursue common projects.[10]

Interpretation facilitates an understanding of human rights that can expose the weaknesses of competing accounts that claim to be absolute and universal in their validity. Like all normative perspectives, human rights are culturally and normatively relative with respect to source, meaning, and practice. To view moral systems as socially constructed is not to deny that society is prior to any individual's experience and understanding. It is to affirm that "whatever an agent seeks to do will be continuously conditioned by natural constraints, and that effective doing will require the exploitation, not the neglect, of this condition" (Goffman 1974:23). It is to affirm that, as perspectival, a human rights style is always already embedded in particular cultural and historical traditions.[11]

From a sociological standpoint, my universal statement that there are no normative universals (but only less-than-universal social constructions) is not self-contradictory. For rule-governed social behavior can begin with cognitive and normative standards immanent to a community's cultures, understandings, and practices, and eventually exceed them as well. In exceeding them, normative behavior neither ceases being situated nor starts being universal. It never ceases being situated because it cannot escape the conditions of collective life, including those that discourage perception that gets beyond parochialism. It is unlikely to achieve moral universalism for the same reason. But even if they are less than universally valid, norms can span disputes and communities within society, and they can span different societies.[12]

Second Presupposition: Human Rights Are Morally Relativist and Perspectival

A cognitive style is perspectival. In Goffman's compelling terms, it "provides a way of describing the event to which it is applied. When the sun comes up, a natural event; when the blind is pulled down in order to avoid what has come up, a guided doing. When a coroner asks the cause of death, he wants an answer phrased in the natural schema of physiology; when he asks the manner of death, he wants a dramatically social answer, one that describes what is quite possibly part of an intent" (Goffman 1974:24–25).

With respect, for example, to the question of whether children should have a human right to be free from labor (and, say, to pursue education instead), students might ask: How might a human rights style best respond to the cultural and regional perspectivalism of this or that definition of *child*? Or definition of *child labor*? Or to competing accounts of what drives child labor? Or to the diversity among claims about the potential harms of child labor?

A human rights style addresses these questions with a kind of "human rights pluralism." It proceeds pluralistically as it navigates the morally relativistic qualities of any given human community. And it proceeds pluralistically as it traverses the sometimes profound differences among various communities. Students learn not to draw self-defeating conclusions from the moral relativism that defines the mundane contexts within which human rights are advocated in theory and advanced in practice. Why should they be defeated? On the one hand, *pluralism* does not mean *anything goes*. It acknowledges that no set of rules of any sort is possible in a cultural and political vacuum. It recognizes that any such set depends, in interpretation as in deployment, on its cultural and political contexts. Hence a human rights style always seeks a kind of "conversation" with local cognitive styles.

On the other hand, a human rights style does not take a black-and-white, absolutist approach. It is open to the possibility that at least some prominent forms of child labor are best understood as mixtures of harm and good: some are harmful under some conditions, and in some cases, while others are harmful under all conditions, in all cases. Students profitably explore various possibilities supported by recent empirical research, as follows.

First, whether a particular form of labor is harmful in some cases may depend on the age of the child—for example, where the negative effects of entering the labor market outweigh the positive effects for children under twelve, say, and the positive/negative relationship becomes reversed between the ages of twelve and fourteen. The negative effects of child labor on schooling are not static; they are amplified the younger the child, and increasingly muted as the child ages. The same can be said of the impact of having been a child laborer on someone's later earnings as an adult: negative before ages twelve to fourteen (lower adult earnings might follow from lower educational achievement) but in some cases positive thereafter (Emerson and Souza 2011:348, 374–375, 367–368). (To be sure, that positive impact may simply reflect poor school quality or limited access to physical capital and technology in preceding years.)

Second, school enrollment in some agrarian contexts is strongly gendered: how an individual child fares may be sex specific. For example, in the areas observed, families tend to enroll their young sons at a higher rate than their young daughters. Even though girls tend to enter school at an earlier age, they spend fewer years enrolled. For them, "enrollment is delayed or canceled because of the direct costs of schooling"; "parental behavior involves the opportunity cost of delaying the girls' marriage" (Cogneau and Jedwab 2012:528).[13] School enrollment in some agrarian contexts is also age sensitive: if fewer boys in the twelve to fifteen age range are enrolled in school, then perhaps because more children are working, or those children who are working are working longer hours (ibid., 529).

Third, some forms of children's economic participation may allow the children to accumulate human capital, with positive consequences for their later life. The older the child, the greater the possibility that he or she accumulates human capital.[14]

Finally, some forms of labor may provide valuable experience to some children without precluding their school attendance. Many children who begin to labor early in life continue with their education (Emerson and Souza 2011:374–375). In these ways, college students work out how a human rights style best responds to these empirical findings with a notion of rights as morally relativist and perspectival.

How Human Rights as Cognitive Style Might Approach Child Labor in General

Not unlike the activist in the field, the student in the classroom is challenged to interpret and apply human rights standards under any number of very different social, political, economic, and cultural circumstances. In the proposed curriculum, students have already seen that a locally effective, because nondogmatic, approach seeks ways to construct an understanding of human rights theory and practice in thoughtful conversation with local cognitive styles. How is that conversation to be configured? For example, is the liberal democratic form of government widely favored in the West more likely than other forms to facilitate the realization of one particular conception of human rights—namely, those conceived by analogy to civil rights for the individual?[15] If so, what is the student to make of the fact that many Islamic, or East Asian, or African cultural communities frame human rights more as economic, social, or cultural rights, and as group rights that sometimes trump individual rights? Western students in particular ask themselves: Does a human rights style necessarily champion individualistic liberal legalism? Should it? Students also ask: Particularly in parts of the developing world, is the human rights project best advanced along more communitarian lines? Students need to consider a range of voices not often heard in the West; for example, a Nigerian scholar (speaking of his country): "Abstract legal rights attributed to individuals will not make sense for most of our people; neither will they be relevant to their consciousness and living conditions. It is necessary to extend the idea of human rights to include collective human rights for corporate social groups such as the family, the lineage, the ethnic group" (Ake 1987:9).

To engage such unfamiliar voices, students might first reassure themselves of the plausibility (also for Westerners) of the notion of collective rights, in some cases at least. They do so by examining some of the more communitarian aspects of Western life—the idea of the welfare state, say, or workplace regulation in line with extra-economic standards of employee health, safety, and welfare. But the analysis should flow in both directions. That is, students might also identify elements of cultural individualism in aspects of positive law—such as an individual's right to contract—or in attitudes influenced by the institutionalized norms of science. One such norm directs a researcher to challenge prevailing theories on the basis of his or her own research.

In this way students come to realize that a human rights style is neither inherently individualistic nor innately communitarian. They ask themselves whether the notion of nondiscrimination on the basis of age (advanced age in particular) offers a starting point to argue for a complementary notion of nondiscrimination on the basis of sex (female sex in particular). In these ways students become more receptive to examples of traditional cultures that honor their elderly members.

Conversation between competing approaches can flow in both directions if students look for possible overlaps between individualistic and communitarian approaches. They could challenge social differences such as sex-based inequalities by appealing to forms of antidiscrimination already at work.[16] On the one hand, the idea of the rights of the elderly might be made more plausible to the student on the basis of cultural practices foreign to his or her own cultural or political community. On the other hand, some of the individual rights highly prized in the West emphasize personal freedom and agency *as well as* the individual's dignity and self-control. Rights so conceived instantiate the idea of an individual's having a say about the political arrangements of his or her community and the idea of having access to those arrangements as a participant. This particular cultural conviction contrasts with Islamic cultures that accord rights to the dead, but also with Buddhist cultures that revere nature and the environment in ways that preclude, or at least qualify, the notion of an individual right to private property.

Could an agency-centered human rights style speak to both the Islamic and Buddhist contexts? Might it do so by supporting the granting of a birth certificate (and not only a death certificate) to the parents of a miscarried fetus, for example? The Western student should ask him- or herself: Could the respective cognitive styles that carry some aspects of some versions of Buddhist or Islamic cultures possibly speak to the agency-centered style widely favored in the West? A traditional right of local cultural communities to the places, practices, and preferences of their ancestors might speak to the Western notion of, say, Native Americans having a right to use otherwise proscribed drugs in traditional religious practices.[17]

With regard to child labor, students should analyze the perspectives taken by major Western NGOs such as Human Rights Watch, Amnesty International, and Freedom House. These NGOs typically focus on violations of formal civil rights and do so to the relative neglect of the material conditions perhaps necessary if some of the various formal rights are to be enjoyed concretely. Human rights as a cognitive style, in critical conversation with local styles in targeted areas, confront local contexts in their economic aspects and not solely in moral terms, let alone in absolutist moral terms. Students examine how economic rights and individual rights are in tension with one another. They might begin with Amartya Sen's argument that, "because development involves much more than mere economic growth, the instrumental contribution of political liberty and civil rights goes much beyond the connection with economic growth. The importance of political and civil rights in guaranteeing economic security and in preventing major disasters is particularly relevant" (Sen 1999b:93).

In tandem with primary and secondary education, economic development may sometimes empower the poor more than any particular political and legal arrangement would—whether more individualistic, as in political liberalism, or more communitarian, as in many parts of the world. In light of a region's poverty, a human rights style might eschew the immediate, blanket eradication of child labor.

It might favor schooling or vocational training together with—rather than in place of—work and, wherever possible, "ensuring the payment of adequate wages to adults so that their children are not forced to work" (Monshipouri 2003:198–199). It could favor safe and healthy working conditions rather than no working conditions. Students ask: Does a human rights style possess an instrumental capacity to generate cultural norms and political support for an entire community's economic welfare and development?

The American college student learns to view a human rights style itself as a product of the modern, secular, rationalist individualism of Enlightenment provenience. But now the student realizes that, to the extent that Enlightenment individualism is not shared in many parts of the world, its distinct merits for conceiving of human rights as analogous in some ways to individual civil rights need not preclude expressions of the human rights idea in terms of group rights and economic rights.

I have argued that teaching human rights as a cognitive style teaches an approach nuanced and morally relativist rather than undifferentiated and absolutist.[18] But I do not mean that a human rights style embraces local styles in all of their parts (to do so defeats the purpose of human rights advocacy, after all). Rather, the student entertaining a human rights style imagines and develops locally plausible forms of the human rights idea. In doing so, he or she provokes—and needs to provoke—local understandings. The student hopes to persuade local interlocutors that those understandings are culturally embedded perceptions, no less than a human rights style is itself a culturally embedded perception; and that perceptions are interpretable, criticizable, malleable, and replaceable. Persuading local interlocutors in this way is one step, among others, in advancing human rights locally, with local participation, toward a local embrace.

Communal Features of Agrarian Economies That Encourage Child Labor

What about perceptions? Toward advancing human rights consciousness in communities driven by powerful imperatives that discourage particular human rights, students examine the local context for perceptions that may motivate local behaviors problematic from a human rights standpoint. To repeat this chapter's refrain: local perceptions are core to the human rights project. Indeed, a cognitive style is itself a way of perceiving, such that styles that differ from each other do so perspectively. *Perception* corresponds to the "organization of what is perceived" (Goffman 1974:26), and *organization* refers to how something is "framed."[19] A human rights style reframes relevant aspects of local beliefs and behaviors in ways more human rights friendly, toward altering perceptions that discourage human rights practice.

Even facts are not perspective free, or at least they require contextualization in terms of meanings, goals, and norms. Consider these facts: in the first decade of the twenty-first century, the International Labour Organization estimated the number of children engaged the world over in one form of labor or another at about 182 million (Emerson and Souza 2011:345). Approximately 150 million children labor in Asia; in many parts of Africa, more than 30 percent of the local children work (Canagarajah and Nielsen 2001:72). Political communities frame such statistics one way or another. Framing begins with the most basic definitions: How is *child* best defined? At what age does childhood end? Cultures and communities tend to treat childhood as a kind of natural state. But in labor-relevant respects, childhood is socially and culturally constructed. Expectably, that construction varies across cultures and communities and local responses to the question "What counts as 'child labor'?" will vary. Just as sites of labor range from household work to family business, from farming to street vending, to wage work in various types of enterprise, so the term *child labor* encompasses a broad range of economic activities, some for cash, others in kind, some with nonwage incentives. Many communities may agree that certain forms of child labor are unconditionally unacceptable, usually on the basis of one or more moral claims, such as notions about an individual's moral worth and dignity, including any form of labor that leads to the child's psychological distress, as well as slavery, indentured servitude, prostitution, use in pornography, or deployment in armed conflict.[20] There is much less agreement on the most prevalent forms of labor, however.

One can imagine just how much disagreement when one considers that girls in many developing countries are more often employed in various forms of "household services" than in any other sector. They perform full-time housework more often than boys (as in the West). Disagreement begins with competing definitions of *household services*. What of activities that are unpaid, such as cooking, taking care of siblings or older persons, or collecting water and firewood? Is the distinction between those household services that discourage or preclude school attendance and those that do not objective—or is that, too, perspectival? What forms of labor, if pursued in tandem with school, will harm the child's ability to learn? What types of labor impact the quality and quantity of what the child learns? How are those forms that impart valuable lessons to the child, and that provide him or her with human capital, to be distinguished from those that do not? For the student and activist alike, these lines of inquiry suggest perspectives that guide a human rights style in its work. Like the activist, the student explores a series of questions that, even when they do not lead to definitive answers, helps a human rights style to position itself initially: at the point at which it takes up its work in any particular community, there ideally to engage local cognitive styles in critical conversation.

How does such engagement operate? Students might explore local factors on which a human rights style could orient itself. To resume the example of previous pages: students could analyze child labor and possible harm to children; dependence on an agricultural economy that fosters child labor; economic strategies of families, strategies fostered by poverty and encouraging child labor; and factors other than poverty that foster child labor.[21]

Child Labor and Possible Harm

How does a human rights style best respond to the most basic definitional issue: What, exactly, is the harm caused by some forms of child labor? What is distinctive about those forms? Students begin by connecting, in initial ways, the local cognitive style to a human rights style. One obvious starting point: the child's health and well-being. Easily imaginable is a human rights style that rejects any labor hazardous to the child's health. In an agricultural context, for example, this could refer to labor that exposed children to pesticides.

No less plausible is a human rights style that draws moral conclusions about various differences between children and adults. A moral conclusion could be drawn from children working in the same conditions as adults. They are no less exposed than adults to workplace dangers yet are "more seriously affected because of their different anatomical, physiological, and psychological characteristics" (Canagarajah and Nielsen 2001:72). In fact, children often labor in conditions more dangerous than those in which adults work, for longer periods and for lower wages. That children endure such conditions is explained in part by the fact that they are far less able to oppose such conditions (for example, by agitating for a right to unionize).[22]

Students should confront the ambiguity in the definition and understanding of child labor. They read scholars who argue that certain forms of labor are not necessarily detrimental to learning per se and are not associated with slower learning (Dumas 2012:775, 790). They study research that suggests that certain forms of labor, at least at certain ages, may actually benefit the child even as it decreases the amount of time and energy the child has for schooling. The child might improve his or her mathematical skills, say, or skills in oral communication (among other forms of human capital), by "selling home-produced goods, food, or crops in the market or services (e.g., making customers pay in buses)" (ibid., 790–791). Some forms of child labor may generate income to cover some schooling costs, including books, transportation to and from school, and lunch outside home.

While no one denies that child labor always poses troubling questions from the standpoint of the child's best interests, empirical research is inconclusive on core questions relevant to the effect of child labor on school attainment, school attendance, school progress, work and wage outcomes in later years, as well as the leisure time necessary to any healthy childhood. Kathleen Beegle, Rajeev Dehejia, and Roberta Gatti (2004) link child labor unambiguously with lower school attendance and achievement. Sudharshan Canagarajah and Helena Nielsen (2001:72) find that "school attendance is forgone in favor of work" and that "learning is inefficient because the children are not allowed to spend time doing their homework or because they are unable to pay proper attention in school because of fatigue."

If in this context poverty and school attendance are always factors, the magnitude of their respective effects remains unclear. What if the magnitude is moderate but not severe? And what is the effect of a primary school within the community? Of passable roads and the costs of transportation? Could the very presence of a primary and passable road significantly increase school attendance? Could it decrease the daily length of child labor?[23] Might something as straightforward as basic repairs to classrooms not useable when it rains have a marked positive effect? A human rights style approaches these questions situationally, according to how relevant empirical questions can be answered in any given case. It does not approach these questions in terms of absolute or universally valid norms.

Dependence on an Agrarian Economy

Individuals can deploy cognitive styles to understand their local environments, whether physical, biological, or social. *Understanding* refers to "activity interpreted by the application of particular rules and inducing fitting actions from the interpreter"; it means "organiz[ing] matter for the interpreter" in that local environment (Goffman 1974:247). Given their particular cognitive style, "individuals fit their actions to this understanding and ordinarily find that the ongoing world supports this fitting" (ibid.).

In the context of child labor, a human rights style might investigate the agrarian economy that, in many parts of Africa and other low-income regions of the world, employs a majority of the workforce. Whether for cash crops or subsistence crops, the agrarian sector engages more child labor than any other sector of the economy (Canagarajah and Nielsen 2001:72). In various ways, local cognitive styles likely reflect the community's dependence on an agrarian economy.[24] And they likely reflect strategies of coping with risk. Economic dependence entails risk along several dimensions: volatility in income due to contingencies in production and price that cannot be predicted, such as pests, droughts, or commodity price falls; inability of informal risk-sharing mechanisms within communities to cope adequately with such contingencies (especially given limited credit and insurance markets); and limited capacity for savings and borrowing that constrains a household's capacity to adjust its income and its capacity to finance basic investments in children's schooling.

We find another example in the lack of economic diversification that leaves local economies, including many in Africa, at the mercy of continuously shifting international prices. In Côte d'Ivoire, the world's top producer of cocoa, "more than 25% of the population produces cocoa and is directly affected by fluctuations in the price of this commodity. The rest of the population is also indirectly concerned, through market and nonmarket linkages" (Cogneau and Jedwab 2012:531).

Significant features of the local context shape local cognitive styles relevant to perspectives on child labor. In the current example: the fact that dependence entails chronic economic vulnerability that directly impacts farmers' capacity to finance their children's schooling. Further, if the price of that all-important crop falls, the expected returns on the investment that education represents fall accordingly. Insofar as child labor discourages school attendance—in poor harvest years, a reduction in demand frees up time for attending school—education within an undiversified economy built around a crop that confers little human capital is more likely a strategy to escape that economy than an investment in it (ibid., 525).

What kind of cognitive style emerges from such anxious calculations? This is something students need to puzzle out. For example, they might consider how dependence on an agrarian economy encourages a sexually biased cognitive style. Wherever investments in human capital are pro-cyclical, with tight liquidity constraints, investment in health care and education typically is biased against young girls (ibid., 532).

Economic Strategies Fostered by Poverty

I have emphasized that all cognitive styles are perspectival. But perspectivalism —and the moral relativism it entails—does not imply the moral equivalence of all perspectives. It implies a certain humility. By urging that each perspective forgo regarding itself as a kind of "unmarked marker" that measures other styles against itself as if against something whose moral status were somehow self-evident, perspectivalism urges the college student (no less than the activist) not to frame his or her conception of human rights as a moral universalism over against the various moral particularisms of various local traditions. The critical and informed quality of the engagement with local cognitive styles depends on a human rights style capable of critical self-reflection about its own historical and cultural embeddedness, its own particularity.

So what does a human rights style need to learn about factors that encourage child labor and how such factors feed into local cognitive styles supportive of child labor? A style might be shaped by its carriers' need to strategize in a precarious economy or, in agrarian economies, to adjust child labor to seasonal demands. It could argue in terms of the perceived advantages of child labor. Child labor can be cost-effective because children are paid so poorly (if at all). Children cannot compete with adults in terms of productivity or quality of product, and they possess no irreplaceable skills, but their general pliability and low resistance to the conditions of labor make them attractive to employers: "Children are less aware of their rights, less troublesome, more willing to take orders and to do monotonous work without complaining, more trustworthy, less likely to steal, and less likely to be absent from work" (Canagarajah and Nielsen 2001:74). Such are the strategies of poverty.

Further, child labor as an element in strategies of managing the household budget, especially in households living close to subsistence, can foster local cognitive styles characterized accordingly. By augmenting household income, for example, child labor may reduce the risk that a household might fail to meet even a subsistence level of consumption given a poor harvest, say—or exogenous price fluctuations, or adult job loss. Child labor can do some of the work in household enterprises and even replace some of that labor or replace household labor, in this way freeing up adults to work elsewhere. College students learn a great deal about the challenges confronting a human rights style by tracing out the lines of strategizing that likely inform local cognitive styles in significant and enduring ways.

Factors Other Than Poverty That Foster Child Labor

Even in poor communities, a local cognitive style that encourages child labor is affected by factors quite aside from poverty. One factor is household composition, along various dimensions. One of those dimensions is sex.[25] Where the ratio of girls to boys is high, for example, boys tend to work fewer hours.[26] A significant proportion of laboring girls labor in the household rather than in the market (Emerson and Souza 2011:352). In straitened circumstances, one strategy of household management is to substitute the mother's household labor with that of female children so that the mother can then work outside the house. Correspondingly, the "presence of more females in the 15–59 age group decreases child labor and increases school attendance" (Canagarajah and Nielsen 2001:84). A local cognitive style is shaped, for males as well as females, by such gendered calculations and experiences.

Local cognitive styles are influenced by the presence of siblings, another dimension of household composition. If a child has older siblings—and the more he or she has—the less likely he or she will labor and more likely attend school.[27] If siblings are integrated into the workforce, the child is less likely to work (Canagarajah and Nielsen 2001:77). But if children ages six and younger are present in the household, the child is more likely than otherwise to be engaged in household work.[28] If persons sixty and older are present, the child is more likely to work and less likely to attend school.[29] In some cases the dimension of sex intersects with that of sibling: the more siblings between seven and seventeen years of age a girl has, for example, the less likely she is to work and the more likely she is to attend school.[30] Such factors cannot but impress themselves, one way or another, on local cognitive styles.

Cultural traditions of child labor and education are also major factors, in addition to poverty, that mark local cognitive styles that foster child labor. For example, ethnicity, understood as a cultural phenomenon, likely plays a role; children of one ethnicity are more likely to be involved in labor than children of another.[31] The same may be said of religious affiliation. In Côte d'Ivoire, for example, rural Muslims and adherents of traditional faiths are more likely than Christians to engage in child labor; children from Christian households are more likely to attend school.[32] In Ghana,

> children from Protestant households are much more likely to attend school than those who practice traditional religion; in between are Catholics, other Christians, and Muslims. In rural areas, Protestants have a probability 22 percentage points higher of attending school than those who practice a traditional religion, whereas in urban areas, the similar number is 9 percentage points. In rural areas, Protestants seem to be most likely to use child labor, whereas in urban areas those who practice traditional religion are most likely to use child labor, although the differences are only a couple of percentage points and are not always significant. (Canagarajah and Nielsen 2001:86)

Rather than focus on "religious consciousness," a human rights style engages the consequences for child labor of membership in this or that community of faith and then explores possible explanations of specific correlations between denomination and patterns of school attendance.

Human Rights Cognitive Style Furthers
a Kind of "Groupness"

I advocate a human rights style that "thinks" both with and against local cognitive styles in the venues where it is deployed. It rejects all forms of child labor that have wholly negative consequences for children, such as prostitution and armed warfare. But it does not advocate a complete ban on all forms of child labor, or the blanket sanctioning of all countries that allow the practice, or Western foreign policy interventions seeking to eradicate all forms of child labor in developing countries.[33] It pursues instead a locally sensitive search for plausible points of resonance between a human rights style and aspects of local cognitive styles. But it pursues points of resonance only to the extent that local styles offer potential for the human rights idea. Tensions between targeted local styles and a particular human rights style are not tensions that necessarily defeat the project that promotes a free embrace of human rights. The project has prospects if it can encourage forms of child labor that are relatively positive for children. And it has prospects if it can discourage negative forms.

This "both/and" approach fights child labor wherever child labor threatens children's health, welfare, and overall education. It does not assume that solely a childhood free of labor is a worthy childhood. It recognizes that, for poor households, approaches that ban all child labor cannot be viable in the short run (even if a viable aspiration in the long term). Forms of child labor may be morally acceptable if they neither degrade the child nor hinder his or her physical, intellectual, or social development.

This perspective is neither new nor particularly radical. Instruments such as the International Labour Organization's Minimum Age Convention[34] of 1973 defend it. The convention stipulates: "National laws or regulations may permit the employment or work of persons 13 to 15 years of age on light work which is (a) not likely to be harmful to their health or development; and (b) not such as to prejudice their attendance at school . . . or their capacity to benefit from the instruction received."[35]

The normative basis of a human rights style is moral. It is also, in part, economic—even though eliminating poverty cannot, by itself, eradicate child labor. Eliminating poverty would certainly require substantial subsidies to a very significant proportion of children who labor. Subsidies of this sort are not only economic calculations but political commitments as well, generated in reaction to adverse economic incentives. Daily or weekly income subsidies, food-for-school programs, stipends for completing a grade, or stipends conditional on school attendance can reduce poverty and provide additional incentives (such as adjusting the costs of school and transportation to and from school) for households to choose school attendance over child labor.

Expectably there are no straightforward solutions. Research indicates that "sectoral interventions aimed at boosting product demand or expanding production by lowering costs, for example by affecting import or export tariffs or through targeted aid, might have unwanted effects on child labor" (Manacorda and Rosati 2011:773). It offers "evidence that the incidence of child work increases as child intensive sectors expand." Consequently, "sectoral policies aimed at limiting the spread of child intensive industries or policies that promote the adoption of technologies that are substitutes for children in child intensive industries" might "reduce the incidence of child labor" yet leave households "worse off at the same time" (ibid.).

A human rights style finds further support in "human rights pluralism." This is the idea that there is always more than one plausible conception of human rights. As long as any one conception—in thoughtful, critical conversation with local cognitive styles—advances the embrace and practice of human rights and can do so locally *for local reasons*, human rights as a cognitive style can spread in practice regardless of differences among various conceptions of, or theories about, human rights. This approach accommodates competing conceptions and theories, and differences among them need not defeat the deployment of any particular account.

With respect to child labor in particular, a human rights style can pursue a two-track approach. One track acknowledges that poverty is the single most significant reason why some children are working instead of attending school. It focuses on ways of maximizing school attendance by addressing poverty through insurance or safety nets, such as protecting against negative income shocks. This track promotes improved access to credit, given that households with physical assets such as land or business "use less child labor than other households do" and that "households can sell the assets instead of withdrawing children from work if they experience a sudden drop in income" (Canagarajah and Nielsen 2001:87).

A second track does not advocate the immediate and wholesale elimination of child labor. It recognizes local economic incentives. It promotes legislation that does not require standard school attendance in all cases, so that subsistence households would not be imperiled by a poor harvest, for example. It allows flexibility for deploying child labor in such circumstances, at least temporarily. For affected households, subsidies, taxes, or consumer boycotts might not imperil the household economically the way a strict prohibition of all child labor or an inflexible compulsory schooling policy might.[36] In some cases this track combines school and farm work—for example, by fitting school calendars to an agrarian economy's periods of harvest and periods of slack.[37]

As a kind of risk management for subsistence-level households, a human rights style attempts a trade-off between potential harms of child labor and potential benefits. On the one hand, child labor is harmful if it significantly impacts the child's health, welfare, and dignity, or the quality and quantity of a child's education. On the other hand, labor may benefit a child in the sense of vocational training or the acquisition of other workplace-related experience, skills, strategies, and human capital.[38] Labor could provide an economic means to education otherwise unavailable, and education often offers a means to a better childhood and adolescence.[39]

A human rights style aspires to what may always remain impossible: a universally valid normative basis.[40] It seeks that basis as an element of solidarity, what I will call "groupness," a kind of solidarity necessary for collective political action.[41] A human rights style does not offer group membership along dimensions of race, language, or national origin. It offers a cognitive repertoire deployable as a collective act of political and social self-determination. The groupness that a human rights style constructs is not some essential group identity. A cognitive style implies no essence of the individual carrier or group of carriers.

A human rights style is not an identity, in contrast to the individual's experience of belonging to a concrete group or to an abstract category (racial, national, ethnic, social class, tradition, and so forth). Unlike a human rights style, identity in this sense is publicly represented in narratives of some sort. It is often manipulated by political entrepreneurs who, for certain purposes, would persuade certain persons that they are fundamentally identical with each other in important respects. Such respects could be almost anything, from interests, grievances, conceptions of historical fate, or legitimate claims to currently unrecognized rights.

Rather, the groupness sought by a human rights style is motivated by moral values. These values derive from a sense of self in relation to others. They do not depend on the support or approval of outsiders. They are integrated into the individual's sense of self, potentially through the conversation between a human rights style and local styles. A human rights style constructs the individual human self in a social or group context where "the other" enters into or informs the individual's moral self-understanding.

Groupness of this sort differs from groupness as the "formalized, codified, objectified systems of categorization developed by powerful, authoritative institutions," above all, the contemporary nation state as the primary agent of the individual's social and political identification (Brubaker and Cooper 2000:15). That state is a "powerful 'identifier' not because it can create 'identities' in the strong sense—in general, it cannot—but because it has the material and symbolic resources to impose the categories, classificatory schemes, and modes of social counting and accounting with which bureaucrats, judges, teachers, and doctors must work and to which non-state actors must refer" (ibid., 16). By contrast, a human rights style is no product of the nation state's doings, let alone a political entrepreneur's manipulations. It is not some kind of implicit or tacit groupness. It is an explicitly articulated groupness. This is groupness as an active process performed by its participants as a matter of collective self-representation and self-understanding.

The groupness of a human rights cognitive style, shared, for example, by members of a metaphorical human rights state, does not require the "emotionally laden sense of belonging to a distinctive, bounded group, involving both a felt solidarity or oneness with fellow group members and a felt difference from or even antipathy to specified outsiders" (ibid., 19). By rejecting the nation state's exclusionary logic, groupness of this kind offers an alternative to the nation state's territory-based authority. Because of its inclusionary logic, groupness is a political particularism (the local sources of human rights) that aspires to political universalism (a validity of universal extent). A local human rights initiative can spread across borders and among different localities, each advocating its own conception of a human rights style. A parochial groupness, as a widely participatory, nonexclusionary groupness, could become a cosmopolitan movement.

The notion of a human rights state orients the student as he or she moves between local cognitive styles—with all their particularities—and a human rights style, which aspires to the widest possible embrace. The student can imagine local human rights advocates in terms of their own human rights state as a basis for their advocacy vis-à-vis their nation state. Those advocates might construct a human rights state as they come to realize what they share with other members of their community in terms of local problems, kindred struggles, and similar needs requiring local solutions. If local struggles become inflected with goals that aspire to universal validity and embrace, as they do for the participants in a human rights state, then local struggles also remain deeply embedded in their local context and history.

Teaching human rights as a cognitive style leaves a number of questions open, questions best answered on-site and in light of particular circumstances. Where does the authority of local cognitive styles stop? In what cases might the ideals and practices of human rights best be served by working with the local community to minimize the local community's objections to the content human rights—even when local preferences seem, from a human rights perspective, incompatible? Under what circumstances, with respect to which issues, might they justifiably trump a human rights style? To what extent can human rights accept local cognitive styles that compromise human rights?

In addition to responding to these questions, students need to consider what guidance is best provided by general principles. For example, a human rights style might follow two principles to determine when it must oppose the majority wishes of the local community. It would follow a principle of prevention: the community and family are not to allow child labor to destroy the child's eventual participation in debates about and decisions concerning competing conceptions of what is best for the child and best for his or her community. And it would follow a second principle of prevention: preventing child labor from excluding the child "from an education adequate to participating," later, as an adult, in the "political processes that structure choice among good lives" (Burtt 1994:59–60).

To be sure, a human rights style and the local cognitive style may well differ on what constitutes the child's educational interests. But in most cases a human rights style and local cognitive styles likely share a concern with basic skills such as reading and writing. Few parents are likely to reject education for their child because they reject the value of the child's intellectual growth and maturation.

From a human rights standpoint, schooling usually appears as a question of the child's right to self-determination and a self-determined life. Still, students would do well to consider a family that seeks, through child labor (together with parental labor), to provide itself with the economic resources necessary to survive in a subsistence economy. In this case, some parents may view schooling as a threat to the family's economic survival.

To be sure, in seeking to provide "children with the sense of the very different lives that could be theirs" (Ackerman 1980:139), the college student deploying cognitive styles should be careful not to impose on local communities the liberal assumption that a "marketplace of ideas" best serves the end of individual autonomy. At the same time, the student will reject local cognitive styles not open to examination and debate, especially styles open to forms of child labor that "deprive children of the opportunity to be informed, educated citizens," or deprive them of fundamental skills such as basic literacy, or involve "physical harm, abuse, or maltreatment" (Burtt 1994:68).

I turn now from one context of persuasion to another. I turn from formal education in the democratic West to informal, political education in the newly democratizing countries of Eastern Europe. The human rights state contributes to both, but in different ways.

Chapter 5

Developing Human Rights Commitment in Post-Authoritarian Societies

Chapter 4 explores ways in which Western youth at university might deploy human rights thinking as a cognitive style. The current chapter turns to a very different venue of deployment. It discusses citizens of newly democratizing communities interested in transforming widespread political resignation into a domestic human rights commitment. It focuses on Central and Eastern European countries as well as Russia for case studies as particular examples of post-authoritarian societies.[1]

For more than two decades now, Central and Eastern European countries, as well as Russia, have been transitioning from authoritarian pasts to somewhat more liberal forms of social and political organization.[2] I ask: how does their East bloc legacy impact prospects for advancing human rights in each of these countries by means of civic education and a developing civil society (by which I mean a sphere of social organization positioned between the state and the economy)? To begin to answer this question, I first define three key terms. How can one *generalize* across such different cases? What does *civil society* mean in these cases? And how can *civic education* in this context transform communities?

Regarding the first question, on generalizing across very different cases: While some analytic purposes are best served by distinguishing among the various countries, I identify across countries several important common features of the experience of transitioning from authoritarian to more liberal polities. Any generalization is problematic. Generalization treats diverse countries in ways at once vague and totalizing; it draws on them selectively as illustrative examples; it does not specify each country with respect to its particular institutional context and history; it does not treat the influence of its particular mode of exit from communism; it does not treat of each country's particular postcommunist international relations (for example, whether it joined the European Union). As a group, these twenty-four countries do not constitute a distinctive set of cases. They vary widely among each other along various dimensions, including their current forms of society and citizenship and their respective histories before and after 1989. And as a matter of practice, efforts to advance human rights need to be context specific because they are deeply influenced by local contexts.

But generalization aids both understanding and human rights practice by identifying characteristics sufficiently shared by a set of countries to highlight historical patterns and possible future trends. Members of this group certainly display a shared heritage: common phenomena that characterize several of the core challenges faced by the human rights project as it confronts the shared legacy of twentieth-century communism. By *legacy* I mean path dependence in the sense of beliefs and institutions inherited from the past that, in their continuity with the present, constrain and codetermine the space available for potential change in targeted directions.[3]

Regarding the second question, on the meaning of civil society: I examine legacy and change in the context of civic education, primarily as provided by schools. In most countries, schools have long educated for civic membership. One form of membership, conducive to a free embrace of the human rights idea, involves active participation in civil society. Participation here refers to citizen-to-citizen relations distinct in nature from the citizen-state relationship. Historical legacy, among other factors, discourages civic participation in Eastern Europe. Some of the people who lived through the communist era today regard that system with conflicted emotions. They view it as politically oppressive and economically weak but also as a system with features that functioned well and, to that extent at least, was legitimate. This legitimacy was "attained by trading political democracy for an egalitarian social welfare system and by the regime's tacitly tolerating the existence of a 'second society,'" that is, private niches and cliques (Illner 1996:163). Some "social groups and strata profited from such conditions and were, for quite a long time, interested in maintaining them" (ibid.). While certainly not wishing to resuscitate the socialist state, today they are likely to have high expectations for social welfare and social services.

Though the communist system is often remembered for its repressive nature, many people fondly remember the social welfare aspects of that system (such as promises of full employment, free health care, inexpensive housing, and education). Indeed, civic educators often cite nostalgia for the control and social welfare of the former state as a key obstacle to the creation of civil society in Poland. The protective side of communism has caused some Poles to continue to view the state as a caretaker. Such an opinion of the role of the national government inhibits citizens' adoption of active and participatory stances that are essential for the type of liberal democracy that Poland has outlined in its constitution (Wojcik 2010:397).

In this way, among others, historical legacy influences current efforts to develop greater civic participation. In part the legacy is cohort related. For example, "older people display more of the expectations and value commitments inculcated during the communist era, and they also constitute a relatively disadvantaged group in transition economies" (Evans 2006:263). Civic participation sufficient to contribute meaningfully to a local embrace of human rights, in the face of such legacies, requires a robust civil society. I define civil society as the social, legal, and political contexts for such participation. The term *civil society* already has something of a history in Eastern Europe.

The notion of civil society played a limited role among domestic opponents of some authoritarian regimes. According to Elisabeth Buk-Berge (2006:540), the "actual term did not come into common usage until 1980, but an idea of it evolved during the 1970s, when the expressions 'independent cultures,' 'parallel structures' and 'the independent society' were introduced. The term 'civil society' was used most in Poland and, to a lesser degree, in Hungary and Czechoslovakia. Common to the democratic opposition in those countries was the understanding that civil society was an antipode to the communist state."[4]

Regarding the third question, on the transformative capacity of civic education: To seek social transformation through civic education is to attempt social change through the practical consequences of ideas for the behavior of people who hold them. Education so understood makes significant political claims, above all, that social change is best pursued through persuasion, not coercion. It implies several things: that schools themselves can be part of the transition away from authoritarianism;[5] that schools can affect the community to some extent and be affected by it; that policies of education both reflect and condition the political culture that generated them. Further, education in a broad sense extends beyond the institutional format of education along the various stages beginning with children aged three to seven and ending with youth between fifteen and nineteen years of age; it extends beyond formal settings. Other spaces for education include secondary group associations such as labor, church, or trade organizations. Other spaces include nongovernmental advocacy groups, collective political mobilization, and adult civic education. Finally, civic education toward political socialization and the transmission of values is possible beyond classrooms. It is possible in the "peer group, the mass media, religious institutions" (Slomczynski and Shabad 1998:753). And it is quite possible in the family. Indeed, "family and peers provide the strongest learning relationships and the most effective community for citizenship learning"—for example, in the form of peer-led education for citizenship, or through the involvement in schools of politically active parents (Hoskins, Janmaat, and Villalba 2012:442).

My answers to these three questions anticipate my proposal toward advancing human rights by overcoming authoritarian legacies. I propose the local development of a human rights consciousness, in part by means of citizen-to-citizen relations. I refer to relations as they became possible after 1989 with the introduction of significant freedom from state control; as they derive from pluralism and tolerance; as they develop out of voluntary associations and social movements.[6] In part I would develop human rights consciousness by encouraging independent, critical thinking by stressing alternatives to the centralized-state legacy of uniformity in curricula, textbooks, and teaching methods.

Developing human rights consciousness in this way confronts three challenges posed by the legacy of twentieth-century communism: associational life reduced to niche or clique; lack of trust; and discouragement of individual personhood. I meet these challenges through a new approach to civic education, what I call *cognitive style*. In several steps I address these challenges, emphasizing the importance of path dependence for the success of civic education driven by a human rights cognitive style. Rather than focusing on variations among the various countries, I analyze the role of several institutions in developing potential for a human rights culture. I do so (1) by developing an approach to human rights advocacy by building on the notion of cognitive style introduced in the Chapter 4; (2) by situating that notion in the context of civic education and (3) by considering forms of civic education toward encouraging active civic participation. (4) I sketch three models that deploy this approach in diverse educational settings in liberalizing communities today, showing that (5) a cognitive style can fold human rights into civic participation.

Before proceeding with the analysis, I should note that the education I have in mind here differs from the kind I examine in Chapter 4. Here I intend a human rights cognitive style that advances liberalizing education in John Dewey's (1966) sense of a "pedagogy of democracy." That pedagogy develops capacities for civic participation. To be sure, democracy is not cosmopolitan and it can be narrowly nationalistic. It cannot be globally inclusive, like human rights; it is inherently exclusive, as in proffering voting rights for citizens but not for noncitizens. (Thus in Chapter 8 I argue for a human right not to democracy but to the rule of law. Even as I draw upon liberal democracies as one possible model for transitional democracies, I do not assume some faultless Western liberal template for the rest of the world.) Moreover, citizen education pursues one form of socialization and human rights education pursues another. Democratic education is based on the citizen; human rights education, on the individual regardless of membership in any particular political community. Legitimacy in the democratic project refers to the will of the majority of a particular people, within the territorially delimited nation state. In the human rights project, legitimacy refers to standards not tied to any particular state. Often enough, such standards directly challenge some national norms, preferences, understandings, and priorities. Human rights education pursues values regardless of—even against—national boundaries, identities, and commitments.

Democratic education may well champion certain values that are distinctly anti-cosmopolitan. First, it might support the value of a settled community, with a putative right to preserve a way of life, hence also a right to reject would-be immigrants. By contrast, human rights education aspires to breaking down barriers to immigration. Second, citizen education is well situated if situated within a nation state. After all, citizenship today can only be citizenship within a particular state. By contrast, human rights education seeks to exceed the national setting, first of all by advocating some rights—namely, human rights—not of national origin or limit. This aspiration harnesses the metaphorical human rights state, with its metaphorical citizenship, as a practical means.

Cognitive Styles

Education is only one of many means to address the specific challenges that an authoritarian legacy poses to the human rights project. Civic education in particular bears no necessary relationship to a human rights–driven curriculum. But civic education remains particularly promising[7] in generating receptivity to the idea of human rights.[8] It can affect communities significantly—in decision making, in social responsibility, in conflict resolution—and effect political change specifically by reframing relevant standpoints.[9] Education is a prominent venue for reframing. I urge human rights advocates to regard this or that particular frame as a particular cognitive style, which I define below. By constructing human rights consciousness as a cognitive style, my focus on relevant phenomena is sharper than competing conceptions of human rights, which suffer from a certain fuzziness, whether as "belief" (a feeling of certainty in the truth of a claim), "worldview" (a comprehensive, normative way of regarding social and political life), "morality" (a system for the normative evaluation of behavior), or "ideology" (systematically distorted communication).[10]

Before mapping the deployment of cognitive style, I define its meaning. As I sought to show in Chapter 4, cognitive styles are ways of attending to the world. Each is specialized for some purpose or another; each has its own criteria for determining how well it functions and whether it achieves its goals. But none is a homogenizing groupthink that precludes individual perspective; each allows for ranges of interpretations. I use the term *style* to mark designed, recurring patterns that orient perceptual and intellectual activity and inform a way of doing something. This particular way of doing something becomes typical of an individual as a member of a group that shares this style (no matter how small or fragmented the group).

As for a human rights cognitive style in particular, it approaches human rights with respect to the consciousness that motivates someone to embrace human rights and that orients that embrace in practical ways.[11] I propose deploying it in classrooms as a pluralistic, anti-authoritarian alternative to a legacy of systematic ideological indoctrination controlled by state power in "schools, the mass media, the military, companies and institutions, art production" (Pastuović 1992:410). I propose it as an alternative to communist-era conceptions of monistic "socialist pedagogy" that promoted what authoritarian systems called the "comprehensively developed personality" (ibid., 411). I propose it as an alternative to a "political educational goal aiming at the political homogenization of the population based on communist ideology" (ibid).

Above all, however, I propose a human rights style with an eye more to the future than to the past. After all, the "fact that education increases all forms of participation, many of which are deeply apolitical," underscores the fact that pupils and students of any age are not simple-minded or uncritical receptacles of the information purveyed (Glaeser, Ponzetto, and Shleifer 2007:85).[12]

A human rights cognitive style is oriented to both local circumstances and cosmopolitan goals. On the other hand, human rights are cosmopolitan: they aspire to global embrace and universal validity. Cosmopolitanism in its strongest form seeks to be free of local, domestic, and national convictions, prejudices, commitments, and other attachments. Yet human rights have their greatest practical purchase precisely at the local level: to be effective, they need to be effective locally, in terms that resonate locally.[13] They must always work with, and adapt to, local circumstances.[14] Hence the importance of identifying the local *habitus* in its distinctiveness.[15] Activists need to understand why the local population sees the world the way it does. And they need to consider how aspects of one *habitus* might be exchanged for those of another, toward a *habitus* more human rights friendly.

A human rights cognitive style pursues cosmopolitanism in just this sense: adaptation of cosmopolitan aspirations to particular contexts and venues.[16] *In its local orientation*, then, it shifts education away from an overriding concern with the sovereign state; away from traditional preoccupations with citizenship; away from state-based goals of fostering *national* citizens. It focuses on membership of a different kind, in a human rights state, toward changing membership in the nation state to include an embrace of human rights. This effort is cosmopolitan in another sense as well. Each human rights state aims to transform the corresponding nation state and, in bringing about human rights–friendly domestic change there, aspires to an eventual global community in which individuals everywhere become human rights bearers.[17]

In its cosmopolitan orientation, it loosens the tight territorial focus that characterizes modern nation state citizenship. It loosens that focus toward a citizenship oriented more on human rights. *Citizenship oriented more on human rights* means legal membership in which human rights are an internal feature of national belonging rather than something external and in tension with it.

Changing Behavior by Changing Ideas

A human rights cognitive style works on developing civic education toward civic participation. The style will be more effective with some members of the community than others, sometimes in expectable ways. For example, it will be more effective among persons with higher levels of education. Indeed, "highly educated citizens in more repressive countries are more likely to hold a critical view of their country's human rights conditions" (Carlson and Listhaug 2007:467). And a human rights style will be more effective among persons better integrated into their local networks and among persons "more active in other secondary groups and associations" (Finkel 2002:999).[18]

A human rights cognitive style differs markedly from competing approaches.[19] It grounds human rights in a basic epistemic position. By *epistemic position* I mean an "ideational" approach: it assumes that the individual's beliefs and behavior are determined in part by the individual's ideas about his or her political community. Ideas are not the only things that matter in doing human rights politics, of course; my approach examines this particular factor among others and seeks out ways of deploying it effectively. Other factors relevant to increasing, say, the individual's civic participation in light of an authoritarian legacy that discouraged or precluded participation include a person's occupational status, education, and sex (among other variables of social stratification); the nature of political discussion (open or closed); relationship to the relevant political community (rooted or transient); and quality of the local media (high or low). The individual's skills and knowledge are also relevant to civic participation, such that a lack of knowledge affects the "quality of the political choices made"; for example, "uninformed citizens tend to base their decisions on the personal and social characteristics of political leaders rather than on the content of party programs. Knowledge has also been associated with wider horizons and a stronger engagement with societal issues" (Hoskins, Janmaat, and Villalba 2012:423). Below I show how a human rights cognitive style, in developing the individual's skills and knowledge, might contribute to civic education that encourages civic participation with respect to human rights goals.

Delivering the Model to Its Addressees

How does the proposed cognitive style effectively deliver human rights consciousness, or human rights thinking, to its addressees? It does so by developing that consciousness and thinking locally and in several different ways. *Developing consciousness locally* means regarding human rights as socially constructed and regarding members of one's community as potential co-constructors. To view human rights in this way—as socially constructed—is to assert that a human rights style is always already embedded in particular cultural and historical traditions, locally.[20] Upshot: local actors are core to the human rights project, which proceeds locally even as it aspires to an ultimately global reach. Consider the local approach along three dimensions.

First, because human rights are socially constructed, so is a human rights cognitive style; both are relative not absolute, perspectival not "objective." To say that any cognitive style is perspectival is to say that, to some extent, perception corresponds to how the perceived has been cognitively framed by the perceiver. Thus earlier I spoke of pursuing political change specifically by reframing relevant standpoints.

Second, a cognitive style is shareable because it springs from ways of life shared within a community and sometimes across communities. A human rights cognitive style is not something given universally, metaphysically or theologically. In each case of deployment and in each community of deployment, it is constructed by members of particular communities at particular times, and concerns common experiences, common problems, common goals.

Third, a cognitive approach construes the individual not simply as a bearer of rights but also as an empowered social actor with agency and responsibility to construct rights. It outfits the individual with social and interpersonal competencies relevant to civic participation. On the one hand, by de-emphasizing collective and corporate society, national heritage, and the exclusive sovereignty and authority of a nation state, a human rights style teaches the individual to regard these phenomena as available for critique in the public sphere and as plausible targets of reform. (Other targets include subnational institutions—from the family, to the religious community, to schooling.) On the other hand, this individualistic emphasis of a human rights cognitive style reflects my emphasis on individual human rights in distinction to group rights or socioeconomic rights. While individual rights in a liberalizing society must be balanced with social responsibilities, my proposal shifts that balance more toward the individual.[21] Once I make the model sufficiently plausible at the level of the individual, I can adjust it in ways appropriate for groups as well as for economic dimensions of securing human rights.

Human Rights Cognitive Style via Civic Education

Schools across diverse political regimes promote the teaching of social cooperation. A "primary aim of education is socialization—teaching people how to interact successfully and productively with others" such that "schooling lowers the costs of social interactions more generally"; "indoctrination about political participation" constitutes a major component (Glaeser, Ponzetto, and Shleifer 2007:82). In particular, every political community today to some extent utilizes education to legitimize its social order. Every community seeks to inspire in individual members some degree of identity with the nation and to assimilate individuals into that identity. One form of education is childhood socialization. It can determine the individual to such an extent that the displacement of one set of learned attitudes with another sometimes is possible only through the natural replacement of an older generation by a younger one.[22] Other forms of education target adults, who in any case must constantly relearn what childhood socialization no longer provides—means of coping with changing social, political, and economic circumstances.[23] Civic curricula may be present in all of these various forms.

In their more traditional forms, whether in liberal or authoritarian communities, civic curricula emphasize duties and authority, loyalty and patriotism, nation and family. The socialist countries sought a variation on this traditional approach: "authorities expected schools to help build a new social order by instilling loyalty to the Communist Party and inculcating youth with communist values" (Wojcik 2010:387) toward developing the "good, socially minded citizen of a socialist society who would exemplify in his or her private life the values of a classless, egalitarian, and collective society" (Kozakiewicz 1992:92). After 1989, the various governments "turned again to schools to assist the process of societal transformation" to "dismantle communism and cultivate a democratic citizenry" (Wojcik 2010:387). Yet current efforts to overcome tradition are stuck in the past. In some cases, "civic education follows a centralized and standardized pattern. Students are obligated to study given topics in specific years, students learn about human rights and responsibilities and textbooks often make extensive references to international and national legal texts" (Suárez 2008:496). Yet the "study programs and the textbooks make few references to minorities, marginalized populations and topics involving cultural issues" (ibid.).

Within the legacy of associational life controlled by the state through mass organizations, citizens learned not to trust; this lesson has left them with an abiding suspicion of public organizations. People learned to trust instead the private sphere in the sense of informal social networks among friends, relatives, and colleagues. Networks helped participants acquire goods and services not otherwise available—not because they were illegal but due to scarcity and other economic problems.

These networks encouraged social trust[24] beyond state control just as they discouraged trust and engagement in public networks. They constituted a kind of "second society" or clique, an informal social community operating sometimes inside social institutions and sometimes outside. They marked a "retreat from the public sphere into privatism, a distrust of those outside one's immediate family and close social circle, and an emphasis on personal favors and ties" (Slomczynski and Shabad 1998:750). They integrated individuals at the micro level toward offering the individual member some degree of autonomy from the party-dominated state. Cliques generally pursued their own goals, irrespective of their relations with formal institutions. They had many clienteles, including citizens who felt compelled to act in illegal ways to defend what they took to be their rights, or at least their legitimate interests. Research indicates that the cliques' "informal, unofficial values and norms" in many cases were incompatible with "pluralistic politics, civil society, and a market economy" (ibid.).

Public spheres today are not easily established in the face of cliques that exercise informal rules and personal power rather than, say, popular agreement and the rule of law. Russia in particular struggles with this particular legacy. Lyudmila Filipova, Sergey Patrushev, and Elena Kondratieva (2012) report that the majority of Russian citizens regard themselves as unable to influence public institutions, let alone transform them: the formal right to vote does not necessarily entail its capacity to be effective. Citizens' associations cannot overcome this problem as long as the persistence of cliques discourages the emergence of public spheres. Russia today displays little differentiated political space for the articulation and coordination of interests and values of various social groups through political parties, social movements, and other organizations. It displays little differentiated political space toward formulating common objectives and toward political action to achieve them. Not surprisingly, Filipova, Patrushev, and Kondratieva find that many Russians have a negative image of Russian parties. Many believe that the elections are unfair and the results rigged and that parties do not reflect the views of citizens or otherwise function as institutions of popular representation. The problem with cliques and niches is that nonformal, personal relationships in private life are unlikely to be oriented toward civil rights or human rights, both of which flourish only with broad public commitment and participation. The "persistence of friendship networks" in post-authoritarian societies likely feeds off the "lack of trust towards others outside of those networks," as well as off the "legacy of distrust towards communist organizations," leading to levels of civic and political engagement lower than in more established democracies in the West (Smith 2009:488). The persistence of private networks also goes hand in hand with contemporary mistrust of, even cynicism about, the possibility of good government, including government constitutionally limited in its powers. Although residents of Central and Eastern Europe today "may understand better than many West Europeans the importance of limiting the power of the authorities in ways that help guarantee respect for individual human rights, there is little practical experience and confidence in such mechanisms" (Tibbitts 1994:368–369).

Civic Education Toward Civic Participation

What can a human rights cognitive style contribute to civic participation that would contribute to a local embrace of human rights? First, it encourages the individual to view himself or herself as a "sovereign protagonist of rights claims" (Meyer, Bromley, and Ramirez 2010:113). To view oneself this way is all the more important for weaker members of the community, often women in general, the elderly, indigenous persons, homosexuals, the disabled, and minorities of various kinds. A human rights style provides its carrier with reasons for taking up the role of civic protagonist: to be an active participant in civil society and to value participatory rights. Allowing carriers to view themselves as human rights bearing allows them to regard themselves also as claimants to other rights, such as equal membership in political community.

Second, complexity requires a society to individuate its members beyond levels adequate for older, more traditional societies.[25] Individualism of this sort is a resource for developing what might be called "participatory personhood." Communist Romania, for example, was a "mass society. The individual was not taught he was an individual with rights and responsibilities"; rather, "everybody was taught they were part of a collective, with collective rights" (Dakmara Georgescu, cited in Tibbitts 1994:368). Social engineering under authoritarian regimes discouraged individualism, personal responsibility, and self-initiative. Socialist states provided few if any civil and political rights and did not promote rights for many social groups that sometimes found some support in some parts of the West (women, say, or homosexuals; Jews and other religious minorities). But they did provide social rights, in the form of welfare, and they promoted workers' rights, as well as rights of the poor, certainly more so than Western countries.

The human rights project confronts this legacy today. Residua of the communist period include a "fear of speaking freely," a fear "deeply rooted in the political experience of countries with a long history of suppression" (Molnár 2009:466).[26] Residua also include inadequate encouragement of the individual to "take initiative and to develop his or her unique ideas and actions" (Bianchi 1997:116) or to take "personal responsibility for socially just behavior concerned with the welfare of the society" (ibid.). And residua include conservatism or embeddedness, a preference for "maintaining smooth relations within the in-group and not standing out," for "maintaining the status quo of mutual obligations," for harmony or "avoiding interpersonal conflict and fitting into the environment rather than trying to change it" (ibid.).[27]

Many of these residua concern an underdeveloped sense of individualism. The underdevelopment discourages an authoritarian community from transitioning to a liberalized one. It perpetuates individuals' civil passivity and their self-protective survival strategies. It hardly spurs people to civic participation and it does not encourage them to assert their individual rights.

By contrast (and as I noted above), a human rights cognitive style emphasizes individual rights; it offers an interpretation of human rights that stresses individual rights over group rights. Individual rights contrast with "second wave" human rights that animated various socialist and labor movements in the last decades of the nineteenth century and the first decades of the twentieth, and also by contrast to "third wave" human rights following from decolonization after World War II: notions of collective rights such as a community's right to socioeconomic development, a right to a safe environment (for example, one free from malaria), or a people's right to political and cultural self-determination. Of course, individualism does not necessarily preclude solidarity; citizenship does not have to exhaust personal identity; an emphasis on each person's unique identity need not preclude citizenship.

With this individualistic thrust, a human rights cognitive style resists a postcommunist agenda of state cohesion, cultural unity, and unconditional loyalty to state and nation. It resists discourses of patriotic education that drive agendas in which nation building trumps democratization, individualization, civic attitudes, pluralism, and tolerance. It promotes "individual autonomy, respect for diversity, challenging authority and standing up for one's rights" (Janmaat and Piattoeva 2007:532). It pursues a de-ideologization of civic education, away from a unitary perspective, toward a pluralist approach—but also away from past curricular policy "adjusted to fit predominant political forces" and nationalist goals or even traditional religious education (Tibbitts 1994:370). It does so in part by giving regional authorities and parents more say in educational matters. It pursues a pupil-centered pedagogy and promotes general humanistic values that stress the individual's primacy in more liberal forms of society.

My proposal departs markedly from traditional education for state citizenship that emphasizes "responsibility, conformity, national loyalty and service to the community" (ibid.). When pursued in postcommunist contexts, education in a human rights style encourages persons who are as distrustful of the contemporary state (and their fellow citizens) as they were of the communist-era state. For post-authoritarian communities, education in a human rights style offers an alternative to intolerant ethno-national identities that substitute for the now defunct, unifying public belief system of state socialism. In these various ways, a human rights cognitive style facilitates education for an antiauthoritarian, non-nation-building attachment to human rights. It replaces a pedagogy of conformity, loyalty, and patriotism with one of pluralism, individual autonomy, active citizenship, and independent thinking.

Different Models of a Human Rights Cognitive Style

Given its localist orientation, a human rights cognitive style does not entail a single form or model of human rights advocacy. Among many possible forms of persuasion by means of different models of education, I conclude by sketching three forms of a human rights cognitive style to spur civic education and participation.[28]

One human rights cognitive style, for professional activists, provides skill development. It targets various kinds of relevant professionals, from legal professionals (police, lawyers, judges, prosecutors) to journalists to health and social service workers, from civil servants to military personnel. It targets them for training in monitoring violations, registering grievances with national or international organizations, bringing legal cases, accessing media outlets, lobbying public officials, and promoting accountability in public and private institutions. This model motivates professionals to deploy their knowledge, skills, and networks in procedures defending human rights, in legal contexts and in other venues. It helps them to see their capacity to realize the human rights–relevant potential of their skills in ways likely not anticipated by their formal training or much of their professional experience.

A second human rights cognitive style serves nonprofessional community activists. Perhaps more difficult to implement than the other two styles, it addresses vulnerable populations such as victims of abuse and trauma. It seeks to change beliefs, practices, and institutions that are human rights violative (in the family, in the workplace, in the public sphere, in religious communities). It does so by training participants in leadership, conflict resolution, human rights–relevant vocations, and in other forms of activism. It is community based and focused on changing and building the local community (for example, in school settings, refugee camps, women's shelters, soup kitchens, and ghettos of the socially marginalized). This style operates through the therapeutic thematization of participants' experience as victims of human rights abuses. It can equally focus on violators and those at increased risk of becoming future perpetrators, such as young men in a country engulfed by civil war. It focuses on framing traumatic experience in ways to render it a resource for motivating restorative self-regard for victims in a larger context of human rights–supportive behavior.

A third human rights cognitive style seeks educational deployment. It engages in social critique toward identifying the human rights–relevant aspects of institutions, understandings, and practices—toward analyzing social, political, cultural, and policy issues in terms of a human rights framework. It attempts to generate widely shared support for human rights within a political community and to generate opposition to institutions and authorities that violate human rights. Activists transmit it by teaching about human rights (history, for example, or institutions such as international courts, or examples from human trafficking, to child labor, to violations of an individual's bodily and psychological integrity). Participants advance it by integrating the idea of human rights into local public values and understandings (through school curricula, popular culture, and public awareness campaigns). This model is largely cognitive; unlike the other two, it does not aim at developing relevant skills for human rights activism and conflict resolution. It offers itself as a tool of analysis and persuasion, in the manner of Chapter 4's proposal for teaching human rights as a cognitive style.

Two Examples of Antiauthoritarian Education with a Human Rights Component

This third cognitive style is particularly relevant to youth born after the communist period. For this style, we have (unlike the other two, as far as I can determine) concrete examples of particular instances of good practice. Consider two examples, both pedagogical projects of the European Union, each a conception of education for democratic citizenship and human rights education for students, particularly in the later years of secondary education but capable of variations appropriate for children even at kindergarten level, children not yet able to read and write (Krapf, Gollob, and Weidinger 2010:21 n.4). Both projects display a robust antiauthoritarianism well suited to advancing human rights in post-authoritarian communities through education.

One project, edited by Peter Krapf, Rolf Gollob, and Wiltrud Weidinger, finds expression in *Taking Part in Democracy: Lesson Plans for Upper Secondary Level on Democratic Citizenship and Human Rights Education* (2010). This project resonates with the vision I develop in these pages in several ways.

It teaches that law alone cannot realize human rights: "Rules cannot take care of every problem, so the members of a community must share an attitude of responsibility towards each other" (Krapf, Gollob, and Weidinger 2010:7). Further, "we only learn how to take responsibility under conditions of liberty, which includes the liberty to fail" (ibid., 78).

Krapf and his colleagues convey the deeply agonistic nature of advancing human rights. The movement for human rights thinking can only be one of abiding disagreement, and therefore core to the human rights project is the capacity of participants to cope with disagreement, not to be undermined by it: "In an open, secular and pluralist society, we cannot take for granted that there is a framework of values that everyone will immediately agree to—but for the stability of a community, such a framework is essential. We must therefore communicate and negotiate the basic principles that we share in taking responsibility" (ibid., 61). Further, a "democratic and secular state depends on cultural conditions that its institutions and authorities cannot produce or enforce. A set of collectively accepted and appreciated values, rules and goals cannot be taken for granted. Rather, it is the citizens' responsibility to (re)negotiate and (re)define their values, rules and goals"—and human rights education in particular can "play a key role in meeting this challenge inasmuch as human rights involve the principle of mutual recognition—the golden rule—but do not promote any particular religious belief or philosophy of ethics and morals" (ibid., 79).

Taking Part in Democracy emphasizes that agreement in the human rights project must be constructed by its participants. A human rights perspective simply imposed on those who disagree with it violates my proposal to understand human rights as self-authored, self-granted norms, but also as norms that can emerge for a political community and across political communities only in a spirit of compromise that rejects absolute certainty: "We have to agree on what serves us best. The common good is something to be negotiated" (ibid., 83). Human rights pedagogy so understood entails, I would argue, four distinct features:

First, human rights understood as something constructed by their own addressees rejects any notion of human rights as elite-directed norms imposed, top down, by some moral, legal, or political hierarchy. *Taking Part in Democracy* "points out that human rights not only have a vertical dimension—the relationship between state authority and the individual citizen—but also a horizontal dimension—the relationship between individuals as members of a community" (ibid., 73–74).

Second, the political search for participants' agreement in the process of constructing human rights is best guided by a this-worldly pragmatism (rather than by the absolute, otherworldly certainties of, say, theology or metaphysics): "Pluralism is therefore linked to a constructivist concept of the common good. First all the players articulate their different interests, and then they look for a solution that everyone can accept. . . . [C]onstructivism emphasises that there is an element of learning involved, following the pattern of trial and error. Practice will show how good a solution is, and it may have to be changed or improved—in a new round of discussions and negotiations" (ibid., 83–84).

Third, understood as social constructions, human rights are not otherworldly truths discovered by special persons (in the manner, say, of religions). Rather, participants socially construct human rights for themselves and others, in a fallibilistic spirit, that is, participants must always examine those constructions critically and always be prepared to revise them toward better constructions:

> Young citizens who take part in democracy do so as free individuals with equal rights, but unequal opportunities. As members of dynamic pluralist societies that are globally interdependent, they face increasingly complex challenges (e.g. climate change, exhaustion of natural resources, failing states) for which school cannot provide any concrete solutions, but can offer competence training to equip the young generation with tools with which to develop solutions. How such challenges are to be met is a matter of trial and error and negotiation of compromises between different interests. The outcome of such decision-making processes can be understood as an attempt to achieve the goal of the common good. The result is always incomplete, and immediately open to critical discussion and improvement. (Ibid., 11)

The human rights project is ever open-ended; it will never be exhaustively achieved, and " 'learning for' democracy and human rights therefore means that the students prepare for their roles as lifelong learners, both as individuals and as a community" (ibid., 29).

Accordingly, fourth, the agonistic process of participants constructing human rights for themselves can only be pluralistic: "Pluralism is a form of competition. The players compete with each other to promote their interests, and negotiation involves both power and reasoning. But this kind of competition also ensures that no player in the field becomes dominant" (ibid., 84). For the Central and Eastern European countries transitioning from authoritarian pasts to somewhat more liberal forms of social and political organization, the "rejection of pluralism implies giving in to the 'authoritarian temptation.' The common good is defined by an authority, and whoever disagrees is oppressed as an enemy. Communist parties are an example in point. They claimed sole leadership on the grounds of being able to define the common good by scientific means. Both liberal and egalitarian democracy was rejected" (ibid., 84).

The human rights project is best pursued as a communal effort, and human rights education does well to explore ways in which students might thematize their own schools as microcosms of society. In just this sense,

Krapf and his colleagues conceive human rights education as a "community of learners governed by human rights, but also as citizens engaged in decision-making processes" (ibid., 29). For the human rights project, particularly in the sense of advancing human rights in post-authoritarian communities through education, is deeply participatory; all addressees of human rights should participate in the social construction of those rights: "Citizens should have the opportunity to take part in democracy, and to express their views and interests when discussing any issue on the agenda" (ibid., 29). In this way the pedagogical project reinforces the democratic, participatory features of the human rights project in the former East bloc: "Democracy stands and falls with the promise that every interested citizen can take part in decision making. To do so with responsibility requires educated citizens," and in particular citizens educated in human rights thinking (ibid., 79).

The participatory quality of the human rights project so understood is framed by two concerns for rules themselves guided by principles. First, participation in the project of advancing human rights, and human rights thinking, must be bounded by rules generally acceptable to the participants—acceptable because participants understand the rules and freely embrace them by their own best lights: "students should learn how to exercise their rights to liberty, for example their right to free access to information, and to free thought, opinion and expression. They should also have active experience in interacting with others—for example, promoting their interests, negotiating for compromise, or agreeing on how to define 'the general welfare.' . . . They should be able to act in a framework of rules and accept the limits that may be imposed on them. They should have developed an attitude of responsibility for the welfare of others and the community as a whole" (ibid., 9). This project "depends on citizens who are willing and able to take part in decision making, and to take office in its institutions. Students need these competences and skills to be able to exercise their human and civil rights and to perform their roles as active citizens" (ibid., 19).

Second, to overcome the communist legacy by advancing human rights by means of civic education and a developing civil society, Central and Eastern European polities need to overcome the abiding residue of authoritarian forms of obtaining compliance:

There are two traps in teaching responsibility—abstract moralising and indoctrination. Moralising means talking about being "a good citizen" without looking at a concrete issue. The students are given the message that taking responsibility is only a matter of wanting to or not. They never learn how difficult this task can be, and how important it is to share their reasons for making a choice. The trap of indoctrination refers to teachers who attempt to impose a certain set of values. They have no mandate to do so, and whatever set of values they choose, it can be questioned and deconstructed. To avoid these traps, this approach "gives the students the opportunity to make decisions on their own." (Ibid., 61–62)

That opportunity is pedagogically provided in part where the "teacher is their coach and facilitator. The students discuss how to solve dilemmas. The case stories refer to the students' everyday experience, which puts the students in the role of experts" (ibid., 62).

Another project, pursued by the Organization for Security and Co-operation in Europe's Office for Democratic Institutions and Human Rights (OSCE/ODIHR) in *Guidelines on Human Rights Education for Secondary School Systems* (2012) in Warsaw, Poland, offers an approach that, in six ways, resonates with other aspects of the proposal I develop in these pages. First, the book advances a kind of localism: "Training programmes are adapted to the particular cultural, educational, regional and experiential needs and realities of the teachers and their students" (OSCE/ODIHR 2012:43). Second, it takes a community-wide, cross-institutional approach:

Human rights education in secondary schools is designed in consultation with key stakeholders, including civil society organizations, and with the direct and meaningful participation of youth. Human rights education is implemented in secondary schools in collaboration with a wide range of stakeholders at the national, sub-national/regional and local levels, including policymakers, educational professionals, teacher-training institutions, students, parents, educational institutions, non-governmental organizations, children and youth organizations and the media, in order to foster a wide and multi-faceted range of opportunities for students to engage with human rights in their community. (Ibid., 20)

Third, the guidelines advocate education in both formal and informal contexts, incorporating human rights issues or themes "within existing compulsory subjects," developing "new courses or special subjects," and complemented by "non-formal learning opportunities in and out of schools, such as extra-curricular classes and clubs, and participation in projects, field trips and other activities, such as seminars and round tables" (ibid., 16).

Fourth, this project stresses education toward "strengthen[ing] the capacity of duty bearers (e.g., legislators, policymakers, educational professionals and teacher trainers) to meet their human rights obligations through improvements in policies, legislation, resource allocation and practices supporting human rights education" (ibid., 20–21).

Fifth, this approach gives special attention to the vulnerable: the "special needs or vulnerabilities of students, such as those learning in conflict, post-conflict and post-disaster situations, or those who are at risk of dropping out of school due to various factors, such as poverty, health conditions or violence" (ibid., 16), and "especially persons who are particularly vulnerable to human rights abuse, for example those with disabilities" (ibid., 31). Finally, the guidelines emphasize the importance of the media with respect to the free access to information and freedom of the media, but also ways in which the media can contribute to setting a community's political agenda, by teaching students to "evaluate information sources, including media and learning resources, and recognize points of view, bias and reliability" (ibid., 27).

Folding Human Rights into Civic Participation

My three models of a human rights cognitive style—for professional activists, providing skill development; for nonprofessional community activists; and for educational deployment—associate civic participation with human rights in three ways. First, they represent in concrete ways the abstract claim that social institutions can only be credible if citizens are involved to some extent in the political background conditions for such institutions. That involvement will only become universal when all participants can be regarded as radically equal in ways that exceed the kinds of legal equality offered by civil rights as well as in ways that find expression in human rights.

Second, popular political participation is a means of holding elected representatives to account. Holding national representatives to cosmopolitan account requires a perspective and commitment larger than domestic justice; human rights offer that perspective.

Third, "not all political activity deserves the label "virtuous" or contributes to the commonweal" (Putnam 1993:88). But activity that advances common interests rather than self-interest, that promotes shared benefits rather than merely private interests, follows a logic of inclusion rather than exclusion, which is precisely the logic of human rights. Advancing this inclusive logic depends, of course, on more rather than fewer supporters. It depends on supporters whose personal investment in participation is sufficient to motivate participation even in the face of many, constant discouragements. All forms of a human rights style have practical implications for civic education and civic participation in post-authoritarian communities. The development of each form hinges on the acquisition and exchange of information among citizens. Coordination facilitates exchange, and coordination depends on developed capacities of a group to determine its goals, to understand its tasks, to determine how best to accomplish them, and how best to explain those goals to others, with knowledge of and sensitivity toward local conditions. Better civic-educated citizens are better able to persuade others to participate in human rights politics. Better educated participants can better express the reasoning, goals, and means of a human rights style and can better inform and persuade others. And civic education is furthered when its addressees are able to form increasingly inclusive groups involved in civic participation. As civic education develops and expands, the capacity of citizens to advance a human rights cognitive style increases.

In all three cases, human rights practitioners in education maximize their effectiveness by deploying a human rights style against the legacy of fifty years of authoritarian rule in Central and Eastern European countries —namely, low levels of social trust and social interconnectedness that discourage human rights consciousness. To develop trust and interconnectedness in these societies, practitioners develop civic participation (a) in some cases as a result of a cognitive style and (b) in other cases as a resource for a cognitive style.

(a) Sometimes civic participation *results* from participants adopting a human rights cognitive style.[29] In this "top-down" scenario, practitioners convey human rights consciousness by participating with citizens in various types of networks and associations. Here the focus is not on explicit principles of human rights so much as on some of the "by-products" of human rights, such as norms of generalized reciprocity and trust—norms that encourage civic participation.

(b) Sometimes civic participation is the *source* of a human rights cognitive style.[30] In this "bottom-up" scenario, citizens' human rights impact the quality and stability of civic institutions. Borne by a cognitive style, trust leads to civic participation whereas in the other scenario, civic participation leads to the kind of trust involved in a human rights consciousness. Trust, reciprocity, and related orientations of a cognitive style contribute to citizen participation and the development of civic networks.

I turn now from informal, political education in post-authoritarian societies, and particularly in the newly democratizing countries of Eastern Europe, to persuasion through digital media potentially anywhere in the world.

Chapter 6

Digital Technology as Resource
for the Human Rights Project

One practical method of advancing the human rights project, I argued in earlier chapters, is by discursive appeal to a way of looking at the world. Possible venues for that appeal include educational settings where students learn to associate rights with people, not territory (Chapter 4). They include political settings where citizens learn to trust the liberalizing state and their fellow citizens and to reject intolerant ethno-national identities that substitute for the now defunct unifying public belief system of state socialism (Chapter 5). This chapter extends to the technology of cyberspace my overall concern with how the human rights project can be advanced. I am particularly interested in the human rights potential of uncoupling, in cyberspace, the individual's social and political identity from his or her social and political voice.

In the developed world, but increasingly in the developing world as well, the digital liquefaction of human bodies and national boundaries challenges prevailing notions of the nation state, of private property, and of bodily autonomy. This dynamic technology also contests the standard model of political personhood that connects, in legal categories, bodies with territories. Computer-mediated communication elides national boundaries into nongeographic borders that operate transnationally as well as subnationally. Individuals' legal presence becomes detached from their national territorial jurisdictions. Their legal presence becomes incorporated into other normative regimes. I explore one alternative regime in particular, nonterritorial human rights. As I urge in Chapter 3, what are now state borders can one day become "embedded" in the person him- or herself. The dynamics of liquefaction via digital communication contribute to the freeing of citizenship rights and protections from state capture. These dynamics play a role in denationalizing the connection between membership in a particular political community and the enjoyment of legal rights. They may be able to contribute to the advancement of human rights by bypassing state authorities and facilitating a new type of cross-border politics—one deeply local yet intensely connected digitally.

What prospects might contemporary digital technology offer the human rights project? Research on the Internet in particular has focused on its consequences for cultural diversity and homogenization, its inflection with the economy, and its regulation through domestic and international law. Research has examined the complex problem of unequal access. It has investigated ways in which the user's level of social capital influences if and how he or she goes online. And it has examined its effect on political participation. But this concern with political participation has largely neglected the Internet's possible consequences for the politics of human rights. I analyze these consequences in several steps. (1) I identify the Internet's general potential to advance human rights as well as some of the problems that discourage that potential. (2) In particular, the Internet can advance the cause of human rights by changing civil society by means of digital abstraction from human bodies and national borders (3) but also by facilitating critical public opinion. (4) I then limn the parameters of possible Internet contributions to a human rights state as well as (5) the intersection of culture and nature in digital technology.

Potential and Problems of Advancing Human Rights Digitally

Technology is not inherently political. But technology often influences politics, often profoundly, as military, economic, medical, and communications technology always has. Estimations of the political upshot of digital communication range widely. Utopian narratives of progress mark one end of the spectrum. They imagine computer-based media bringing ever more people into communication with each other in ways participants desire and can control. A more dystopian optic defines the other end of the spectrum. It depicts digital media operating above the heads of most people, often beyond the reach of critical argument in the public sphere, in ways damaging to persons and even to whole communities. On this view, unrestricted commercial interests or a state's excessively centralized controls pose the greatest threats.

In their one-dimensionality, the sweeping assumptions of both ends of the spectrum are easily mistaken. They neglect technology's complexity and the diversity of communities and social sectors in which technology is always already embedded. Utopian and dystopian interpretations alike miss technology's inflection in legal, policy, and economic decisions as it becomes institutionalized. That inflection renders the consequences of technology along many different dimensions. And assumptions of both ends of the spectrum overlook the double-edged quality of any technology: digital methods of reducing barriers of time and distance, for example, enhance communications also among dispersed terrorist cells.

To take the measure of digital technology's political potential, I attend to emancipatory and oppressive dimensions equally, anticipating elements of both, in shifting combinations. Societal disparities in access, or local barriers to free expression and information, or telecommunication sectors consumed by commercial interests or governmental regulation and censorship, accompany unimpeded flows of digital information across territorial borders. It remains, however, that digital technology can advance the idea, and even the practice, of human rights.

I engage negative and positive dimensions alike as I analyze the Internet in particular. It is a global, decentralized, computer-based network of networks that facilitates information flows both public and private.[1] The political dimensions of this technology are immediate and profound. Consider five.

First, the Internet transcends the limits of political communities in its openness to diverse persons and groups dispersed across the world. It facilitates communication in ways that older media cannot match. Television, radio, and newspapers rarely penetrate the national level, and few ever rise to that level. The Internet is less easily controlled by state authorities than are older forms of media. Today more than a few countries escape full penetration because of very low levels of technology and energy (in some parts of the developing world). Others escape full penetration because they are controlled by an authoritarian regime with advanced information technology and strict levels of political censorship (such as China). Still, the general trend is toward ever-greater penetration, whereby the nature of the penetration varies widely.

Second, the Internet is highly decentralized. It supports a large and increasing number of globally dispersed participants with their various sites, blogs, web pages, and networks. By digitalizing information, it renders information hypermobile that then circulates through global networks almost instantaneously. This compression of space and time facilitates the almost immediate interlinking of dispersed individuals, groups, and communities.

Third, the cost of equipment and access to the Internet generally fall, relatively quickly and continuously. Cost reduction removes some barriers to individual Internet access, but only to some. The outsourcing of manufacturing removes others. Although the "headquarters of the major transnational corporations in the computer industry—such as Microsoft, Google, and Apple—are located on the Pacific West Coast," more than a few "computer hardware components and software products are produced in developing and middle-income nations, such as India, China, and Brazil" (Norris and Inglehart 2009:93).

Fourth, to members of a political community—including groups heretofore marginalized because geographically remote from metropolitan centers—the Internet facilitates information acquisition and the self-organization of political groups, improving their possibility of airing complaints or advancing demands on the virtual stage of a digital public sphere. Digital mediation of state and citizen may sometimes strengthen civil society, much more likely in a liberal democratic order than in a more traditional polity, let alone in an authoritarian regime. I also see potential beyond liberal democratic communities for voluntary communication among dispersed, marginalized, or besieged groups and individuals with shared interests and concerns—but not without problems, some of which I detail.

Fifth, by providing domestic and foreign information not filtered by the state, the Internet sometimes strengthens oppositional groups and insurgent organizations in their challenges to state oppression, even though such groups lack many of the traditional advantages of their opponents. Still, persons with the highly specialized technical knowledge to circumvent governmental regulation are found everywhere, even in authoritarian polities. In some cases the Internet levels the playing field for transnational advocacy networks. But such best-case scenarios need to be leavened by attention to profound and deep-seated problems.

Like most technology, the Internet is distinctly double edged. It can lead to a public sphere that disconnects a citizenry's beliefs, preferences, and convictions from policy and other decisions. It may relate actor and audience online but only asymmetrically (such as hierarchical organization through webmasters and moderators, and Internet services that control content, employees, or consumers). Corporations or other private economic powers may capture whole sectors of the Internet—by filtering political claims through market categories, for example, or through private media interests deploying the power that comes with significant property to wield disproportionate influence over public policy or electoral campaigns.[2] The Internet creates privacy concerns where "corporations even more than governments have a strong interest in developing profiles of their customers together with their information and communication preferences" (Gould 2004:241). It contributes to the loss of traditional indigenous culture, minority languages, and ways of life through convergence with contemporary Western culture.[3] The Internet easily polarizes different social sectors, such as global elites and poor, rural populations.[4] And it is marked by inequality. A chasm between the information rich and the information poor characterizes access to the Internet (and to telephones, televisions, and radio, for that matter) within postindustrial countries but even more so between postindustrial and developing countries. Such disparities "have been deepening, not diminishing, during recent decades" (Norris and Inglehart 2009:302).

This last point about inequality is complex. Unequal access occurs along multiple dimensions. One involves economically relevant factors, such as an unreliable electricity supply or the absence of broadband Internet (or speed of access, or availability of advanced computers), or the lack of the economic wherewithal to purchase devices and access. A second dimension concerns political factors, such as control and censorship by repressive states that sharply limit access to information domestically and from abroad. Another dimension involves cultural capital, when social status and cultural background significantly influence the individual's interest in public affairs and his or her use of the Internet. Inequality in cultural capital assumes additional forms: when Internet use favors literacy and sufficient educational attainment to utilize the Internet as a source of information, for example, and when it favors users with an English language capacity, given the predominance of English in centers of technological design and marketing as well as on websites.[5]

Nor is the Internet culturally neutral or indifferent. Its self-selected users tend to have higher levels of education. They tend to share norms positively associated with higher education; to be persons more secular, more politically engaged, and more socially liberal (embracing more liberal sexual moral values, for example, but not nationalism or religious values in any strong way). The values gap between parochial and cosmopolitan societies maintains itself "in the case of liberal social values" or widens "with feelings of nationalism and the strength of religiosity" (Norris and Inglehart 2009:308).[6]

Civil Society Improved via Abstraction from Bodies and Borders

To make the most of the Internet's positive political potential, while avoiding at least some of the many problems it also generates, I propose a human rights–friendly civil society that builds on two things. It would build on a property of digital communication: abstraction. And it would build on one of its promises: public deliberation. I turn first to abstraction and take up deliberation in a later section.

The Internet abstracts from participants' physical bodies and geographical locations.[7] Digital abstraction is politically significant with regard to social spaces. Social spaces are shaped along various dimensions of a community's collective imagination. They are shaped as well by how the community "inhabits" those spaces. To be sure, the physical world is not the only locus of politics or participation. And not all parts of a political system are anchored in the physical world. Consider democracy. Popular participation is central to it. Yet democracy does not require physical copresence. And it need not privilege face-to-face meetings in neighborhood assemblies as a *conditio sine qua non* of authentic democratic politics.

The physical world is never without immediate political import, for example in the individual's physical embodiment. As individuals, humans share an understanding of this phenomenon, for at a fundamental level, every body corresponds to all others. Each person has a resonant understanding of the embodiedness of other persons and most people probably feel an immediate correspondence with the bodies of others. In its vulnerability, for example, each body mirrors the vulnerability of all others. On the basis of such near universal resonance, some types of political association can be reconfigured in the form of human rights. For a shared understanding of the universal correspondence of human bodies allows any person to understand—at a level immediate, personal, even existential—what bodily and psychological harm is. *Having* a body that is vulnerable corresponds with *being* a body that is vulnerable. In identifying with one's body in this sense, one identifies with other bodies as well, precisely because they are no less vulnerable.

Popular sovereignty in modern societies is already uncoupled from the physical copresence of citizens who decide public issues. (It is uncoupled from the physical copresence of citizens' parliamentary representatives.) Sovereignty is one of the ways in which members of a community are related legally and politically to each other; they need not stand face-to-face in those various ways. Popular sovereignty can advance the human rights idea, but only if it facilitates noninstitutionalized opinion-forming opportunities. And the Internet demonstrates that such discussions need not take place in physical space, and that they do not require the physical copresence of participants.

To see how abstraction advances the human rights project, consider cyberspace. It places into question current understandings of private property, rights to bodily integrity and individual authority over one's body, as well as conventional understandings of the national borders I discuss throughout this book. We usually think of property, boundaries, and authority in terms of the physical copresence of all affected persons. We often think of communal membership, some kinds of political practice, and aspects of governability in the same way. So if the individual in cyberspace exists only as electronic data, one wonders: What happens to politics offline? What happens to politics in a context "where embodiment is no longer evident in customary ways, where 'bodies' are made 'visible' only incidentally, if at all, and primarily through practices of inscription (writing)" (Saco 2002:133)?

These questions go to the heart of digital communication. In a *politics of concealment*, cyberspace renders us less visible, "act[ing] on bodies at a distance through a form of disembodied projection" (Saco 2002:206). In a *politics of appearance*, cyberspace renders us more visible, acting in embodied ways. In cyberspace we can isolate ourselves from face-to-face encounters with others. Or we can generate virtual communities, some of which can be as close-knit as any physical community.

The virtual world allows as well for elements of freedom, such as the anonymity it affords the cybernaut. The political freedom that anonymity permits long predates the Internet, of course. The ancient device of the secret ballot, for example, shields the voter from negative consequences for life and limb, liberty and property—for example, when the voter's preferences offend powerful and unconstrained elites. Concealed identity can also protect someone from unwanted repercussions when expressing unpopular or politically risky viewpoints. An online persona is uncoupled from the cybernaut's social and physical identity. It can protect both kinds of identity by constructing in cyberspace a kind of prosthetic self or virtual persona.

Just as a technologically mediated public sphere provides social space in which subjugated groups can agitate for their interests without suffering negative repercussions, so a "prosthetic self" provides safety to the politically engaged person. It affords safety for the individual's off-line or "analog" body. Online, the person has no body. Anonymity also protects against being targeted. In these ways, corporeal presence and visibility are no more necessary for human rights–friendly politics than the physical body is necessary to political agency. What matters for such politics is not the Internet itself. What matters are the *political* circumstances under which the individual employs it, as well as the nature of the space he or she coinhabits on the Internet. To an extent, institutions, including media, can form those who inhabit them.[8] What matters politically is the quality of the shared social space in its accessibility, norms, and openness. For purposes of advancing human rights, private persons who have now come together on the Internet as culture-debating publics should participate in the production of critical public opinion, as I explain in the following section. Critical public opinion challenges forces that threaten or preclude human rights— including rapacious commercial interests, repressive state interests, as well as individual behavior that feeds off the lack of personal accountability in cyberspace.

Creating and Assigning Human Rights in Digitally Mediated Critical Deliberation

The development of networks of peer-to-peer file sharing has political potential. This is the potential of a decentralized dissemination and sharing of information. The development of these networks equally marks significant scope for socially destructive online behavior, undermining political potential. Potential of a positive sort depends on the Internet not becoming entirely independent of the political community in which it is embedded, in several respects.

First, in polities not deeply oppressive, the law should not treat online personas as discrete individuals who exist only online, without reference to their off-line creators who should be legally responsible for their online behavior.[9] Cyberspace confounds the clear identifiability of discrete individuals. A cybernaut might construct multiple personas online, each anonymous, making it difficult to match online activities with actual persons. Anonymity is necessary in authoritarian contexts to protect the cybernaut from the depredations of the state. In all cases, an individual could abandon an online persona after having offended or damaged someone or some group or some site, and so escape responsibility. This person might return with a different persona and offend again.

Second, accountability in cyberspace requires the application to the online sphere of community-oriented off-line laws. Citizenship, conventionally conceived, couples body and territory in legal terms. The citizen, as someone with political presence in a conventional sense, is coupled with geography. That is, the citizen is someone who the nation state apprehends in terms of a body coupled with national territory. So do other institutions as well as fellow citizens. Citizenship or residency status and personal and legal identity are tied to the citizen's physical body—for example, in the embodied political agency of one person, one vote. States, bureaucracies, but also the individual him- or herself, regard the body as the site of the self and its powers and therefore as the locus of the individual's political agency. Where the individual is not present as a body but becomes visible through writing online, the political community's ability to control or otherwise influence the individual diminishes and perhaps sometimes even vanishes.

Third, today's communicative context differs from the pre-Internet era, but not in terms of cross-border information flows as such. It differs with respect to the increased magnitude, scope, and simultaneity of those flows, now as digital communication. As magnitude, scope, and simultaneity increase, the possibility increases for developing "networks for circulating place-based information (about local environmental, housing, political conditions) that can become part of political work and strategies addressing a global condition—the environment, growing poverty and unemployment worldwide, lack of accountability among multinationals, and so forth" (Sassen 2006:370). Local political practice is transformed by digital technologies, institutions, and imaginaries by disputing the nation state's authority. The state's national exclusivity is challenged especially where cyberspace offers novel venues for cross-border politics. By *novel* I mean cross-border communication that challenges the primacy of place-based, in-state activities that a political elite regards as necessary to sovereign, national territory.

For example, because in some respects cyberspace has no territorially based boundaries, it challenges traditional legal concepts of jurisdiction that locate the jurisdiction of courts, and the application of laws, within nation state borders. Cyberspace offers a unique site for cross-border politics precisely where it challenges territorially based understandings of jurisdiction.

Yet even though it is nonterritorial, cyberspace does not escape all geographic authority. The nation state still "exercise[s] authority over digital networks through the indirect venue of hardware standards" and "regulations of content circulation and intellectual property rights" (Sassen 2006:418). Electronically mediated communication does not threaten to eliminate a nation state with its territory-based authority. But it transforms certain qualities of national territory by changing the relationship between the local and the nonlocal. Here the Internet shares one feature of the human rights idea: its aspirations to global validity. Like the human rights idea, the Internet alters the relevant relationship between political particularism and political universalism. It alters the relationship between the local sources of human rights, on the one hand, and a validity ideally of universal extent, on the other. The Internet facilitates localized human rights initiatives becoming part of cross-border networks, generating a network of multiple localities, each advocating human rights. By means of Internet communication, parochial local initiatives can remake themselves into more cosmopolitan movements.

Fourth, realizing the Internet's positive potential depends on a nation state allowing space for human rights within itself. It depends on the nation state allowing human rights as an internal feature of the nation state, hence with some degree of autonomy from nation state territory. The construction of a particular human rights state by some of the citizens of a corresponding nation state is one means of moving the state toward a free embrace of human rights (as I argue particularly in Chapters 1 and 2).

By generating internal space for human rights, the nation state strengthens civic republicanism within itself. As a site for people to come together to pursue human rights for themselves and for others, the Internet creates a widely participatory, *nonexclusionary* space—without the physical copresence of others—to advocate physical, psychological, social, and political well-being in a human rights sense.

From a human rights perspective, the denationalized state is less parochial, more universalist than the typical nation state. To be sure, some conceptions of political universalism are exclusionary.[10] This was the case during the first seventy-eight years of a universalistic American democracy of "all men . . . created equal" that nonetheless permitted slavery and slaves' legal exclusion from all processes of the community's self-determination. But the political universalism to which a human rights state—within or alongside a corresponding nation state—aspires is nonexclusionary. It is nonexclusionary in a way unique to cyberspace. It expands communal rights to all adults based on a norm of equality. Yet it does so without systematically excluding ascriptive, cultural, and other differences among members. Compare nation state and cyberspace. In the nation state, exclusion targets groups defined in terms of their bodies (among many other characteristics), from women and children in general to various ethnic or racial minorities. Cyberspace constitutes a kind of denationalized state. In cyberspace, body exclusion *removes* at least some grounds for prejudice in the political sphere.

Fifth, off-line civic membership combines elements of the private and the public sphere if civic membership becomes a zone in which state authority and individual freedom meet. That is, civic membership combines elements of the private and the public sphere where public power and the private life of members meet. Elements of the public and private spheres also combine if civic membership becomes a zone for a critical, debating public in which people come together *as a public* to confront state authorities over their demands for human rights as an element internal to the nation state.[11] Off-line life can relate public and private in ways that parallel the public/private relation online.

This parallel has negative aspects, in some respects. Negative aspects include a nation state and a government that, as public entities, threaten the private sphere with regulation. Negative aspects include economic interests that, as private interests, threaten the private sphere if those interests are inadequately regulated or unregulated. But in other ways, the parallel has positive aspects. The nation state furthers the private sphere by protecting and facilitating pluralism in viewpoints and ways of life. It might do so by arbitrating among private interests, such as individual privacy, and public interests, such as public security. Correspondingly, the Internet's potential for advancing the human rights idea requires the combination of persons and pluralism in the deliberative processes of political will formation.

Computer mediated deliberation introduces a particular epistemic dimension into political will formation. It introduces that dimension into communal decision making as well. It thereby serves as a mechanism to enhance cooperative learning and collective problem solving. It can address matters from an equal right to marriage for homosexuals, to affirmative action in college admissions, to the awarding of governmental contracts to firms owned and operated by minorities historically discriminated against. It can speak to issues ranging from the distributive justice of flat tax schemes to the risks of cultivating genetically modified plants and animals. It can confront problems such as poverty and unemployment worldwide, and it can confront the lack of accountability among multinational corporations.[12]

The online generation of public opinion distinguishes itself from one possible product of some Internet use: a manufactured form of mass opinion. By *public opinion* I mean opinion that maintains a critical interpretive distance to society, government, economy, culture, traditions, nationalism, and other possible forces that, in some of their forms, discourage or preclude human rights. An Internet experience that produces information for debate, and not merely for consumption, is realistic where cyberspace-based disembodiment and self-abstraction can advance noninstitutional, interactive venues for debate, collective learning, collective will formation, and problem solving. The Internet can use critical information to monitor, identify, and criticize excessive state intervention into the private sphere. It can monitor and criticize mass media that shape public opinion rather than just report on it.

An online debating public, as distinguished from an online consuming public, facilitates the formation of considered public opinion that in turn contributes to processes of deliberative legitimation for human rights.[13] But such a public is not easily created, given that the "*dynamics* of mass communication are driven by the power of the media to select, and shape the presentation of, messages and by the strategic use of political and social power to influence the agendas as well as the triggering and framing of public issues" (Habermas 2006b:415).

To paraphrase a distinction developed years ago by C. Wright Mills, the goal is an Internet that furthers *public opinion* rather than *mass opinion*. Mass opinion is really just a form of *non*-public opinion. It derives from a system of communication in which the "role of mass media is increased and that of discussion circles is decreased," limiting popular participation. This system centralizes the "opinion process" such that "discussion circles are necessarily small and decentralized" and "media markets are huge and centralized," restricting access and voice for ordinary people. In this system, the "way opinions *change* is more authoritative and manipulative," with "little or no self-regulation on the part of the public," such that participants in the media market are "propagandized: they cannot answer back to the print in the column, the voice on the radio; they cannot even answer back to the media in their immediate circle of co-listeners with ease and without fear," in short, where communication flows in one direction only. In this system, the "use of physical and institutional sanctions are involved in opinion process," such that ordinary people have little autonomy from it (Mills 1963:584).

Accordingly, the Internet-mediated generation of *public* opinion needs to "involve as many givers of opinion as receivers (i.e., be the product of a many-to-many communications paradigm)." It needs to be "organized to allow immediate response (i.e., be based on a system of open access and two-way communication)." It needs to be "easily translatable into public action, even against public authorities." And in its operations, it needs to remain more or less autonomous of political and economic forces that might colonize it (Saco 2002:65).

An Internet of this sort finds support in what Cass Sunstein (2007) describes as "deliberative domains," that is, sites where people of very different views are invited to read and participate in discussions of a topic of one's choice, by clicking on icons representing, for example, national security, wars, civil rights, the environment, unemployment, foreign affairs, poverty, children, labor unions, and so forth. Digitally facilitated deliberation would also benefit (following the main lines of Sunstein's analysis) if some governments provided a funding mechanism to subsidize the development of some such sites, without having a managerial role. It would benefit if sites voluntarily adopted an informal code to cover substantive issues in a serious way, avoiding sensationalistic treatment of politics, giving extended coverage to public issues, and allowing diverse voices to be heard. It would benefit if links were used creatively to draw people's attention to multiple views: for example, persons who use websites are, in a sense, themselves commodities, at least as much as they are consumers; and in the context of the Internet, the point of links is to capture users' attention, however fleetingly. Sunstein imagines providers of material with a certain point of view also providing links to sites with a very different point of view—a left-wing site, say, might agree to provide icons for a right-wing site in return for an informal agreement to reciprocate.

Precisely as a mechanism for collective learning and problem solving, the Internet is a mechanism for advancing the human rights idea. It offers itself as a resource for citizens of a nation state who construct a corresponding human rights state. Digitally facilitated deliberation offers itself as a resource wherever it can be more than the expression of unthoughtful, unreflected opinion. It can be more wherever it shapes opinion critically and transcends the current self-understanding of participants. For example, groups and individuals in a particular nation state might come to identify themselves as the addressees of the human rights that they themselves author. (In this way they would contribute to a corresponding human rights state.)[14] The Internet transcends current self-understandings of participants because, by developing and communicating critical information, participants communicate about the communicators. The identity of individuals, achieved in part through communication with others, can foster group identity, as human rights advocates and as fellow members of a human rights state. Cybernauts contribute to the construction of human rights states when they learn to identify themselves as bearers of human rights, who construct their collective political identity as a public of authors of their own human rights.[15]

Parameters of Possible Internet Contributions to the Human Rights State

Digitally mediated communication has future political potential not apparent today. Likely it will always confront the tension between local conditions and local obligations and the extra-local perspectives and connections it generates. That tension is sometimes positive, sometimes negative. I see four ways in which that tension can work itself out in positive ways. First, as a resource for advancing the human rights idea, the Internet contributes to multiplying local human rights–oriented practices to encourage human rights thinking locally and beyond. Second, it works toward normatively universal human rights in local communities, even as it, third, recognizes individuals' special obligations to those local communities. Fourth, the Internet can contribute more effectively to human rights advocacy than to democracy building. I will consider each in turn.

Internet Contributes to Multiplying Local Human Rights–Oriented Practices

In its contributions to a human rights state, cyberspace is not a venue for national sovereignty. It is a venue for cosmopolitan, postnationalist thinking. The principles of a human rights state are postnational: collective allegiance to norms of individual freedom and legal equality—but allegiance also to human rights rather than to a people, culture, language, or territory. A human rights state furthers a local identity (that of the corresponding nation state) by preserving it even as it modifies it by encouraging its embrace of human rights (hence a weakening of its sovereignty). A human rights state abjures the aggressive particularism of a nation state. Its norms are located *beyond* the state's constitution, in an identity larger than national membership: in the identity of a virtual, potentially universal community of human rights bearers. Again, it seeks to establish those norms within the nation state and its constitution, so that the final constellation is a combination of nation state and human rights state, each somewhat limited by the other.

Digital communication can contribute to a postnational community of human rights values within or alongside a particular nation state. It so contributes where a human rights state forms itself not through mass opinion but through critical information. The Internet facilitates access to information and the sharing of information. The Internet can define itself through its embrace of human rights norms but equally by advocating the inclusion of human rights in the corresponding nation state's political and social institutions.

The Internet also offers a means for local struggles to "multiply" aspects of their goals and practices, moving local politics to a register more global. A multiplicity of local political movements together constitute a global context where domestic advocacy becomes a local environment "wired" with extra-local "circuits." In other words, local struggles become inflected with universal goals. Out of local advocacy, extra-local advocacy grows by aggregating different kinds of local struggles. Each local struggle is deeply embedded in its local context and history, each in the first instance pursuing norms local, not global. But local struggles develop an extra-local presence in digital media, gaining wider recognition of local struggles by multiplying local practices.

On-site arguments for human rights expand over time. They can grow to ever-greater scales, indeed through the choices of ordinary nation state citizens. They can enlarge the domestic practices of nation state institutions through human rights advocacy. Local struggles framed in human rights terms win wider recognition for those struggles because the terms of the discussion are now also cosmopolitan rather than only domestic. Framing different local struggles within one nation state, or across several nation states, has an aggregating effect. Digital communication multiplies local factors to identify and develop extra-local affinities and transborder flows of ideas and practices.

Internet Works Toward Normatively Universal Human Rights in Local Communities

Members of a human rights state deploy digital communication to argue for points of resonance between the normatively particularistic force of local struggles and the normatively universalistic idea of human rights. Their self-authored human rights resonate with a conception of the corresponding nation state that makes human rights an internal feature. One all-too-brief phase of the French Revolution offers one historical precedent: article 4 of the French constitution of 24 June 1793 (Acte constitutionnel du 24 juin 1793). The "status of citizens" provides that "every man born and living in France, having achieved twenty-one years of age, who, domiciled in France for one year—and who lives from his labor—or has acquired property—or married a French woman—or has adopted a child—or supports an elderly man; and finally, any alien judged by the legislative body to be well deserving of humanity—is admitted to the exercise of the rights of a French citizen."[16] Note the universalistic quality of this particularistic national constitution: it endows every adult foreigner, resident in France for at least one year, with the same rights as the French citizen's.

A human rights state is similarly universalistic. Each human rights state supports all other human rights states in their respective quests to gain recognition for human rights in the corresponding nation states. Further, any one human rights state endows members of all human rights states with whatever entitlements it offers to its members, binding them to the same duties that its members bear, and advocating support for all human rights states anywhere in the world.[17]

An individual's enjoyment of self-granted human rights in the human right state is congruent with his or her citizenship in the corresponding nation state, such that national citizenship comes to include human rights. A human rights state targets the government and laws of the corresponding nation state, toward transforming them.

One dimension of that transformation is "normatively thin."[18] The individual's attachment to a human rights state is itself normatively thin.

He or she is bound to a human rights state not by points of cultural reference but by a human rights state's cosmopolitan principle of seeking human rights not only for its members but for all members of the corresponding nation state, and by supporting other human rights states in their efforts. Normatively thin cosmopolitan community contrasts with normatively thick national community before it is mediated by a human rights state. Membership in a human rights state has a universal content whereas citizenship in the nation state has a particularistic content. For example, a human rights state offers membership to anyone, whether or not they are citizens of the corresponding nation state. This openness to outsiders is more liberal than even those of article 4 of the Jacobins' 1793 constitution.

Internet Can Recognize Individuals' Special Obligations to Local Communities

But membership in a human rights state is not universalist in all respects. A member retains various special obligations to his or her corresponding nation state. He or she has special duties to compatriots: the needs of one, connected to poverty, say, are different from the needs of others, related to civil strife, for example. He or she has duties that exist only within the social and cultural borders of that community and not within the potentially global community of human rights bearers: not all members of that community struggle with poverty or civil strife.

Further, a member of a human rights state has particularistic obligations to family and, say, to members of his or her parish, or profession, or to groups in addition to his or her political community. And, of course, one's local community may well include persons quite distant from the individual's own nation state. On the one hand, social proximity can hardly define boundaries of particularistic obligations. On the other hand, some special obligations are generated by physical proximity, certainly as a matter of efficiency. The local populace might be assigned specific responsibilities because, for example, one can more easily attend to those geographically near than to those distant. Such an assignment does not morally excuse its addressees from a human rights–based moral obligation to those distant. But it recognizes that local resources and institutions are most efficient when deployed locally.

Special obligations of this sort contrast with a general or universalistic obligation to observe individual rights arguably more fundamental than enfranchisement (as I argue in Chapter 8), such as rights to life, liberty, freedoms of conscience and assembly, and freedom from discrimination on the basis of sex, ethnicity, race, religion, age, or national origin.

Internet Can Contribute More Effectively to Human Rights Advocacy Than to Democracy Building

The Internet offers more promise where human rights are least needed, in democratic regimes; and it offers less promise where human rights are more needed, in oppressive, authoritarian communities. Further, richer communities of any political kind have much greater access to digital media than poorer ones. Richer communities tend to change culturally more rapidly than most countries in the developing world, where normative realignment in a human rights sense generally is more urgent than elsewhere.

By itself, an enhanced communicative capacity promises nothing in the way of democratic process, no more than an enhanced capacity to disseminate information necessarily empowers a political community's members. To be sure, the diffusion of information about human rights encourages a free embrace at the local level, such that some Internet use can be an act of civic engagement, encouraging advocacy, protest, and new values. By itself, however, diffusion does not increase democratic participation or otherwise cultivate "digital democracy." Computer-mediated, web-based debates have unequivocally democratic potential only in limited contexts, such as subverting the censorship of authoritarian regimes that both control public opinion and suppress it.

Even in authoritarian regimes that dominate and suppress public opinion by means of censorship, the Internet has so far displayed little democratizing potential.[19] Between 1989 and 1994 the number of electoral democracies worldwide grew from 69 to 113, yet with no help from the Internet (which at the time was much less developed and accessible than it is today). More recently, the Arab Spring from 2010 to 2012 displayed little evidence that digital technology facilitates political liberalization. To be sure, protesters and rebels did not act in isolation; they took advantage of computer-mediated communications technology to draw inspiration from each other and to exchange tactical information. Sometimes the Internet facilitated the spontaneous coming together of demonstrators. But while the dissidents initiated the movement, the soldiers retained the last word. If demonstrations seemed to appear out of nowhere, then not on the basis of strategizing by digital means but because the conventional political forces were inefficient, spent forces unable to anticipate revolutionary developments, let alone head them off. Protests were limited in scope and failed to bring about any far-reaching change. Only half of the six rebellions (in Tunisia, Egypt, and Yemen) achieved a change in leadership.[20]

The Internet has yet to confront effectively any autocratic institution or coercive apparatus that keeps the opposition at bay. It remains to be seen if cybertechnology will ever contribute meaningfully to reconfiguring a community's political and economic conditions. Democratic consolidation in particular requires what the Internet cannot provide: the reorganization of political and economic conditions. Still, democratic consolidation is not necessary for a human rights state to pursue its advocacy of human rights, even under the difficult and discouraging conditions in the Middle East and North Africa.

The Intersection of Culture and Nature in Digital Technology

Whether the Internet can be a human rights resource in any given case, in any given community, will depend on how it copes with several factors. I see four.

First, digital communication will always need to attend to irreducible and sometimes difficult social dimensions. These dimensions include the material conditions necessary for such technologies; the fact that much of the meaning of what happens in digital space comes from nondigital settings; and the fact that cyberspace can hardly escape the particular values, cultures, power systems, inequality, hierarchy, and the institutional orders in which it is embedded.

Second, the market, among other factors, limits the digital capacity for self-determination inasmuch as the Internet's infrastructure is privately owned; because a large proportion of electronic networks is private and inaccessible to nonmembers; because the Internet's openness and technology leave it vulnerable to indirect control and limitations to access.

Third, the Internet is always vulnerable to different kinds of regulation hostile to human rights, such as governmental authority through technical and operational standard setting for hardware and software. It is vulnerable as well to the power of large corporate interests in orienting the Internet toward privatizing various of its features and capabilities.

Fourth, electronic space is far more accessible in highly industrialized countries than in less developed ones. In developed countries, it is far more accessible for middle-class households than for poor ones.

To develop a strategy to realize the potential of digital media to further the human rights project, advocates need to understand the gap between the Internet's human rights potential and factors that inhibit its realization. That is, they need to appreciate that technology can only be a tool and in itself promises nothing in the way of social justice. Factors that inhibit its positive realization are themselves not technological but rather human.

To illuminate this point, I offer a rather philosophical excursus on the relationship between nature (as in humans) and culture (as in human artifacts, such as technology). Humans are evolved organisms with a capacity for culture. By *culture* I mean inventions of the human mind, such as political, legal, and moral orders. Always in nature, humans also always exceed biological existence by "doing" culture. Central to culture is the activity of interpretation, responding to questions such as: Which rights are properly construed as human rights? What is a human in the sense of human rights? (Does a fetus have human rights, for example?) What role do human rights play in various forms of social justice? What do rights for humans imply or entail about possible rights for nonhuman animals? How do human rights–oriented worldviews best engage and exchange with comprehensive worldviews that compete in part with human rights, including religious faiths?

A very different type of culture is technology, also an invention of the human mind. The political significance of technology flows in part from its cultural interpretation—but in part from the power it offers to accomplish human ends.

The cultural interpretation of cultural artifacts of one sort—technology—can only be guided by cultural artifacts of another sort—social norms. Norms are core elements of any human community. People understand themselves as moral agents, and that understanding is one of many in which nature and culture flow into one another. As one particular concern with norms of behavior, someone who imagines universal human rights thereby imagines man's *biological* membership in a *cultural* category. That is, the person regards all members of a species equally as rights possessors—equally as bearers of the cultural construct of rights. At the same time, someone imagining norms to guide his or her behavior with regard to the bodies of others then engages in *cultural* membership in a *biological* category. For he or she is imagining normative guides—which are cultural—for a piece of nature, the evolved organism that we are.

How is this normative understanding of a biological category—say, our bodies understood biologically—related to a cultural product, technology? After all, technology allows us to "escape" our bodies (as well as national boundaries), at least in the restricted sense of disembodiedness and boundarylessness in cyberspace. The answer concerns *how* nature and culture flow, one into the other, when humans manipulate, through technology, human presence in time and space. That flow, between the categories of nature and culture, is evident in the sorts of questions one could ask about manipulation: Why does it matter, at the level of culture, whether we manipulate ourselves in digital space? What cultural limitations should we place on the mode and scope of digital engineering and why? (I answered one aspect of this question above: we should want to place legal limitations on this technology where doing so prevents abuse.)

The question remains: Where lies the boundary between the natural bodies that we *are* and the technology we *give* ourselves? This is not a question about digital technology as such; it is a question about the mode and scope of its use. It is a political question, one about the technical capacity to transform our political presence: How can we determine, at the level of culture, what kind of presence might be "best" for us if the goal is universally valid human rights? The answer concerns how we relate ourselves to nature and to our bodies in particular. When we so relate through digital technology, nature is not something that limits us. It is not something we are constrained to simply accept, in the sense of something that should not be at our technological disposal.

Culture in the form of technology marks historical practices that, in their plasticity, reflect human will and design. Such historical practices reflect the human capacity to mold and remold ideas, artifacts, institutions, practices, and norms. At the level of historical practice, humans seek to control the double-edged quality of the technology. Humans should seek a politics that deploys technology in ways emancipatory rather than oppressive.

Here we also have one possible relationship between human biology and human culture that creates technology. One's genome determines some aspects of one's "natural fate" (a predisposition to certain diseases or disorders, for example). While political socialization may determine some aspects of one's "cultural fate," political socialization is highly malleable.

By *political socialization* I mean the lineages of historical traditions and the settings of social interactions that form the individual's personal and social identity over the course of a lifetime. Human rights provide one perspective on how best to evaluate cultural fates today and to imagine better fates tomorrow. The task is one of moral imagination beyond all technology. For humans have no objective knowledge of values beyond moral insight, a fact reflected in intractable disagreements about the nature and extent of human rights. The human species has no species-wide normative viewpoint, no cultural guide to how our species might best understand itself ethically. Disagreements are inevitable among competing approaches toward a species-wide ethics. The ethical conceptions of particular political communities do not harmonize with some universal self-understanding of humans. Correspondingly, there is today no universal cultural consensus on protecting the rights, dignity, and self-determination of the individual.[21]

Perhaps any notion of the inviolability of human dignity, as one possible basis for human rights, presupposes moral control of technological capacities to render once again morally inviolable that which technology has made available to human control. Of course, technology itself cannot answer normative questions such as: Where is the line between desirable and undesirable technological manipulation best drawn?

Could the digital manipulation of the human body ever constitute something like a transgression of natural boundaries? Yes, but only if human life is thought to possess some kind of metaphysical essence that endows it with a telos or destiny, as part of a natural order capable of being violated in sacrilegious ways. In fact, this viewpoint erects artificial barriers in terms of taboos that would protect "human nature" from its capture through empirical observation by human technology.[22] If restricting digital disembodiment and digital denationalization are possible only as a re-enchantment of nature—of "human nature" in particular—then doing so "moralizes" nature. To *moralize nature* is to invest it with socially constructed meanings that deny their own social-constructedness, toward sanctifying or enchanting nature on a basis theological or metaphysical. We miss the distinction between nature and culture in technology if we view humans as something essentially "natural," indeed with some kind of human right to "naturalness" in the sense of being free of technical intervention and culturally guided engineering.

This chapter concludes the second part of this book. The first part explored the notion of politics through metaphor—a human rights state—

while the second part deployed the politics of metaphor in various forms and venues of persuasion. The third part, to which I now turn, addresses several of the greatest challenges that a human rights state confronts: How can someone swear allegiance to both a national identity and the cosmopolitan identity of human rights (Chapter 7)? If democratic communities are distinctly friendlier toward the human rights idea than are nondemocratic communities, is democracy itself a condition for the possibility of human rights—in a world much of which is decidedly nondemocratic (Chapter 8)? Can human rights ever be advanced through humanitarian military interventions, even in cases of grave human rights abuses (Chapter 9)?

PART III

Defense of the Human Rights State
in the Face of Challenges

Chapter 7

Human Rights Patriotism

Part I of this book develops the notion of a human rights state. Part II then deploys this theory in three empirical contexts. Part III will now defend the theory against three particularly significant challenges. This chapter responds to the challenges to human rights cosmopolitanism posed by national patriotism. Chapter 8 addresses the fact that, while democratic conditions facilitate human rights, many of the world's nation states are not democratic and are distinctly unlikely to go democratic in the foreseeable future. Chapter 9 examines humanitarian intervention in the name of human rights that all too often threatens to undermine those human rights.

Note that all three of these challenges involve the nation state. To be sure, factors beyond the state also challenge the human rights state, including poverty, as Chapter 3 makes clear, and warfare, as we see in Chapter 9. Moreover, the state is a vague and distant abstraction particularly to some rural populations in some parts of the developing world for which local power dynamics alone are relevant. Still, for the inhabitants of most of the world's regions, life's basic political unit remains the nation state.

Forms of attachment to the nation state are many. Most citizens likely regard their national membership in multiple, overlapping terms of territory and culture; history and perhaps some conception of historical fate; patrimony and or ancestral inheritance; community constituted by family, friends, neighbors; the "imagined community" of conationals, most of whom one does not know. Most citizens probably regard themselves as insiders. Insiders and outsiders typically think that insiders have a discretionary right to exclude outsiders territorially. Insiders usually want to perpetuate some of today's shared institutions and cultural practices into the distant future, to preserve them for future generations.

And they typically want to perpetuate a right to exclude outsiders. National membership is widely understood as a kind of territorial patrimony, as a right of the members of a legal community to exclude others from its territory. Patrimony is a form of favoritism toward those already resident, toward fellow members who share an inherited context along cultural lines, and perhaps even a community of national identity. Members of the contemporary nation state likely regard the exclusion of outsiders as morally and politically acceptable if based on a particular kind of favoritism. The peculiar favoritism of patriotism is allegiance or loyalty to a particular nation state.

I ask: Is patriotism in any form compatible with what might seem to be its opposite, the universalist humanitarianism of the human rights idea? Is loyalty to the nation state congruent with the idea of norms that obtain across national borders? Does favoritism toward one's country fit with the idea of a human right of all persons to be treated in certain ways regardless of national affiliation or place of residence?

Anyone who regards patriotism as compatible with human rights cosmopolitanism probably entertains a fairly positive notion of patriotism. One might construe patriotism as necessary for cohesion even in the constituent elements of a cosmopolitanism beyond those elements: "without some internal support and loyalty, no group, however small, could survive" (Bok 2002:40). Perhaps one thinks that states need "strong identification on the part of their citizens" and a "strong sense of allegiance" (Taylor 2002:119). Some people suggest that patriotism provides a "basis for education, socialization, aspiration, and loyalty" (Falk 2002:54). Some are persuaded that it plays a "humanizing role" as an "identity politics in a deracinating world of contracts, markets, and legal personhood" (Barber 2002:30). Perhaps patriotism, at its best, provides the basis for a "coherent moral education" that can only be "rooted in particular moral communities with distinctive identities" that are not "too bloodless to capture the moral imagination" (McConnell 2002:79).

But the rootedness, localism, and particular cultural attachments of patriotism would appear irreconcilable with human rights cosmopolitanism in obvious ways. Most arguments relate patriotism and cosmopolitanism in one of three ways.

One way is to insist that patriotism and human rights occupy very different domains of belonging. Accordingly, human rights are cosmopolitan because they aspire to universal validity; they articulate a threshold commitment to just behavior and treatment for everyone. Patriotism, by contrast, aspires to very particular attachments to a very limited group of people—namely, fellow citizens. While the patriot might regard his or her compatriots as bearers of human rights, the patriotic relationship is countercosmopolitan. It places country before right (or defines country *as* right) while cosmopolitanism places right before country (or defines cosmopolitan as right). This stark trade-off is jingoistic, easily leading to an impasse.

A second way of relating patriotism and cosmopolitanism is to contrast the concrete emotional immediacy of patriotism with the abstract and distant emotional quality of cosmopolitanism. People sympathetic to this viewpoint argue that cosmopolitanism denies the "givens of life: parents, ancestors, family, race, religion, heritage, history, culture, tradition, community—and nationality," all of which are "essential attributes" and "defining characteristics that go into a fully formed human being, a being with an identity" that is "given, not willed. We may, in the course of our lives, reject or alter one or another of these givens, perhaps for good reason. But we do so at some cost to the self" (Himmelfarb 2002:77). Or people inclined to this viewpoint claim that patriotism ("localized attachments," the "closer ties of nation, community, or religion" and the "very basis of our natural sociality") trumps abstract cosmopolitanism because its goods are greater, its dangers less; unlike cosmopolitanism, it does not "breed contempt for our actual fellow citizens" (McConnell 2002:82). Again we have a rather stark trade-off, easily leading to an extreme rejection of cosmopolitanism. One form of rejection is functional, finding cosmopolitanism simply too "thin" for allegiance: "Like such kindred ideas as legal personhood, contract society, and the economic market, the idea of cosmopolitanism offers little or nothing for the human psyche to fasten on" (Barber 2002:33). Another form of rejection would expose cosmopolitanism as fraudulent: "Cosmopolitan political loyalty" in fact expresses the "Western cultural tradition" (Glazer 2002:64).

I urge a third possibility of relating patriotism and cosmopolitanism. I propose their cohabitation in a sovereign nation state that embraces human rights as internal to itself. This position goes beyond claims that cosmopolitanism and patriotism are both good, such that one need not choose between them because "there isn't just one form of life that is 'good'" (Putnam 2002:94). My proposal also exceeds claims that cosmopolitanism corrects a serious neglect of the "interest of people who are not related to us through, say, kinship or community or nationality. The assertion that one's fundamental allegiance is to humanity at large brings every other person into the domain of concern, without eliminating anyone" (Sen 2002:114).

My argument from cohabitation is not a claim that human rights and patriotism are naturally or internally compatible. It proposes to make them so. It combines the conviction that human rights require a political, territorial space with the view that motivation in political community often requires some degree of emotional affect. Each of the components of my argument is familiar by itself. Thus Hannah Arendt tenders an argument from territory: the "fundamental deprivation of human rights is manifested first and above all in the deprivation of a place in the world which makes opinions significant, and actions effective," such that a "loss of a polity expels him from humanity" (Young-Bruehl 1982:257). For her part, Margaret Canovan (2000) associates the nation state with immediate and visceral emotions by contrast with the coolly reasoned embrace of abstract principles. She regards thick emotions as the pre-political springs of political community even in its formal administrative features of deliberation, legislation, and legal status.

I lace patriotism with human rights by making the human rights point of view integral to a citizen's point of view *as a citizen*. (1) I develop human rights patriotism as a politics of metaphor that (2) leads to a transnational patriotism in the form (3) of a constitutionally supported attachment both national and cosmopolitan.

Human Rights Patriotism as a Politics of Metaphor

I propose a *human rights patriotism*. As a cosmopolitan notion, my proposal is counterintuitive. After all, patriotism, however defined, will always include one element: a deeply particularistic commitment. Cosmopolitanism, however defined, will always include some element of universalism. Toward their reconciliation, I propose patriotism as loyalty to a *nonterritorial* polity, that is, to a human rights state. Patriotism so understood operates by means of metaphor because it operates through the metaphorical human rights state. The device of metaphor makes plausible what otherwise is implausible.

Human rights patriotism is a particular kind of politics. First, it replaces normatively thick social, cultural, and political particularism with normatively thin politics (Gregg 2003b). Human rights patriotism calls for a specifically *political* form of nation state patriotism. The term *political* in this context spans a variety of related meanings. For example, the political is not "natural." Thus persons who find themselves divided into separate, unequal groups do not regard themselves as "naturally" so divided—or as justifiably so divided (if "nature" grounds justification). Or the political has no ultimate, objective or consensual basis or source of validity but is thoroughly contingent—in the form of a public basis for principled critique within a world of competing principles. Alternatively, the political involves trade-offs between or among equally attractive goods. After all, sometimes the conditions of meeting some rights can be satisfied only at the cost of not meeting others. Or the political is nothing timeless: "Many of the threats protected against (e.g., unfair pay, lack of educational opportunity, lack of access to medical care, loss of nationality) arise distinctively in modern or modernizing societies" (Beitz 2013:30). Or the political is nothing static; it can articulate new rights and reject old ones, quite beyond merely elaborating ones already established.

Human rights patriotism, oriented on these various understandings of *political*, will easily resonate with political liberals in the Western mold. But it can resonate as well with conservative patriots of diverse molds, by means of good arguments. Someone convinced that human beings are "naturally" divided into separate and unequal groups might be persuaded otherwise by histories of marginalized or oppressed groups (including groups related to the person in question) overcoming their station to assume one of accomplishment and prestige. That some problems, or some rights, might endure need not discourage the conservative patriot. Justice, for example, as both a problem—where it is thwarted—and a right—as God-given, say—could be understood as a permanent goal requiring permanent effort. The conservative patriot might regard political values as timeless or static. But he or she would be open to ways in which those values are confronted by an ever-changing landscape—for example in technological development or medical breakthroughs, such as genetic engineering that might one day solve Parkinson's yet also pose questions of genetic "enhancement." To see politics as a clash among competing values is possible within a liberal worldview as well as within a conservative one. Politics is then understood as two goods that preclude one another. In this sense of *political*, for example, political conservatives in the United States today support monogamy and the nuclear family yet oppose same-sex marriage.

In short, the political can be addressed to people united in pursuit of a common political goal, in the spirit, say, of Jacques Maritain (1949), who regards human rights as the result of agreement in outcome despite disagreement in justification. The political in this sense describes a shared appreciation of shared political goods, from rights and freedoms to effective administrative institutions. It describes an interest in a common good that allows criticism of social practices and political institutions. But it does not homogenize competing positions even as it tempers them.

For a human rights patriotism, the reconciliation of patriotism and cosmopolitanism does not preclude attachment to, even partiality for, a particular polity. Particularism abides in the form of: "an individual who asks herself, 'Should I be a patriot?' does not typically face the further question, 'If so, then of which country?'" (Keller 2005:568). But cosmopolitanism is no less present because a particular polity can include within itself, as a feature of itself, a cosmopolitan identity. That is, citizens could identify themselves as members of a culture, community, and polity in terms of a unifying principle, such as a commitment to human rights.

The political, so conceived, reconciles patriotism and cosmopolitanism in two ways: through the diminution of state sovereignty and as the exercise of metaphor. I examine each in turn.

Commitment to Human Rights as the Diminution of State Sovereignty

A human right state seeks to diminish the reach or extent of the nation state's sovereignty without extinguishing its sovereignty as such. Here we have the real-world consequence of human rights patriotism. It is a domestic attachment to human rights; it is a patriotic attachment; and, ideally, it is a constitutionally supported attachment, as I argue in later pages. The patriot is attached to his or her nation state—now diminished in its sovereignty to the extent necessary for the domestic recognition of human rights. What extent is that? The following example illuminates a sliver of the vision but hardly its totality. If capital punishment is viewed as a violation of human rights, then a nation state with human rights patriotism would be prohibited by its own constitution from legalizing capital punishment. That prohibition would not be a matter of domestic decision (for example, by legislation, judicial interpretation, or referendum). But it would follow from the *domestic understanding* of human rights.

Note here what makes my approach to patriotism distinct from other approaches. Human rights patriotism is patriotism for a nation state that renders human rights *domestic* rights—citizens must obey them as a matter of national regulation—even as they are also always extra-domestic rights: their ultimate validity is cosmopolitan not national.

Patriotism of this sort renders human rights extra-domestic. Participating nation states freely embrace the extra-domestic entailments of human rights. These entailments include the legal arrangement that domestic legislation, judicial interpretation, or referendum cannot trump the human rights perspective on particular issues.

In each of these nation states, the controlling human rights perspective is the domestic one. Different polities will have domestic understandings of human rights that, at any given time, likely overlap but likely only in part.

But the participating nation state ceases to be the final arbiter of its own boundaries *with respect to human rights*—even as the national understanding of human rights is the controlling one. Such a national understanding does not rule out cosmopolitanism. It marries it to the domestic framework in terms of local interpretations of rights whose legitimacy is not only domestic.

This diminution of state sovereignty does not destroy state sovereignty. It modifies the state-centric model articulated in international instruments such as the United Nations' 1948 Universal Declaration of Human Rights (among other significant examples). My proposal is itself state-centric but not in the same way: each human rights state is focused on a corresponding nation state.

My proposal recognizes that international instruments such as the Universal Declaration of Human Rights locate primary responsibility for protecting human rights in states.[1] But my proposal does not lodge all responsibility for human rights solely in nation states. It locates responsibility also in individuals as potential *protectors* of human rights, as potential *violators*, but also as potential *authors* of human rights. Participating citizens of a nation state make themselves into addressees as authors of their own human rights. They do so in the corresponding human rights state.

Commitment to Human Rights as the Exercise of Metaphor

To say that a human rights state is metaphorical is to say that it pursues a politics of metaphor. To claim simply that metaphors can influence politics is to claim nothing new. Metaphors are ideas; any given politics has an ideational component insofar as it involves aspects of one or more world-views. By *metaphor* I mean a polity without territorial component, hence a polity of the imagination. It "stands" alongside the territorial nation state as a moral commitment. It works toward reorienting a nation state in human rights–friendly ways yet without undermining the nation state as a sovereign entity. By *metaphor* I also intend a means toward a core proposal of this book: social change through ideas—namely, advancing human rights through persuasion, not coercion.

Through metaphor, patriotism assumes a form that does not exclude human rights cosmopolitanism. I offer four arguments in support of this claim. First, a metaphorical state does not replace an actual state in, say, administrative functions or legal responsibilities. To include human rights as part of the nation state's self-understanding and responsibility is not to reject the individual's attachments to the nation state through national welfare systems and distributary mechanisms for other social goods and services. Membership in a human rights state exceeds a client's relationship to a state administration that simply provides services and benefits to its clients. It exceeds a private contract with its clientele.

Second, a human rights state is a metaphorical republic of members practicing self-granted human rights and advocating their inclusion in the corresponding nation state. It entails a republican culture that practices citizenship understood as political commitment and vibrant activism, indeed from the perspective of active participants, not passive observers. By *the perspective of active participants* I mean politics in the first-person plural: the "we" perspective of advocacy on behalf of an entire community. Membership means constant socialization of participants into persons expecting and demanding human rights for themselves and for fellow members of the corresponding nation state. This republican orientation discourages privatism, that is, members' retreat into private life and disengagement from the public sphere as well as from engagement on behalf of others, with special attention to the marginalized and the victims of injustice.

Third, the metaphorical human rights state does not lead to indifference about nation state membership status, especially citizenship; indifference destroys republican culture. Of the rights that a nation state protects, some protect members, such as a right to enfranchisement. But a human rights state certainly encourages the corresponding nation state to be more inclusive, to move toward partial enfranchisement for resident aliens, including local voting rights, for example, in municipal and district elections—not only as part of becoming a citizen but also for persons who will not become citizens. A human rights state also encourages its correlate nation state to embrace such nonmembers as "aliens, homeless foreigners, and stateless persons" with a legal status somewhat "more like the status of citizens" (Habermas 1996:509).[2] Civil rights in a nation state are compatible with human rights because citizenship in the national community is compatible with membership in a human rights state. In a nation state, citizen rights are civil rights. The rights of the metaphorical "citizen" of a metaphorical human rights state are, of course, human rights. The goal is domestic rights in the nation state such that the rights of the citizen include universal human rights.

Fourth, imagine different combinations of these two forms of patriotism. Different domains of authority could be assigned to each. The individual need not hold either form across all possible domains. Thus one might be a nation state patriot with regard to economic matters (the local deployment of local taxes, say) but a human rights patriot in public health, where one advocates taxes for a worldwide inoculation program. Or one might be a human rights patriot with regard to standards for labor but a nation state patriot concerning standards for required educational curriculum. Even then one might be a human rights patriot but only with regard to basic skills of reading, writing, and mathematics.

Human Rights Patriotism Is a Transnational Patriotism

In practice, human rights patriotism constitutes a patriotism that is transnational. *Transnational* refers to a concern greater than the national frame yet less than a world state or global citizenship. A human rights state advocates for human rights by transforming a nation state from within, whereby human rights become an integral aspect of nation state jurisdiction.[3] This is cosmopolitanism from *within* the nation state, nation state sovereignty that recognizes rights of transnational validity.

My proposal amounts to transnational solidarity that allows for particular commitments. Such solidarity might be forged in civic practice and political participation. It might be forged in terms of what citizens *do* rather than in terms of what they *are* (in terms of a common language, shared traditions, common descent, and so forth). This is a distinctly republican vision. It is not a national consciousness but a *postnational* consciousness that features the peculiar solidarity among persons who share not only the same moral convictions but convictions that are cosmopolitan.

Solidarity among participants is then twofold: it rests on universal values held domestically. To *hold universal values domestically* means two things. First, it means that the cosmopolitan norms of human rights monitor relevant domestic norms of the nation state for their compatibility with human rights and attempt to change those found to violate human rights norms. Second, it means that the transnational solidarity at the core of human rights does not rob the individual of all personal and group identities, all public and private interests, and all local commitments.

Transnational solidarity has no geographic boundaries even as each particular human rights state stands alongside a particular nation state.[4] Transnational solidarity has boundaries, just not those of a world state. Its boundaries are those of all human rights states, each advocating for human rights in the corresponding nation state. If entirely successful in its advocacy, a particular human rights state and the corresponding nation state merge. They merge in the sense that the nation state now recognizes human rights as a feature internal to its identity. At that point, the transformed nation state becomes a constituent part of transnational solidarity. Transformed nation state boundaries are no longer boundaries to the validity of human rights. National sovereignty no longer keeps human rights out of national territory. The nation state now recognizes human rights as part of its domestic legal and moral identity.

The individual makes him- or herself a member of a human rights state by embracing the idea and practice of human rights. That embrace is also psychological: if his or her nation state embraces human rights, the individual may feel patriotic about human rights and his or her nation state at the same time. In this way, transnational solidarity involves a moral psychology involved in patriotic feelings focused on a shared domestic culture of human rights. It does not homogenize the participants, for there is more than one form of membership and there are many different forms of belonging. Any given form of membership need not coincide completely with everyone else's to instantiate the ideal of human rights as political. By analogy: it does not undermine the strength of my ties to my fellow citizens that they are not all members of my family.

In other words, the sources of one's emotional attachments can be plural. I draw upon the richness of this word. *Plural* means that the universalistic aspirations of human rights can allow for many identities, locally constructed and attached to local ways of life. *Plural* also means that nation state patriotism does some work (a devotion to a national culture, say) and a commitment to human rights does other work (a devotion to universal rights, addressed here to one's fellow citizens, say). Nation state patriotism is then not so much laced with the universalistic humanitarianism of the human rights idea as it is constrained by that humanitarianism—constrained not to violate it. Finally, *plural* means that human rights patriotism does not require some norm (such as international law) or institution (such as a world state) that transcends or transgresses the political sovereignty of existing nation states.

So why speak of patriotism rather than cosmopolitan solidarity? After all, are not human rights already uncoupled from any particular territory by definition?[5]

First, there can be no international regime of human rights as long as human rights are mostly dependent on local state recognition. And while no form of patriotism is possible in relation to such instruments, it is possible in relation to the nation state. But the goal of a nation state that recognizes human rights as part of its constitutional self-understanding can be advanced by the politics of metaphor. As a human rights state successfully turns the corresponding sovereign nation state into a state that embraces human rights, the work of international politics—among all such nation states, but not between them and nation states that have not embraced human rights as domestic policy—becomes more human rights driven.

Second, constitutionalizing human rights involves not only the international solidarity of human rights but also possible patriotism toward the particular nation state. Along one dimension I would invoke Dolf Sternberger's (1990:13–31) notion, as developed by Jürgen Habermas (1996), of "constitutional patriotism," a patriotism toward a particular state's constitutional tradition that enshrines a set of basic rights. Yet human rights patriotism exceeds the idea of constitutional patriotism, which concerns citizens' patriotism toward their national constitution and not toward the human rights project.[6] If the nation state is a "complex of hierarchically organized capacities available for the exercise of political power," and a constitution "lay[s] down the fundamental rights that free and equal founders mutually grant each other" (Habermas 2006a:131–132), then a human rights state goes beyond patriotism as allegiance to a historically situated tradition that embodies a set of principles. It goes beyond the constitution as a state-based historical fait accompli. It goes beyond both by means of metaphor, in several ways.

In short, a human rights patriotism does *not* require the wholesale renunciation, in any given nation state, of its particular political, cultural, or religious commitments. Rather, a human rights state diminishes state sovereignty as far as necessary for the realization of human rights. A commitment to human rights requires the renunciation of those particularistic cultural commitments that locally violate human rights. The pursuit of human rights within a nation state can harness patriotic attitudes. It can tap into a reserve of energy and commitment that can motivate behavior, individual and collective.

Human Rights Patriotism: A Constitutionally Supported Political Attachment Both National and Cosmopolitan

Human rights patriotism as a politics of metaphor leads to a transnational patriotism. Transnational patriotism takes the form of a domestic attachment to universal human rights. It does so when human rights become constitutionalized in ever more nation states. By *constitutionalizing human rights* I mean the legal indigenization, in a nation state, of human rights. The citizen of such a nation state is a "citizen of the world" without being a citizen of a world state. To be a citizen of the world is more than a legal status; it is a moral status that cannot be reduced to a nation state's laws. A moral status can be legalized (as in the U.S. Constitution's Thirteenth Amendment, outlawing slavery, that is, declaring the moral status of persons, at least on American territory, to be one that excludes given persons the legal status of property).

A moral status exceeds a legal status. If, as I propose, a moral commitment to human rights becomes compatible with a particular form of loyalty to a nation state, then terms such as a "moral point of view" and "moral identity" now exceed the usual application to the idea of a *moral commitment* to human rights. They now extend *patriotism* per se. A member of a human rights state (simultaneously a citizen of the corresponding nation state) shares with a nation state citizen (not a member of the corresponding human right state) a moral or political "duty to be concerned, for the sake of justice," with the "preservation of the state in which one is a citizen (provided it is just)" (Kleingold 2000:329–330). The person shares in a concern for a nation state's flourishing insofar as a "certain degree of flourishing is necessary for the state to secure justice (bankrupt states cannot enforce their own laws)," for example. And he or she shares in a concern with improving of the nation's states institutions "where necessary (including such preconditions for effective political participation as a good educational system)" (ibid.).

Combining the moral and the legal, the constitutionalization of human rights in a nation state leads to a mixed institutional structure. A domestic constitution that upholds the cosmopolitan values of human rights makes the nation state into a "coauthor" of those rights. Individuals give human rights to themselves through a human rights state and the nation state assumes responsibility for enforcing them.

I first address circumstances in which the moral and the legal—that is, human rights norms and national constitutions—cannot be combined, then turn to circumstances more promising.

Circumstances in Which Human Rights Norms and National Constitutions Cannot Be Combined

I advocate the incorporation of human rights into domestic law because I view human rights as moral rights that need to be juridified if they are to be enjoyed by all citizens, or to be enjoyed fully.[7] Because rights can take a legal or moral form, the idea of constitutionalizing the moral norms of human rights is immediately plausible. But the possibility of constitutionalizing them does not by itself recommend doing so. After all, to the extent that human rights have purchase in the world today, that purchase takes place mostly outside any existing legal framework. Amartya Sen (2011a:7) notes the work of human rights without legislation, for example, in the sometimes effective "monitoring of gross violations of what people tend to take as human rights, and other activist support provided by such organizations as Human Rights Watch, or Amnesty International, or Oxfam, or Médecins Sans Frontières, Save the Children, Red Cross, or Action Aid (to consider many different types of NGOs)."

All of the preceding chapters advocate the incorporation of human rights into the nation state's legal structure. But the means of advocacy—namely, the human rights state—operates not by legislation but rather by public discussion, persuasion, agitation, and education, whether through metaphor (Chapter 1), backpack (Chapter 2), body as boundary (Chapter

3), cognitive style (Chapter 4), civic commitment (Chapter 5), or digital abstraction from physical embodiment (Chapter 6). In this sense, advocacy is political work on behalf of human rights without the coercion of legal rules. Human rights have their source in politics and moral intuitions. They can assume a legal form, and can be more effective in legal form, without being reducible to narrowly legal terms. It is not law that guides human rights norms. It is moral imagination that inspires and sustains human rights norms. In some ways those norms exceed any juridified form they might take. For example, the extension of legal protections to women and children within the family provides help for some of the most vulnerable members of society, in one of the most vulnerable venues—the private sphere. But the logic of familial relationships, the moral obligations mutually owed within the family, cannot be realized by legal means. When domestic tort law must be invoked to protect victims, the moral qualities of the familial relationship have already been grievously damaged and may be irreparable. These moral qualities cannot be replaced by legal rules.

Other areas of life enjoy legal protection from particular moralities offended by the action, including abortion, sex outside of marriage, same-sex marriage and other rights for homosexuals, let alone particular religious beliefs and practices and other forms of expression. In these cases the offending behavior is not criminal. It may have been decriminalized and, if so, in the name of rights to privacy and expression and personal autonomy.

In short, for moral norms to inspire specific legislation, moral norms need not be parasitic on positive law. Such norms can motivate legislation and judicial enforcement. For Jeremy Bentham, rights can only be a "child of law." But for H. L. A. Hart (1984:79), the idea of a right not yet a law can inspire corresponding legislation, and inspiration can motivate: people "speak of their moral rights mainly when advocating their incorporation in a legal system."

Circumstances in Which Human Rights Norms and National Constitutions Can Be Combined

In other contexts, law ensures effective support and realization of moral norms, including nonlegal rights. Law extends from the legal enforcement of legislatively or constitutionally created rights to a political community shaped by a constitutional culture of rights and legal consciousness. That culture exists quite beyond formal legality, not only among legal professionals but among the general populace.[8]

Cosmopolitan patriotism does not reject constitutionalism "in favor of unanchored good will that can be summarized under the heading of generous imaginings," bypassing legal provisions and constitutional procedures and thus erasing authorizing bases for human rights norms (Scarry 2002:99). Nor does it pursue a bright-line division between legislation and formal legal enactment, on the one hand, and informal, nonlegal strategies, on the other. Instead it relates the legal and the moral to one another in ways that do not damage or diminish either but rather change the institutional structure of both.[9]

Consider a right guaranteeing freedom of expression. In the United States, the First Amendment right of expression protects the expression by ordinary citizens and private organizations of slanderous, bigoted, racist, misogynist, deliberately deceitful, and otherwise hateful and hurtful expression. But a different clause of the same amendment prohibits governmental speech that favors or disfavors any particular religion (the prohibition applies, for example, to state officials speaking in an official capacity). In this example, the law protects the particular moralities of private citizens and groups. And it prohibits the state from advocating or criticizing these moralities.

Now contemplate the different example of courts of law that sometimes facilitate the realization of certain social rights in areas such as housing, health care, elementary education, and minimum wage. In this case, constitutional law supports norms in the shape of *imperfect* obligations. These are obligations of the state. They do not imply a right to compel performance; they do not entail a legal sanction for nonperformance. They allow exceptions in the interest of inclination, or to adopt certain ends but not to do certain acts.[10] Horacio Javier Etchichury (2006:111) notes that, in 2000, the Argentine Supreme Court confirmed a lower court decision ordering the "national government to grant timely and appropriate medical treatment, including the allocation of required drugs, to all patients affected by HIV/AIDS. The court enforced the state duty as described in a national law and as framed in the right to health care, now included in the Constitution." Etchichury then extrapolates a vision for a generalized judicial enforcement of various social rights. He urges judges in Argentina to "combine and improve the concepts of 'reasonableness' and 'minimum core,' in light of their institutional mission, namely, to protect the citizens' rights."

He encourages them to "analyze the resources really available, going beyond existing budget allocations, and requiring the state to demonstrate the impossibility of reaching the 'minimum core'" (ibid.,123). He recommends that the judiciary replace the notion of minimum core with what he calls an "adequate" or "proportional core," in light of the "prevailing social and economic conditions of the country as a whole" (ibid.). And he advises the judiciary to transform state policy into legal obligation. In that case, the "court declares that what the state did was not a policy choice, but rather a duty under a constitutional provision, a statute, or even an international law treaty or covenant" (ibid.).

And what about instances where the legal supports the moral? The legal supports the moral by interpreting constitutional provisions to entail, in their penumbra, certain directly enforceable social rights. Peter Quint (1999:307–308) observes as much in the German Constitutional Court's holdings that "various statutory programs of social welfare insurance —such as those providing for old age pensions, health benefits, and unemployment compensation—create protected property rights in the beneficiaries." Quint observes the legal supporting the moral in the court's interpretation of article 14 of the German Basic Law (*Grundgesetz*), which states that "property has its obligations. Its use should also serve the well-being of the community." The court, says, Quint, thus "allows the limitation of certain property rights for the purpose of furthering goals of social welfare." And Quint observes the legal supporting the moral in the court's claim that the *Grundgesetz* "requires that financial disparities among the [federal] states be mitigated through compensatory federal payments, coupled with a complex system of allocating certain tax revenues among the state governments," toward equalizing the "ability of the states to provide a broad range of services, including social welfare."

Finally, I would note that even as authoritarian states reject rule-of-law and executive accountability, they may still support limited rule by law for reasons of social order and stability. Courts in authoritarian regimes are not always mere pawns. Some judiciaries operate within illiberal contexts to promote some social norms, in some cases functioning as sites of resistance. Courts in some authoritarian states sometimes rule in ways that promote more liberal agendas contrary to regime interests and goals. Sometimes dictators may empower courts that then sometimes contest aspects of regime rule (Ginsberg and Moustafa 2008). Evidently authoritarian elites, and not only democratic ones, sometimes feel compelled to trust courts if courts are to have any power (Hirschl 2004), as did the Egyptian leadership to facilitate economic development—only to find that critics were able to use courts to lance claims against the state (Moustafa 2009). In China, lower courts have developed into fora for contesting rights-based claims. They are not solely defined by top-down control and coordination by state and party, even as contestations of rights-based claims increase tensions with state and party (Liebman 2007). These examples indicate that even in political environments distinctly hostile to the rule of law, courts sometimes may support some social norms, and even some nonlegal rights. Courts do so not in the sense of constitutionalizing human rights domestically. They do so in the sense of providing openings, however limited and tenuous, for promoting some human rights norms to some extent.

In Chapter 8 I turn to another challenge for the human rights state: arguments that tie human rights to democracy. Such viewpoints claim that, without democracy, human rights are not possible. Yet developing democracy in these areas is much more difficult than developing some rule of law, itself no easy undertaking.

Chapter 8

———

A Human Right Not to Democracy
but to the Rule of Law

Depending on the nation state, for many people it is either the most important possible protector of an individual's life and liberty—or the greatest single threat. It is not only the default form of political and legal authority for most people. In many cases, the nature of that authority determines whether or not a person enjoys human rights.[1] The nation state is a strong authority, the strongest most people will ever confront. Observers tend to think of human rights accordingly. From one angle, Thomas Pogge (2002:57–58) frames human rights as grants from authority: "Human-rights postulates are addressed, in the first instance at least, to those who occupy positions of authority within a society (or other comparable social system)." From a different angle, Mathias Risse (2012:69) casts human rights in terms of their violation by authority. Of "two otherwise identical acts, only one might violate human rights, namely, the one that amounts to an abuse of authority" (ibid.). Pogge and Risse are typical of analysts who suggest (implicitly if not explicitly) that one can assert, without invoking a human right to democracy, that states abuse their authority when they abuse the human rights of citizens.

Democratic self-determination entails the right of participants to expression and assembly, dissent and opposition. It entails that right on behalf of all members of the community and not just for various elites. Is democracy a plausible candidate for inclusion on a list of possible human rights? Is equal access of citizens to participation in the democratic self-determination of a political community a fundamental human right?

I respond in several steps. (1) To determine what might best be constructed locally as a human right, I propose the capacity of the candidate norm to be freely embraced by its addressees. (2) I argue that the rule of law is the better alternative to constructing democracy as a human right. I then examine (3) the noncosmopolitan quality of democracy and (4) the rule of law and the possibility of self-determination without democracy to propose, toward advancing the human rights project, (5) the legalism not of democracy but of the rule of law.

Before I begin, I want to emphasize that, in any given case, a human rights state assumes a shape relative to the corresponding nation state. There is no human rights state *as such* because there is no nation state as such. Just as each nation state is unique, so each human rights state is singular. For that reason I speak in this book of *a* human rights state and rarely of *the* human rights state.

To be sure, nation states can and should be grouped plausibly along certain dimensions, depending on the criteria of interest. Along one dimension, Chapters 4 and 5 fit one category (democratic or newly democratizing polities) and this chapter fits another (nondemocratic regimes). Chapter 4 pursues human rights–oriented pedagogy in a democratic community. Chapter 5 analyzes countries in transition away from authoritarianism toward democracy (with case studies ranging from the robust, such as Poland, to the imperiled, such as Russia). By contrast, this chapter examines nondemocratic regimes hostile to democracy. It argues that democratic communities are distinctly friendlier toward the human rights idea than are nondemocratic communities. But democracy is not itself a condition for the possibility of human rights. Consequently a human rights state working with nondemocratic communities would emphasize the development of the rule of law, not democracy. That recommendation in no way vitiates my advocacy, in Chapter 4, of a pedagogy aimed at students in democratic states. Nor does it undermine, in Chapter 5, my ideas about facilitating the goals of democratization in newly democratizing communities.

Free Embrace of Public Decisions by Their Addressees

How might we determine what should count as a human right? As one condition, necessary but not sufficient, I propose the capacity of the candidate norm to find *free embrace by its addressees*. This proposal corresponds with a social constructionist understanding of human rights (Gregg 2012b). Accordingly, norms whose validity is a matter of social construction have practical purchase if their addressees freely embrace them. This embrace depends on publicly acceptable reasons capable of freely persuading participants in public discussion.

From the standpoint of social construction, which regards all norms as constructed, a free embrace by addressees is plausible as a test. The "better" the construction, the stronger the validity. To understand what makes construction stronger rather than weaker, consider criteria of construction.

First, all the problems of communication in general are relevant here. This approach depends on measures to ensure that the communication is not systematically distorted, whether willfully through propaganda or unintentionally because of inadequate information.[2]

Second, the potential validity of human rights is a matter of authoritative opinion or conviction. It is not a matter of empirical truth in the sense of natural science. Nor is it a subject of logical entailment in the sense of mathematics.[3] Unlike validity in natural science or mathematics, the validity of authoritative opinion cannot be nonpartisan. It cannot be nonparochial. It cannot be "invariant with respect to local conventions, institutions, culture, or religion" (Risse 2012:69). Validity here is always perspectival. It is embedded culturally and in time, without any culturally neutral point of reference. This relativist perspective contrasts with validity as understood in natural science, which measures propositions against an external world the same for all persons. And relativism contrasts with those religious faiths that measure propositions against sacred texts understood within the faith to be divine (indeed, divine even for persons outside the faith and even for persons with competing sacred texts).

Third, on a perspectival approach, a decision may be regarded as freely embraced even if only at one time; even if not on a continuing basis; and even if only some persons embrace it but others do not. A perspectival validity is not absolute. It is not absolute over time nor is it absolute as consensus among its addressees.

There is a flip side to these limitations. The greatest single merit of relativism is this: if human rights are social constructs rather than prepolitical metaphysical or theological givens, then constructs that addressees can freely embrace have greater promise of being practiced and protected than constructs that addressees are likely to reject. By *greater promise* I refer to the project of persuading as many people as possible to be guided by human rights, and to be so guided because participants freely regard them as valid norms. I advocate persuasion not coercion as the primary means of advancing the human rights project.[4]

The Rule of Law as a Plausible Alternative to Democracy as a Human Right

A democratic polity offers prospects for advancing the human rights project that are distinctly better than the prospects offered by nondemocratic polities, for reasons I address shortly. Here I want to suggest two things: first, that the human rights project can be advanced without construing democracy as a human right; and second, that it cannot be advanced without construing the rule of law as a human right. By *rule of law* I mean political power subordinated to established law whereby all people and institutions are subject to and accountable to enforceable law applied fairly.

To render democracy a criterion for the possibility of human rights is to render human rights impossible in many parts of the world that are undemocratic today and that will remain undemocratic for the foreseeable future. To make democracy a criterion for the possibility of human rights would make human rights impossible precisely in areas of the world where the need for them is the deepest and the most urgent. Better then, I argue, to decouple the human rights project from the project for advancing democracy. Better to pursue each project separate from the other, so that the difficulties of establishing a democratic way of life do not impede the prospects for advancing human rights even in nondemocratic polities.

This is a nonideal approach: human rights are more likely in a democratic community than in any of the variety of nondemocratic communities. From a human rights standpoint, ideally all communities would be democratic. With regard to the considerable benefits of democracy to advancing human rights, consider the following.

First, addressees of rules who are simultaneously the authors of those rules will embrace those rules freely. They are likely to embrace the organization of community that follows from such rules. Democracy is not the only way in which author and addressee can coincide, but it is the way most direct and compelling. Democracy and the criterion of free embraceability are not only compatible; they are mutually reinforcing (a community embraces its own self-determining choices). Democratic majorities will embrace decisions where they prevail, but minorities will embrace decisions even as they do not prevail, given the procedural legitimacy of the decision-making process, that is, if their minority status follows from procedurally correct decision mechanisms.

Further, democracy contributes to a free embrace of human rights if it includes values and orientations shared by participants—values of freedom of expression as well as wide access for individuals' participation in the public self-determination of political community.

The parliaments of democratic polities are interested in preserving such freedoms. But they are also interested in preserving maximum sovereignty. To that extent they are disinclined to legislate human rights. The advancement of human rights in democratic contexts does better to rely on wide-open discussion and debate in public fora. Here advocates assert the importance of freedoms necessary for such discussion and association—freedoms of speech, assembly, conscience, and opposition. These are core freedoms of a democratic polity. But not all of them are necessarily impossible in all nondemocratic contexts. Some nondemocratic orders would certainly limit such freedoms but not necessarily exclude all of them altogether.

Consider one of the most urgent of human rights: freedom from torture. Is a human right to be free from torture plausible only if universally valid? If torture is fundamentally violative of human rights, is it not violative without exception? If such a right is an absolute right, then its validity is independent of whether corresponding freedoms are available, such as a right to participate in the selection of legislators who could outlaw torture domestically. Its validity is independent of a right to freely express opposition to torture or of a right to organize citizens into political parties that would advocate against torture.

In other words, to argue against torture and any legislation that would either allow or not prevent torture, interlocutors need not be able to offer a claim as to what ideally should be legislated. A human right to be free from torture would not require a nondemocratic polity to meet the significant standards of a democratic polity in which assertions must be able to withstand public scrutiny if they are to retain a rational persuasive power (rational because based on discursive argument). Democracy is more likely to offer public scrutiny, and scrutiny more robust, than any nondemocratic form of political organization. (To be sure, actual democracies fail in various degrees to live up to the potential and promise of the democratic ideal.) From the standpoint of liberal democracy, norms can be regarded as valid within the polity only if they can survive ongoing processes of open and unhindered questioning and contestation.[5] Open critical scrutiny is no less important for confirming a normative claim as for disconfirming it. These are standards no nondemocratic polity is ever likely to meet.

Even though a right to freedom from torture is more likely in a political community that allows public opposition than in one where public and even private opposition may be forbidden and punished, freedom from torture does not require the more liberal type of community for its very possibility. What a right to be free from torture requires is an obligation of compliance. Immanuel Kant's distinction between perfect and imperfect duties helps us to see that the relevant obligation benefits from the rule of law (heightening the likelihood of enforcement) but not necessarily from a democratic order. According to Kant (1998), a *perfect duty* admits of no exceptions. All persons in a position to affect the matter bear an *imperfect obligation* to discourage or hinder torture (Kant 1956). Whereas the duty of the torturer is specific enough to be legislated (do not torture!), the corresponding obligation is so lacking in specificity as to ways or means that it cannot be legislated. While an imperfect obligation is still an obligation, it is easily overwhelmed by its indeterminacy and threatens to slide into no obligation at all. Hence while compliance with any obligation is more likely if the obligation is freely embraced rather than coerced—and free embrace is more likely if the norm to be complied with is the product of open scrutiny and democratic decision—compliance with some human rights is still possible in some nondemocratic communities.

Further, the common correlation between democracy and human rights is not unproblematic. Above all, democracy in a nation state is not transnational. It is countercosmopolitan: the sovereignty of democratic polities excludes everyone not a member of the demos, which is always most people in the world. Yet if human rights are to realize their aspiration to transnational validity, they must bind not only the domestic democracy that chooses human rights democratically but authorities *outside* the state as well. Mathias Risse (2012:214) captures this aspect of human rights: "for a right to X to be a human right" in distinction to any other kind of right, "it must involve duties (beyond nonviolation) on the part of entities in the global order other than a person's own state."

Democracy is an implausible candidate for inclusion among transnational norms binding on all states. It does not fit any plausible paradigm for duties of global reach.[6] It does not fit any number of paradigms. For example, even in legal communities guided by law, democracy does not fit common notions of a "responsibility to protect" that refer to norms prohibiting genocide and other grave violations. (I analyze the idea of a responsibility to protect in Chapter 9.) State failure to prevent genocide on its own territory triggers other states' responsibility to protect victims. By itself, the absence of democracy triggers no obligation to intervene in a sovereign state. Consider another paradigm: democracy fits no principle of universal jurisdiction whereby a state is entitled to assume jurisdiction over certain kinds of criminals even if it has no particular relation to them.[7] Or another: the International Criminal Court prosecutes crimes of genocide and war crimes but not a state's rejection of democracy.[8] Democracy does not fit the following paradigm either: the idea of making a state's "international legitimacy" contingent on its observation of its citizens' human rights usually refers to a right to life, not a right to democracy. The idea of making a state's legitimacy contingent on its minimal justness is no alternative. *Minimally just* in this context refers to bodily security and individual liberty, not to a democratic political system.

A human right to democracy is implausible on other grounds as well. David Held (1998) frames contemporary international relations in terms of "overlapping communities of fate" in which the needs and interests of one political community cannot be satisfied without engaging other communities. If, from a human rights standpoint, democracy in one form or another were the only acceptable form of political organization, then a (violated) right to human rights would outweigh the sovereignty of nondemocratic communities. A human right to democracy could entail international relations as centrally concerned with attempts to change nondemocratic states into democratic ones. It might destabilize a world of many nondemocracies that do not recognize human rights. The democratic states of the world then lie on a perpetual collision course with nondemocratic states because a core feature of the relationship between the two would be fundamentally antagonistic.

Three factors bear closer scrutiny. I examine each in the remaining pages of this chapter. First, a democratic polity that determines, through public debate, that a particular norm (such as a human right) is valid, finds it to be valid only for the participating *demos* but not for *demoi* beyond national borders. Second, many countries in the world today are not democratic. Some of them are without prospects for democracy in the foreseeable future (the Central African Republic, Equatorial Guinea, Eritrea, North

Korea, Saudi Arabia, Somalia, Sudan, Syria, Turkmenistan, and Uzbekistan, among others). Third, some communities are not strongly organized along formal legal lines, such that a legalistic understanding of human rights would have little purchase—even as nonlegal approaches often are unpromising.

The Noncosmopolitan Quality of Democracy

A domestic embrace of human rights clearly advances the human rights project. But domestic biases and the myopia of local moralities confound the aspiration of the human rights project to an embrace that crosses national borders to a global purchase. Global purchase begins locally with critical public reasoning toward a free embrace of the idea and practice of human rights. Global entry to public reasoning may advance that free embrace even further.

But global entry does not require modern democratic circumstances. One of the earliest proponents of global entry, Adam Smith, advocated it under circumstances of a society riven by socioeconomic class structure and a hereditary nobility, plus a morally myopic ruling class not easily challenged.[9] *Global entry*, entry not confined to one community, would allow for phenomena currently difficult to imagine, such as human rights advocates outside Afghanistan and Pakistan critically reviewing the Taliban practice of stoning adulterous women, and for Afghanis and Pakistanis critically evaluating the practice of capital punishment in the United States, China, and Iran. *Global entry* so understood refers to a process of attempting to be free of group or individual bias as far as possible. Elsewhere I have developed this approach as one of enlightened localism in distinction from unenlightened parochialism.[10] The approach is local because the venue of the action being judged is particular. It is enlightened because the standards of evaluation exceed that venue.

Global entry in its strongest possible sense would require a world state, in particular a state in which the constituent nations or peoples would enjoy a legally enforceable right to participate in a global public sphere. But talk of a global state is unrealistic today, for reasons I discuss in the Coda. My alternative, a human right to the rule of law in one's domestic community, requires no such state.

Rule of Law and Self-Determination Without Democracy

Democracy is hardly a global preference today; it may never become one. It is far distant from many of the political traditions, values, and cultures of some authoritarian political communities. That distance is structural and deeply rooted.[11] From a liberal democratic perspective, an authoritarian regime cannot be legitimate in any robust sense. Authoritarian regimes see things differently. Consider China.[12] The Communist Party of China explicitly rejects "civil rights, political and religious freedom, and Western democracy" in the sense of a division of executive, legislative, and judicial powers and a system of multiple parties holding office in rotation (Wang 2012:11–12). The "China Model, or Beijing Consensus, features an all-powerful political leadership that effectively manages social and economic affairs" (ibid., 10). This elite believes that "China's development model provides an alternative to Western democracy and experiences for other developing countries." It claims that "many developing countries that have introduced Western values and political systems are experiencing disorder and chaos" (ibid.).

Needless to say, authoritarian regimes do not entertain a politically liberal view of human rights. And China is not alone in viewing "many American activities in the world as violations of the principle of noninterference in other countries' domestic affairs" (ibid.,19). On this view, American "promotion of democracy and human rights are in reality policy tools to achieve goals of power politics" (ibid., 11), where the "ultimate goal of the United States in world affairs is to maintain its hegemony and dominance" (ibid., 10–11). Authoritarian regimes like China regard human rights with strategic distrust—as a means for liberal polities to achieve long-term strategic goals quite beyond human rights and to achieve these goals at the expense of the core interests of authoritarian regimes.[13]

At the same time, liberal democratic and authoritarian polities are equally attached to the notion of national self-determination. While all democratic forms of politics are forms of self-determination, not all forms of self-determination are democratic. I argue that, for purposes of advancing the human rights project, setting the standard higher than nondemocratic forms of collective self-determination is setting the standard too high in terms of what is realistically possible today.[14]

The relevant difference here is not between democracies and nondemocracies as much as between authoritarian communities and nondemocratic, nonauthoritarian communities organized through collective self-determination. Self-determining communities may offer any number of ostensible human rights, such as freedoms of expression, assembly, press, and political participation—even if not democracy. Authoritarian communities offer far fewer, if any, of these freedoms and thus render their citizens politically and legally equal to each other in fewer ways.

Politically and socially repressive regimes reject open public reasoning. Such regimes are unlikely to recognize human rights. They might not recognize the rule of law to any degree. But they are more likely to recognize some degree of the rule of law—to the extent it does not threaten a self-selected party's monopoly on power—than any degree of democracy. Rule of law in private and civil matters, in matters of contract and tort, may not threaten the state yet still contribute to social order. But the same cannot be said even of low-level, local democracy. Core features of democracy—the competition among different viewpoints, the organization of power outside state control—threaten an authoritarian state, whereas limited rule of law need not.

Even a limited rule of law offers some prospects for advancing at least some human rights (even if rejected by the authoritarian elites). Consider forms of legal equality possible in some authoritarian communities. To the extent that citizens enjoy equal legal standing in most day-to-day matters of civil and criminal nature, in access to medical care and primary education, in housing and welfare, they are part of a system in which subordination is unacceptable in those spheres. Subordination in any of these spheres can be challenged by appeal to law. Even a community that is less than fully just (or unjust yet beyond reproach) could provide equality in this sense.[15]

The rule of law is much more likely than democracy to find wide embrace across the globe. The benefits of the rule of law are clear: safety, order, and protection from many harms, if not from political harms perpetrated by the elite. The disbenefits of the rule of law may confront elites more than ordinary citizens. Thus resistance to the rule of law is more likely from authoritarian elites than the masses they rule over. In a legal system that allows people to sue for civil and criminal wrongs, for example, courageous legal professionals and others could deploy the system to challenge injustices committed by the elite.

Even in the most discouraging of circumstances, the goal of the project is a human rights–recognizing nation state (or other forms of governance where the nation state does not exist or is irrelevant to human rights conditions in local communities). The conditions in an authoritarian state are certainly difficult and discouraging. The task of developing a human rights state within or alongside such a polity is much more difficult than the task of a human rights state within or alongside a liberal democratic polity, which will be friendly to some human rights. Yet the members of the former human rights state self-determine no less than those of the latter one. For members of any human rights state are equally the authors and addressees of the human rights. In any human rights state, participants are related to each other in terms of formal reciprocity, as individuals free and equal to each other. They enjoy equal rights to participation in this metaphorical community of human rights–granting members. *Freedom* in this context is the freedom to participate in the metaphorical community's collective self-determination. *Equality* in this context means equal access to participation within that community.

Human rights advocates find little guidance for advocacy in the United Nations' Universal Declaration of Human Rights, article 21, which regards democratic representation, universal suffrage, periodic elections, and genuine proceduralism as the standard features of the nation state to which the declaration is addressed. The declaration either addresses itself to democratic polities in particular, or it implies that a democratic form of organization is the default form in a world of human rights: "Everyone has the right to take part in the government of his country, directly or through freely chosen representatives. Everyone has the right to equal access to public service in his country. The will of the people shall be the basis of the authority of government; this will shall be expressed in periodic and genuine elections which shall be by universal and equal suffrage and shall be held by secret vote or by equivalent free voting procedures."[16]

Democracy includes the rule of law but promises much more—for example, with respect to the distribution among citizens of social, economic, and political status. In Chapter 9 I advocate a human rights minimalism that guarantees life and individual liberty but not democratic conditions. These guarantees do not require a democratic political community; they are possible under nondemocratic conditions. So what *do* life and individual freedom require? Consider the possible perspective of persons denied them. No one would be surprised if persons denied respond by freely embracing resistance. No one would be surprised if they granted themselves a *right* to resist. History records examples of communities authoring their own right to resistance against oppressive institutions and practices—for example, in the Déclaration des droits de l'homme et du citoyen of the French Revolution. Persons who author their own rights to resist are engaged not in democracy but in resistance to oppression. They assert a right not to democracy but a right to be free from oppression. Resistance to oppression creates a political space that is defensive and reactive in nature. Democracy creates a space that can be defensive and reactive, but, more important, it creates a space that can be offensive and constructive. Freedoms of conscience, expression, and assembly, for example, exceed rights to life and individual freedom. Such freedoms are internally related to a democratic form of political community. A right to democracy is plausible as a right of the citizen operating at a very high level of moral agency. But it is implausible as a right of the human being as such at a lower level of moral agency.

Further, the citizen who enjoys a right to democracy is probably already a citizen of a democratic political community. Such a person cannot be viewed as simply a member of the species. We observe the high level of normative agency involved in a right to democracy by its extensive requirements vis-à-vis the political community. For example, a rights-bearing woman is gravely hindered in realizing those rights if she is afforded only a poor education. She is stalled if obstacles such as poll taxes, literacy tests, or extralegal intimidation are placed in her way to register to vote. The same is true if she is discouraged from participating because she is a woman (or dark skinned, or poor, or an immigrant, or a lesbian, or a member of a disfavored confession or a despised national heritage). She may be discouraged from registering to vote simply because she lives in a chronically economically depressed region that the authorities supply with a higher-than-usual number of faulty voting machines.

From my perspective of human rights minimalism, advocates are better guided by the International Covenant on Civil and Political Rights, article 1.[17] It provides for nondemocratic self-determination: "All peoples have the right of self-determination. By virtue of that right they freely determine their political status and freely pursue their economic, social and cultural development." Providing a right to self-determination is not necessarily providing a right to a specifically democratic form of self-determination. A right to self-determination does not entail the equality of the individual members of a self-determining political community. It entails only that different political communities are equally entitled to a right of self-determination.

Further, the process of self-determination need not be based on collective decisions. Nor need it equally represent the interests and opinions of all members of the community. It can be compatible with domestic laws and regulations that generate or preserve various kinds of legal and other inequalities among groups and individuals, even to the point of infringements of other fundamental interests of particular members, such as favoring members of one religious faith with regard to occupying positions of authority in the state.

John Rawls imagines human rights in just this sense when he speaks of human rights within "decent, hierarchical communities." Even as nondemocratic, such communities could still offer the "right to life (to the means of subsistence and security); to liberty (to freedom from slavery, serfdom, and forced occupation, and to a sufficient measure of liberty of conscience to ensure freedom of religion and thought); to property (personal property); and to formal equality as expressed by the rules of natural justice (that is, that similar cases be treated similarly)" (Rawls 1999b:65).[18]

In other words, group membership organized around a shared common good may still exclude individual rights—for example, by allowing the common good to trump individual preferences. This understanding of human rights, for example, allows for restricting freedom of religious belief but not precluding it. It allows for privileging one confession over others.[19]

Narrow conceptions of human rights—such as mine, or Rawls's, or that of the International Covenant on Civil and Political Rights—regard all individuals as inherently worthy of being treated as legally free and equal. More expansive conceptions—the Universal Declaration of Human Rights offers one example; Seyla Benhabib, another—render individuals not only free and equal but beneficiaries of an "equal individual right to political participation" (Joshua Cohen 2006:236). Benhabib argues that *self*-government can be nothing other than *democratic* self-government. Hence, self-government requires human rights because "without the right to self-government, human rights cannot be contextualized as justiciable entitlements" (Benhabib 2013a:89–90). In fact, human rights *can* contextualize justiciable entitlements under nondemocratic circumstances if a legislature so legislates. Above, I give reasons why even some authoritarian polities might welcome some degree of the rule of law, and why some justiciable entitlements could fall within that degree, including some rights that are plausible candidates for human rights, such as the legal equality of men and women. If even some authoritarian polities welcome some degree of the rule of law, then a citizen need not be the "author" of entitlements to enjoy those entitlements.[20]

To be sure, narrow or minimal conceptions of human rights do not preclude deep and urgent aspirations to democratic forms of community. They do not undermine advancing the possibility of some human rights in nondemocratic communities by insisting that, without a human right to democracy, no human rights are possible. Laura Valentini (2012:589) points to one version of these terms. She speaks of a very particular kind of nondemocratic state, one "where an enlightened elite is doing all it can to protect human rights, but cannot quite yet introduce democratic institutions because the necessary social conditions are lacking."

On a more narrow conception of human rights, the provision of equal liberties to all members of the political community does not require political liberalism. Rather, the provision of equal liberties requires individual liberty and equality, which can be available without democracy. But they can be available only with a minimally effective rule of law, as I describe it in earlier paragraphs.[21] Still, liberty and equality do not require the social conditions necessary for democracy, including economic, infrastructural, and administrative conditions, or conditions sufficiently free from natural disaster or armed conflict. Neither does the rule of law.

So if democracy is not construed as a human right, and if human rights do not require territorial sovereignty but rather a self-determining community of another, lesser sort, then such communities might still practice some human rights. Human rights are possible if collective self-determination can be more than merely group domination even if not rising to the level of democratic self-determination.[22]

I would add that justice in international relations—understood as a nation state's equal right among nation states to self-determination—need not entail or require justice as equality among the members of a self-determining community. Equality is *external* to community where communities are externally equal to each other. Such communities need not be communities of *internal* equality. It follows that a community's standards for its international relations need not resonate with its own internal cultural preferences.[23]

Legalism Not of Democracy but of the Rule of Law

Democracy is a legal arrangement; it constitutes a legal community. But some of the world's political communities, in Africa and Asia in particular, do not deploy law as the primary means of social organization and the provision of justice, fairness, and dignity. In communities organized more along nonlegal lines of religion, kinship bonds, cultural forms of obligation, or communal duties, actionable legal rights are probably an ineffective means of advancing human rights.[24]

A distinct advantage of my proposal is that it offers the motivational force of local worldviews if harnessed to the human rights project: "since people are more likely to observe normative propositions if they believe them to be sanctioned by their own cultural traditions, observance of human rights standards can be improved through the enhancement of the cultural legitimacy of those standards" (An-Na'im 1992:20).

Tom Zwart (2012:556) identifies a range of possible alternatives within existing local social structures and institutions, such as kinship systems in some parts of Africa. Zwart pinpoints nonlegal aspects of social and normative organization and orientation that may serve as receptors for the idea and practice of human rights. These institutions encompass roles and norms, beliefs and practices that contribute to stable patterns of daily interaction reproduced over time: "the support generated by membership of an extended family; the performance of duties by others; religious charitableness; and the stimulation of self-help. Membership in the extended family provides a number of human rights, like the communal right of succession to family property; the right to be supported in times of scarcity; the right to claim social and psychological help in moments of need; and the right to social welfare, including benefits, social security, and old age pensions" (ibid.). What Zwart neglects are possible dangers to the human rights project sometimes possible in some of these alternatives. Private organizations and institutions may deploy coercion in their control of membership and exclusion from membership. In some cases the extended family can be a resource for nonlegal forms of human rights advancement. But in other cases they may be the chief carrier and defender of beliefs and practices violative of human rights, such as female genital cutting (Marasinghe 1984:33–34).[25]

On the one hand, traditional moral systems might advance some human rights insofar as these systems already articulate rights with obligations to observe them, as well as rights with duties that *others* are obliged to perform. Such duty-based normative systems offer openings for human rights advocacy wherever the individual's rights correlate with duties incumbent on others.[26] On the other hand, traditional religious faiths, among other examples, can motivate human rights behavior. But they can motivate human rights–violative behavior as well.

Such possibilities alert us to the limitations of nonlegal forms of advancing human rights. But where legal forms will not work, some nonlegal forms might. And if they work, they do not require an institutional context of democratic political community. They do not require any human right to citizenship. To the extent that any of these alternatives work, a human rights bearer need not be a member of a particular political community to enjoy human rights. One needs to be a member of a community, however, and whereas a human right to citizenship is plausible because the state is a legal community that could be bound by such a right, nonlegal communities cannot be bound to extend membership to outsiders.

One could argue that states have some kind of duty to prevent statelessness. One might contend that states are obligated to grant asylum to persons rendered stateless. But nation states cannot be obliged, in any democratic sense, to accept outsiders into residency and even citizenship. No democratic regime (let alone any nondemocratic regime) supports the individual's unrestricted right to relocate according to preference.

I would make a final point as I advocate the legalism not of democracy but of the rule of law. Nonlegal means to human rights in communities organized in chiefly nonlegal ways are disadvantageous with respect to the human rights–relevant imperative of juridifying rights in general. Human rights can best achieve sustained, consequential purchase on human behavior if they become law. Norms with a social steering capacity require juridification if they are to be of direct, sustained, predictable consequence in a community. *In a community* means that, if human rights achieve juridical form, then that form will be valid not universally but only within this or that nation state, for it can take such form only within a particular political community.

Absent a global state governed by a world legislature, only the local legislature of each national community can effectively juridify human rights norms. For no domestic legislature, above all no democratic legislature, can feel bound by any claim to a human rights norm with which that legislature or a majority of its constituents disagree. Yet anyone who agrees with that norm would regard that democratically constituted majority as human rights abusive. Hence only the constitutionalization of human rights leads to laws not open to majority preference. An undemocratic but not authoritarian government can bind itself to the rule of law as it constitutionalizes some human rights.

Despite these various problems with nonlegal ways of advancing human rights, communities not strongly organized along formal legal lines may have no option more viable. To be sure, the transformation of such communities into ones that recognize a human right to live under the rule of law is ambitious. But it is still less ambitious than the goal of creating a democracy.

The extraordinary conditions that might call for humanitarian military intervention to stop grave abuses of human beings challenge a human rights state in a different way. In Chapter 9 I consider what a human rights state might contribute in such conditions.

Chapter 9

———

Human Rights and Humanitarian Intervention

This chapter is the last of three examining some of the greatest challenges faced by a human rights state. I ask: From a human rights standpoint, what conditions of brutality and oppression justify coercive intervention in a sovereign nation state? I argue that humanitarian intervention has no normative deep grammar; that its grammar is pragmatic and opportunistic; that intervention can be humanitarian at best only in part.[1] Each case must be evaluated individually because principles guiding the evaluation of agents, means, and ends of coercive intervention cannot be unconditional. Even under the best of circumstances—which are never particularly good—exceptions to principles, standards, and guidelines should always be possible.[2]

In this chapter I address (1) the goal of humanitarian intervention and (2) the paradoxical status of state sovereignty. (3) I argue that sovereignty is necessary for human rights and (4) suggest a realistic understanding of state sovereignty in the context of humanitarian intervention. (5) I advocate a human rights minimalism, one neither value neutral nor nonpartisan, whereby (6) the minimalist goal of intervention is to stop the killing, nothing more. (7) For intervention cannot do the work that only domestic politics can do, including the work of a human rights state. (8) I argue for unilateralism rather than multilateralism in most cases and (9) find no universal a priori responsibility to protect.

The Goal of Humanitarian Intervention

The goal of any particular intervention must be evaluated in light of its peculiar circumstances. Interventions are complex, messy, conflicted, and often unlikely to meet the first operational principle of what the International

Commission on Intervention and State Sovereignty (ICISS 2001: xiii) calls the "responsibility to protect": a "clear and unambiguous mandate at all times." The doctrine states: "Where a population is suffering serious harm, as a result of internal war, insurgency, repression or state failure, and the state in question is unwilling or unable to halt or avert it, the principle of non-intervention yields to the international responsibility to protect" (ibid., xi).

Humanitarian intervention, and any putative responsibility to protect, will never be a matter of pure motives. The costs and risks of intervention are so great that the intervening party acts only if it believes that it stands to gain sufficiently to justify the certain costs and risks of intervention. Hence analyses of intervention in terms of ideal cases are unlikely to generate usable insights. They will not heighten understanding if they fail to take account of the actual political motivations of interveners. And if they take motivations into account but only as something unfortunate but ultimately irrelevant in determining whether intervention is justified by human rights–compatible criteria, analyses fail their task. I regard the self-interested motivations of states as a core facet of humanitarian intervention, for reasons I explain below.[3]

But first I propose a variation on a theme that, in its standard form, is also unhelpfully ideal. According to this theme, any nation state should be held to some threshold of domestic human rights observance as a condition of other states' recognizing that state as a sovereign entity. The responsibility-to-protect doctrine advocates as much: "State sovereignty implies . . . responsibility for the protection of its people" (ibid., xi). So do many scholars. John Rawls (1999b: 4) distinguishes between nondemocratic communities above that threshold ("decent" peoples) and others below it ("outlaw" states). Laura Valentini (2012:588) recognizes a state's "right to govern its population undisturbed only so long as it respects human rights. When it fails to do so, it loses part of (or all) its moral standing vis-à-vis both insiders and outsiders." Michael Walzer (1977) measures political communities against a minimal conception of human rights to distinguish between those deserving of recognition and those not.[4]

The Paradoxical Status of State Sovereignty

Sovereignty is a core feature of nation statehood. In its conventional form, it is the single greatest barrier to the realization of human rights wherever nation states reject them. The responsibility-to-protect doctrine challenges sovereignty fundamentally. A right to national sovereignty and self-determination is forfeit—temporarily diluted or transferred—if deployed in ways that violate human rights, whether actively (with purpose) or passively (the state is unable to prevent abuses it does not condone).

Humanitarian intervention proceeds by way of violating sovereignty. Violation is necessary to stop the killing (*killing* in the sense of genocide or ethnic cleansing). Violation of sovereignty also constitutes a punishment for killing on sovereign territory. From a human rights standpoint, the only acceptable form of national sovereignty is one that neither commits nor allows such killing.

I would argue that a state that freely binds itself to observe the prohibition on such killing has not made itself any less sovereign.[5] But I immediately note that a state that so binds itself likely does not regard itself as so bound simply because it signed this or that international instrument. It so binds itself only in the conviction that doing so somehow furthers its own national interests.

Hence the International Commission on Intervention and State Sovereignty engages in unhelpful because unrealistic formalism when it asserts that the "state itself, in signing the Charter [of the United Nations], accepts the responsibilities of membership flowing from that signature. There is no transfer or dilution of state sovereignty. But there is a necessary re-characterization involved: from *sovereignty as control* to *sovereignty as responsibility* in both internal functions and external duties" (ICISS 2001:13).

I raise two objections. First, nation states sign instruments for many different reasons but usually only for mainly self-serving reasons. They do not necessarily abide by treaty obligations.[6] Being a signatory to international instruments is no guarantee of compliance. In many cases, national sovereignty trumps formal obligations entered into by states.

Second, there is no permanent, unambiguous, clearly defined international community that might restrain murderous states. Neither an association of human rights states, nor an association of human rights–embracing nation states (which I discuss in the Coda), constitutes an international community.

Some nation states enable the murderous activities of other states or regimes or elites. For example, some developed states transfer arms and money to developing states, fueling local civil conflicts while potentially destabilizing the "developed world in everything from globally interconnected terrorism to refugee flows, the export of drugs, the spread of infections diseases and organized crime" (ICISS 2001:5). Here there is no restraining international community to observe. Instead we observe that "some states are becoming reluctant to accept any internationally endorsed preventative measures at all. . . . Their fear is that any 'internationalization' of the problem will result in further external 'interference' and start down a slippery slope to intervention. . . . [F]or international policy makers to be sensitive to it [is] to recognize that many preventative measures are inherently coercive and intrusive in character" (ibid., 25). The ICISS is not naive. It acknowledges the likelihood of coercion on the part of donors: "Economic direct prevention efforts may . . . be of a more coercive nature, including threats of trade and financial sanctions; withdrawal of investment; threats to withdraw IMF or World Bank support and the curtailment of aid and other assistance" (ibid., 24). And the commission concedes that assistance might exacerbate issues of conflict. But even what it calls "development assistance . . . to help address the root cause" is likely to be part and parcel of a donor's self-interested strategy (ibid., 19).

Sovereignty Is Necessary for Human Rights

Human rights are possible on a regular basis only through a nation state. The nation state is the single most import guarantor of human rights. The ICISS recognizes as much: "key to the effective observance of human rights remains, as it always has been, national law and practice" (ibid., 14). It also acknowledges that, "in a dangerous world marked by overwhelming inequalities of power and resources, sovereignty is for many states their best—and sometimes seemingly their only—line of defense" (ibid., 7).[7] Yet the commission is undone by its formalistic understanding of nation states. It seeks to "reconcile two objectives: to strengthen, not weaken, the sovereignty of states, and to improve the capacity of the international community to react decisively when states are either unable or unwilling to protect their own people" (ICISS 2001:75). Strengthening state sovereignty, or at least not weakening it, is an objective of the human rights movement when the state has some promise—hence, not where a regime kills, perpetuates killing, acquiesces in killing, or is unable to prevent killing as I define it in this chapter.

But the imperative of "improv[ing] the capacity of the international community to react decisively" presupposes not only an international community; it presupposes a community willing and able to "react decisively." Again, I ask: What "international community"? The United Nations is not an international community. And it certainly cannot react decisively, either because it is internally fraught with divisions (at various levels, including the Security Council) or because it is too slow and cumbersome to respond to the urgency of genocide or ethnic cleansing. So when the International Commission on Intervention and State Sovereignty states that the "very term 'international community' will become a travesty unless the community of states can act decisively when large groups of human beings are being massacred or subjected to ethnic cleansing" (ibid., 75), it declaims against a straw man.[8] In later pages I argue that unilateralism is the most realistic and effective form of humanitarian intervention, to the extent that any form can be effective, and not multilateralism in the sense of some "international community."

A Realistic Understanding of State Sovereignty in the Context of Humanitarian Intervention

The perspective of a realistic doctrine of humanitarian intervention urges a different understanding of the imperative of state sovereignty. Toward constructing that alternative understanding, I note, first, that for purposes of weighing possible intervention, it is outsiders, not members of the violated community, who here define *violation*. Insiders—involved, for example, in a civil war—may not in particular cases understand killing in the way outsiders may understand it. Thus validity of human rights cannot properly lie in the eyes of its local addressees in the case of genocide and ethnic cleansing (whereas other human rights are indeed best defined locally).[9] Citizens' respect and support for a nation state do not automatically render any intervention into the state unjust.

State sovereignty is related in paradoxical fashion to human rights that prohibit killing. On the one hand, the nation state can be a source of human rights. But, on the other hand, particular states reject human rights. Intervention to stop the killing destroys a sovereignty that did not protect parts of the population anyway. But outside intervention cannot itself create, in the invaded state, a sovereign government and state that respects human rights. Only insiders can construct such a state and government.

Indeed, military intervention cannot establish a human rights order, even if it can build a state and government. By the same token, war cannot establish legality; coercion cannot establish justice.[10] Coercion as a means of politics is so explosively unstable that any intervention whatsoever should always be subject to critical scrutiny. If at all possible, it should also be subject to some sort of outside supervision and regulation. Establishing such scrutiny will be difficult in the best of circumstances; more often than not, it will fail. Note that the scrutinizers, regulators, and supervisors are themselves outside powers no less conditioned by self-interest. They are no less limited than the interveners by partial knowledge and restricted means.

The kind of sovereignty that might pass the no-killing threshold is sovereignty that is less than full. It would be sovereignty subject to critical outside scrutiny and influence. Let me explain. From the standpoint of self-determination, citizens' respect for the state and agreement with practices within the community justify state sovereignty to some extent, as long as respect and understanding are widely held. To be sure, no state should ever be regarded or treated as immune from critical scrutiny by outsiders.

This argument holds in the other direction as well. The state's respect for its own citizens, its respect for their political preferences, is necessary to the legitimacy and justification of state sovereignty. What if some force intervenes in a polity that respects its citizens' political preferences, and those preferences oppose or undermine or preclude human rights? It should recognize the right of the citizens to hold such beliefs—with two immediate qualifications.

First, intervention is warranted when a nation state's violations are severe enough to make humanitarian intervention plausible yet where the citizens of that state are unable to voice dissent. Otherwise intervention assumes forms unhelpful to human rights. It is unhelpful if limited to instances where the population is in open rebellion against the state or government. It is unhelpful if limited to instances where people have enough freedom to criticize the government. Such conditions do not begin to capture repression of the sort practiced in, say, North Korea, where rebellion (let alone dissent) is impossible.

Second, if a nation state is prepared to intervene at all, it might be motivated most powerfully when the target state violates the lives of masses of its people. By contrast, a population compellingly rejects outside inter-vention if it regards many social and cultural rights as undesirable—in the conviction, say, that political dissensus is too destabilizing in a weak civil society. Or a population plausibly rejects outside intervention if it regards political dissensus as "unaffordable" at present: for a polity struggling with poverty, illiteracy, disease, famine, war, or other scourges. Here, too, poten-tial invaders must recognize the anti–human rights convictions of the population.

But a state makes itself vulnerable to outside intervention where it fails to observe and guarantee putative human rights to life and individual lib-erty. In such cases, outsiders are justified, from a human rights standpoint, in intervening regardless of insiders' or citizens' own perspectives on human rights.

This standpoint is paternalistic: it is untroubled by the possibility that the intervened-upon may not share the values of the interveners, including interveners who would save them from oppression. Intervention is then justified even where there is "little reason to believe that the victims all share the values that the oppressors think justify their conduct" (Beitz 2001:273). To be sure, victims of genocide and ethnic cleansing will hardly agree with any of the unfathomable justifications and preferences of their victimizers.

In other words, to argue that intervention is not justified *from a human rights standpoint* is to speak to non-life-threatening conditions of what might be described as "ordinary" cruelty, violence, inhumanity, and oppression.[11] Such daily conditions are best dealt with within the commu-nity itself, by its own members locally—no matter how difficult to accom-plish, no matter how unlikely the prospect of success. (For this reason, the mundane, long-term work of a human rights state takes place in the local context of a corresponding nation state.) To say that intervention is not warranted speaks to the "ethical significance of local disagreement over political values" (Beitz 2001:279). It speaks not so much to a government's violation of its citizen's rights as to violations that occur at the substate level, within citizen populations. Such violations are unlikely to trigger out-side intervention.[12]

In this context I think of a *human rights standpoint* as the narrowest possible understanding of human rights: a right to life as well as a right to individual liberty.[13] Human rights so understood focus on genocide and ethnic cleansing because both violate "urgent principles that persons in any culture would have reason to accept" (Cohen 2008:582).[14] If ethnic cleansing and genocide did not qualify as justifying coercive intervention, then life and liberty would not count as human rights.

From this minimalist stance, the relevant human rights standpoint excludes the legal equality of individuals. It also excludes rights to pluralism, liberalism, democracy, or to a particular kind of economic order. Instead it seeks to establish minimal conditions that are nonlethal, nonbrutal, nonvicious, noncruel. No matter how unrealistic securing such conditions may be in any particular instance, that effort will always be more realistic than the attempt to secure, through coercion, a more expansive list of human rights.

Human Rights Minimalism Is Not
Value Neutral or Nonpartisan

Human rights minimalism does not intend to prevent interventionism as such but only intervention unjustified in terms of a minimalist approach. Even that approach yields a comprehensive view of the world, or of the human good, or even of human rights as they might be imagined in contexts of "ordinary" daily brutality and oppression. But it yields them only in the sense that the prevention of suffering is a fundamental good that trumps competing goods.[15] This approach is neither neutral nor nonpartisan. It does not pursue a better world in the sense of bringing perpetrators to justice. It does not seek to establish a regime committed to human rights in any sense broader than whatever is needed to justify the intervention: preventing genocide and ethnic cleansing and securing conditions minimally necessary for life and individual liberty. The realization of a human right to liberty requires less than the realization of a right to democracy. From a human rights standpoint, a duty to secure conditions under which individuals can enjoy a right to liberty is not a duty to provide democratic conditions. As for the self-interested intervener, unacceptable grounds for intervention include: to overthrow a government; to support a group's claim to a right of self-determination or succession or some other means to statehood; to change national borders.

Indeed, human rights conceived as intervention triggers are vulnerable to political abuse. They could be abused by powers that would instrumentalize human rights declarations or the idea of human rights as such for ends not themselves guided by human rights,or even for ends contrary to human rights. My position makes sense only if intervention itself and the regime constructed after intervention has ended do not create a situation worse than the genocide it would replace, even given the intervener's self-interest.[16] But as the International Commission on Intervention and State Sovereignty concedes, "even when the goal of international action" is "protecting ordinary human beings from gross and systematic abuse, it can be difficult to avoid doing rather more harm than good" (ICISS 2001:5).[17]

Minimalist Goals of Intervention: Stop the Killing, Nothing More

By restricting the relevant list of human rights to life and liberty, I configure humanitarian intervention as an effective effort to end the carnage and unfreedom—but no more than that. So configured, human rights as intervention triggers can be more than moral aspirations only if they can suspend an offending state's sovereignty through military intervention. Human rights can be more than moral aspirations only if they can "specify limits to a regime's internal autonomy" (Rawls 1999b:79–80).

But a minimalist definition of conditions that call for military intervention does not establish limits to pluralism and toleration of difference in international affairs. Of course, toleration for cultural diversity could include toleration of cultural practices that violate human rights—but only at a price. In cases where the intervention is opposed by a majority of the invaded community, intervention subordinates the community's self-determination to the plans and decisions of outside agents, as long as the occupation lasts. Rights of any kind are likely to be "withheld from a person in any social context in which coercion is exercised" (Cohen 2008:599). Intervention may violate possible domestic rights to individual dissent, to free expression, to appeal, or to the public justification of policy (to be sure, such rights pale vis-à-vis victimization by ethnic cleansing). Deciding on a case-by-case basis allows for intervention in some cases, cases in which the cultural practice in question can hardly be understood as something embraced by all members of the community or as something desirable for all members. Intervention is justified in all cases as extra-local intolerance toward intolerable local practices. Thus debates on the question of intervention are debates about what is tolerable. Genocide and ethnic cleansing are never tolerable, whereas violation of free expression, for example, in some cases may be.

Clearly intolerable from a human rights standpoint is violation of free expression if it is more than a matter of expression—where it masks significant violence against the general population. Further, if a government engages in mass brutality against a minority population, and the majority supports that brutality, majority support should be discounted in consideration of whether to intervene. If a dictator deploys violence against the general population, yet outsiders hear no voices of dissent, that silence should be discounted in determining whether to intervene.

Intervention Cannot Do the Work of Domestic Politics

Intervention is inherently paternalistic. It is not possible to intervene non-paternalistically in someone's liberty to advance his or her liberty (even as the intervener may claim nothing less). Intervention restricts the liberties of some members of the community to protect other members' human rights.[18] In that case, human rights–motivated interventions, in preventing harm to citizens threatened by the state (or by groups within the community), may actually perpetrate human rights violations, even if unintentionally. Intervention then restricts the liberty of those invaded. It does so with the claim that, under the circumstances, persons so restricted are in fact better off with such restrictions.

Interventionism justifies itself in part by falling back on what it paternalistically regards as a "judgment about what it would be rational for people to want if they were in possession of full information and able to reason freely" (Beitz 2001:279). The grounds for intervention so understood bind those intervened upon, even those who reject it. By rejecting intervention, the addressees of intervention show themselves incapable of making human rights–compatible choices for themselves. Such a view, defended by Charles Beitz, is deeply problematic. His political liberalism supposes what cannot be supposed: that superior reason can illuminate all values and exhaustively resolve all conflicts among competing values in ways that all affected persons will freely and consensually embrace. The view is vulnerable to charges of a hegemonic construction of social or traditional preference, cultural imperialism, perhaps even a colonial style of thought. I face the problem of paternalism by taking seriously the normative values of the coerced—at least when it defines those values as life and individual liberty. I reject establishing democracy as grounds for intervention even where the citizenry would prefer democracy to the undemocratic status quo and voices that preference.

Of course, the meaning of the term *human rights compatible* depends on how one understands human rights. If understood to include a right to democratic political community, then certain additional human rights are necessary to realize democratic community (a topic I address in Chapter 8). Prominent among them is free expression in political forms of competition among viewpoints, but also the individual's enfranchisement to choose his or her preferred viewpoint or at least to choose what he or she prefers from the viewpoints on offer in a particular election or referendum.

One might argue that participants' incapacity to make human rights–compatible choices follows from the participants' lack of adequate information. Or one might claim that the inability follows from preferences they otherwise would not hold: "One would want to know . . . about the nature of the evidence that many people reject democratic values, whether the society has any past experience with democratic forms, and whether there have been occasions for public political deliberation about forms of government" (Beitz 2001:279). One might say, with Beitz against Beitz, that citizens of this or that democracy simply do not properly perceive the benefits of having a strong, authoritarian leader. Hence these citizens are ill prepared to discern the ways in which political authoritarianism might be preferable to political liberalism. Beitz neglects the possibility that a significant portion of the community may be unsympathetic to the idea and practice of democracy for any number of reasons. On the basis of some of those reasons, a domestic democratic insurgency could hardly argue that the goal of democratic reform justifies military intervention.[19]

So I reject the claim that any human rights violation whatsoever justifies armed intervention. With Michael Walzer (2002:449) I argue that the "common brutalities of authoritarian politics, the daily oppressiveness of traditional social practices," do not justify humanitarian intervention; only genocide and ethnic cleansing do. Beyond Walzer I argue that political authoritarianism (among other forms of antidemocratic governance) does not justify humanitarian intervention.

This answer presupposes my conviction that human rights–friendly change is best pursued locally, by the addressees themselves. In many if not most cases, local participants are better placed than foreign policy makers, foreign politicians, and intervening soldiers to know the local conditions. On average, they can better perceive and interpret with the requisite sensitivity the current local situation. They can better estimate the force necessary to reduce oppression and brutality.

I describe local knowledge of this sort as a kind of "enlightened localism."[20] Enlightened localism values internal political process over external manipulation, whether political, economic, or military. It champions the critical capacity of communal members to determine their preferences as to forms of political organization and legal rights and to judge for themselves the legitimacy of their government and laws. In this specific regard I agree with the responsibility-to-protect position, that the "domestic authority is best placed to take action to prevent problems from turning into potential conflicts. When problems arise the domestic authority is also the best placed to understand them and to deal with them. When solutions are needed, it is the citizens of a particular state who have the greatest interest and the largest stake in the success of those solutions, in ensuring that the domestic authorities are fully accountable for their actions or inactions in addressing these problems and in helping to ensure that past problems are not allowed to recur" (ICISS 2001:17). Enlightened localism embraces the capacity of ordinary men and women in political community to participate in the learning processes of political and social struggles. It supports and facilitates their capacity to participate in the learning processes of interpreting laws and rights and to advocate for political processes more inclusive and just. Localism so understood agrees with John Stuart Mill (1867:177) that a people builds moral fiber by liberating itself rather than being liberated by outsiders.[21]

Intervention is paternalistic if it provides a security that sacrifices a community's sovereignty. It is paternalistic if it restricts political agency rather than expanding it. (And it expands political agency by championing human development—for example, by providing or enhancing access to food, employment, and environmental security.) Intervention should not defeat the national sovereignty necessary for a community's self-government, self-determination, and autonomy—both internally, within a nation state, and among nations. The "recognition of sovereignty is the only way" to establish an "arena within which freedom can be fought for and sometimes won" (Walzer 1980:214). This view entails recognizing a state's sovereignty even if members' rights are being violated. To respect a nation state's sovereignty is to respect the "members of a political community even when the latter's moral rights are violated by their own government" (Cohen 2008:588). Intervention in such cases would be nothing less than usurpation: the violent taking (whether unilaterally or multilaterally) of another nation state without justification (even if to defend human rights) in terms of the minimal list of human rights I propose.[22]

From a minimalist human rights standpoint, armed intervention is justified only when the state, the government, or domestic groups have destroyed the possibility of local politics through brutal behavior at the level of ethnic cleansing or other forms of massacre.[23] Before that point is reached, intervention should assume only forms that allow for a continuation of local politics and that urge changes in local politics by local actors. Intervention in such forms engages the offending powers without destabilizing them. It includes trade sanctions, pressure through diplomatic channels, and international media campaigns.

To be sure, the local level of politics is fraught with problems no less than is politics at the international level. Localism is not "good" simply because it is local; there are "bad" forms of localism, such as human rights–violating forms.[24]

Unilateralism Rather Than Multilateralism in Most Cases

Which entities and forces intervene justifiably and which not, and by what criteria? A compelling answer will have to be better than Gary Bass's. He provides no criteria of selection other than being a "free" country when he argues that the "prevention of mass atrocity is the responsibility not just of the United States, but also of a formidable coalition of free countries: Europe from west to east, Latin America much of Africa, Japan, and rising democratic powers like India, Brazil, and South Africa" (Bass 2008:382). He neglects examples of nondemocratic states intervening to the same end, such as Vietnam in Kampuchea under the Khmer Rouge (1978) or Tanzania in the Uganda ruled by Idi Amin (also in 1978).[25] Because neighboring states are more likely to intervene than distant states, and because in many parts of the world the neighboring state is unlikely to be democratic, "unfree" states often enough are the best bet for humanitarian intervention.

In considering which entities and forces intervene justifiably I would note that, in practice, military interventions are more likely to be unilateral than multilateral; and they are more likely to target neighboring states than states far away. I agree with the International Commission on Intervention and State Sovereignty that "geographic proximity comes into play, simply because what happens nearby is more likely to endanger nations, to raise significant security concerns, and to result in refugees, economic disruptions and unwanted political spillovers" (ICISS 2001:70).[26] Further, "cultural affinity can mean particular concern for the plight of co-religionists, or fellow language speakers, even in small countries far away" (ibid.). Finally, liberal democratic interveners are not less likely than authoritarian interveners to be self-interested; nor are they more likely to be altruistic.

To be sure, this answer raises difficult questions about the moral status of intervention by states with terrible human rights records.[27] And even intervention warranted from a human rights standpoint may find no advocates. After all, even though humankind has distinct interests, above all life and liberty, in addition to other human rights, humankind as such has no advocates, no agents who work on its behalf, no representatives at bargaining tables of powerful states (or even of weak ones). No state, not even a strongly democratic state, acts in the interest of humanity. Further, the balance of self-interestedness and altruism among multilateralists is not likely to be much different from that among unilateralists. Finally, states strongly prefer controlling their own forces to sharing command with other states, even allied ones.

For these reasons, the urgency of stopping genocide or ethnic cleansing in many cases is probably best met unilaterally rather than multilaterally.[28] Urgency of this sort probably is best met by individual states rather than by police forces of the United Nations.[29] Making intervention allowable only when all members of the UN Security Council agree that peace is grievously threatened, if not already breached,[30] might justify intervention in the form of sanctions or blockades. But it will hardly work for genocide or ethnic cleansing, atrocities best confronted with the quickest possible intervention, a response time any organ of the United Nations is unlikely to achieve.[31] So I disagree with a particular claim of the responsibility-to-protect doctrine. I disagree with its unrealistic claim that "Security Council authorization should in all cases be sought prior to any military intervention action being carried out" (ICISS 2001: xii) because "there is no better or more appropriate body than the United Nations Security Council to authorize military intervention for human protection purposes. The task is not to find alternatives to the Security Council as a source of authority, but to make the Security Council work better than it has" (ibid.).

Nor will it necessarily matter if, as is likely, the intervener's motives are mixed.[32] At best, motives will always be mixed; at worst, motives will be insufficient to motivate intervention in the first place. The most likely victims of genocide or ethnic cleansing will have little in the way of economic or political incentives to offer possible interveners. From a consequentialist standpoint, possible victims would be better off if they could attract even the imperial,[33] let alone the benign, interests of states with impure motives.

Indeed, noninterventionists are not less likely to be self-interested than interventionists, nor more likely to be altruistic.[34] But noninterventionists will never halt genocide and ethnic cleansing. They will never restore the possibility for continued life and individual liberty. Nonintervention in the face of murder is not neutrality toward murder but rather its indulgence.

In cases where victims are effectively served only by intervention, whether intervention is unilateral or multilateral will hardly matter. Here I speak of interventions in the least questionable sense. But abusive, exploitative, or brutal interventions must be expected as well.[35] Perhaps the most that can be hoped for is some kind of international public scrutiny that generates some degree of internal or external regulation, if not supervision. (In this context, multilateralism is distinctly preferable to unilateralism, which I argued for in earlier pages. But principles that should guide intervention cannot be unconditional.)

No Universal A Priori Responsibility to Protect

This realism about intervention leads me to reformulate my initial question as follows: If evaluated in human rights terms, what conditions of brutality and oppression not only *justify* coercive intervention into a sovereign nation state but *require* it in the sense of moral duty? To think of human rights as imposing a duty is to think of human rights as triggers to intervention. A number of prominent authors contemplate human rights in just this way. For Charles Beitz (2001:280), human rights could "state conditions for political and social institutions, the systematic violation of which may justify efforts to bring about reform by agents external to the society in which the violation occurs." John Rawls (1999b) views human rights as norms of extra-domestic validity that warrant intervention on their behalf. So does Joseph Raz (2010:328): as rights whose "violation is a (defeasible) reason for taking punitive, compensatory or enforcement measures against the violator," that is, not as an automatic trigger but one that initiates a line of questioning for determining the apposite reaction. Joshua Cohen (2006:234) also imagines a chain of escalating measures leading, "in extreme cases," to "sanctions and intervention." So conceived, human rights are not only a means of criticizing the behavior of states and governments and civil societies. They are springs of military intervention.

To be sure, no human rights declaration obligates any state, or any group of states, to intervene in other states (no *human rights declaration* in distinction, for example, to the Genocide Convention).[36] One proposal that continues to provoke impassioned discussion was never adopted by the United Nations General Assembly; it remains without legal status. At the initiative of its secretary-general, the United Nations in 2001 issued the report of the International Commission on Intervention and State Sovereignty, whose merits and weaknesses I evaluate in this chapter. Its rhetoric of an "international responsibility to protect," in the sense of a broad community of nation states, rings hollow. No political elite altruistically sacrifices its people and resources for global common goods of international peace and order, let alone for the collective good of some other people. Nor do the political elites of several states collectively sacrifice altruistically.

Indeed, the notion of a human rights–based responsibility to military intervention in cases of genocide or ethnic cleansing runs up against the plausibility of a state's right to freely determine whether or not to take upon itself the considerable risks of foreign intervention. Beyond death and maiming of its forces, risks include involvement in intractable, interminable conflicts that yield no clear victory. Risks include conflicts beyond the control of those forces. They include the intervener's becoming indistinguishable from the enemy, at least in the eyes of the civilian population.

The idea of a limited right, perhaps even based on some conception of human rights, to intervene militarily is not defeated by the notion of a possible intervener's right of refusal. To defend one's own political community from significant risk entails the strategic reasonableness (if not moral wisdom) of declining to defend other populations at risk. And if, in this sense, too, the grammar of humanitarian intervention is pragmatic and opportunistic, morally relativist and not universally valid, by what means should agents pursue it, and to what end? If humanitarian intervention is normatively justifiable coercion, then those who practice it pursue military victory—and they do so legitimately.

Often enough that pursuit will be deeply problematic along multiple dimensions. One of these dimensions is practical and strategic in nature. It weighs the risks and costs of interference against prospects for success. It does so not only for the short run but for the long run as well. It weighs the risks of unintended, unwanted collateral harm. It evaluates the feasibility of an intervention at least somewhat constructive instead of purely destructive. *Somewhat constructive* means, for example, facilitating the empowerment of local officials who might be able to govern. It means facilitating persons acceptable, as officials, to much of the populace. Ideally the ability to govern and popular acceptability become wholly independent of the invader.

Another dimension along which the pursuit of military victory is problematic concerns the aftermath of intervention. Does a right to intervene in the sense I've developed entail an obligation of the invader to reestablish authority? Does that obligation require authority that corresponds with some aspects of the invaded state's political culture and traditions? The question arises inasmuch as "all interventions are to bring about a change *in a.* regime: if there was no imperative to change a regime's policy, there would be no need for intervention in the first place. The question has been: will change be made *by* the regime, or will there be a change *of* the regime?" (Trim 2011:393).

In many cases, humanitarian intervention constitutes a charge that the invaded community is a failed state in the sense of minimally acceptable governance. Here *minimally acceptable* is defined in terms of my minimalist list of human rights, the violation of which justifies intervention.

Another problematic dimension concerns withdrawal: When and under what conditions? What if either the human rights atrocity or the intervention itself has left the country without an institutional basis sufficient for self-rule toward reconstruction? What if it has left the country without police force or courts of law, without central bureaucratic administration or a national economy? What if it has only left regional factions, or warlords, or paramilitary forces? What if abiding ethnic, religious, linguistic, historical, or other divisions are so deep-seated and so toxic that withdrawal could only pave the way for new killing fields?

Yet another dimension involves a slippery slope leading from critiques of tyrannical regimes, first to reasons for changing regimes, then to justifications for invasive coercive expansion. While critiques of tyranny need not slide down slippery slopes, any putative "responsibility to protect" individuals' human rights to life and liberty could: it could all too easily lead to a *duty* to intervene.[37] *Slope* is a metaphor for international relations as military interventionism. It likely begins with misjudgments by possible interveners in determining whether any given state is unwilling or unable to protect its citizens adequately.

These various problems do not admit of general solutions because humanitarian intervention has no normative deep grammar providing unambiguous, generalizable guidelines for use in concrete situations. Its grammar is pragmatic and opportunistic, without absolute principles: "intervention amounts to a promise to the people in need: a promise [too often] cruelly betrayed" (ICISS 2001:1).

Intervention is incapable of doing humanitarian work without also generating at least some inhumane consequences. At best, humanitarian intervention might be managed in the sense of self-restraint on the part of the intervener. Bass finds possible techniques even in the very troubled nineteenth-century experience of humanitarian intervention: "delineating spheres of justifiable intervention for each of the great powers, delegating to regional powers, putting time limits on humanitarian interventions, restricting the size of the military force, foreswearing diplomatic and commercial advantages from a humanitarian mission, and, above all, multilateralism" (Bass 2008:360). The International Commission on Intervention and State Sovereignty adopts these nineteenth-century means: the

> effective and legitimate states remain the best way to ensure that the benefits of the internationalization of trade, investment, technology and communication will be equitably shared. Those states which can call upon strong regional alliances, internal peace, and a strong and independent civil society, seem clearly best placed to benefit from globalization. They will also be likely to be those most respectful of human rights. And in security terms, a cohesive and peaceful international system is far more likely to be achieved through the cooperation of effective states, confident of their place in the world, than in an environment of fragile, collapsed, fragmenting or generally chaotic state entities. (ICISS 2001:7–8)

Perhaps the best one can hope for is to make intervention somewhat safer—even as it can never be made safe. *Safer* means reconciling realpolitik with humanitarian concerns where they are simply not possible without realpolitik. If the use of force in and of itself does not render an act unjust, then realpolitik may be reconcilable with humanitarian concerns. By rough domestic analogy to the international arena: "It took federal marshals to enforce integration in Arkansas and Mississippi, but that does not make the civil rights movement an act of police brutality" (Bass 2008:378–379). As a difficult mixture of coercion and humanitarian empathy, reconciliation will always be morally fragile. It can only be fragile if it involves governing other people, even though only temporarily, toward stopping and resisting atrocity.

In the context of military intervention, then, human rights are a tool both necessary and dangerous: without human rights, intervention may be abusive or unjustified; with human rights, intervention as one possibility in some cases threatens to become intervention as a duty in all cases. Constructing human rights[38] with an interference-triggering capacity, or with an interference-justifying role, could well undermine the very possibility of human rights. That happens if urgent and legitimate concern to stop murderous behavior merely transforms the human rights idea—including opposition to armed coercion except where necessary to stop murderous, state-perpetrated violence—into one more instrument of contemporary warfare.

A human rights state cannot help here; it is not an element of intervention. Intervention creates extraordinary circumstances, whereas a human rights state operates in the ordinary circumstances of advancing the human rights project on a gradual, daily basis over time. It becomes relevant in the aftermath of invasion with the reestablishment of a nation state that a human rights state can target in its advocacy.

This chapter pushes my notion of human rights as social construction to its real-world limits. The somber limitations of a human rights state with regard to intervention contrast with the happier prospect of state-based cosmopolitanism. In the Coda I limn the possibility of a group of nation states. I imagine each transformed through the advocacy of their respective human rights states. They form a voluntary supranational community based on a shared embrace of human rights. Participating states, each enjoying constitutionalized human rights domestically, relate to each other horizontally. They form a union not itself a state. I turn now to that vision.

A Community of Nation States Practicing Domestic Cosmopolitanism

A human rights state seeks the embrace of human rights in the corresponding nation state. It advocates human rights as cosmopolitan standards for domestic institutions. The satisfaction of those standards is a matter of both domestic and international concern. If the notion of a human rights state is coherent, even conceivable, could it ever be viable in practice? Are there sufficient empirical grounds to entertain it? Or does it rest on unjustifiably high expectations for the participating nation states?

The theory's viability depends on the existence of at least some nation states that would make for plausible correspondents of human rights states. That many nation states today are implausible correspondents of human rights states is no wonder. A nation state is no plausible correspondent if it undermines rather than secures legal guarantees of rights. It is implausible if it cannot navigate the globalized forces of market economy and political power that otherwise escape nation state control to become functionally autonomous. It is implausible if it cannot practice sovereignty in the face of global forces of injustice, from rapacious global capitalism to reactionary religious movements.

The idea of a human rights state finds a measure of support in observers such as David Held. He sees significant opportunities for cosmopolitan norms at a time when the "main corollaries of the classic system of sovereign law" are now open to "reassessment" and cosmopolitan transformation (Held 2004:138). How so? Some state leadership today is sometimes exposed to international criticism, not always and not entirely without some effect, in ways that sometimes challenge its claim to legitimacy. Unlike earlier in history, leadership today can be "subject to scrutiny and tests with respect to human rights and liberal democratic standards" (ibid.), even if the consequences of scrutiny and tests are often uncertain. And many organizations relevant to national and transnational life are growing ever closer today. Advocates of cosmopolitan politics might find succor in the general "growth of regional and global governance, with responsibility for areas of increasing transborder concern from pollution and health to trade and financial matters" (ibid.).

I find support for my proposal of a human rights state in observers such as James Griffin (2008:104) who views nation states as *necessary* agents of human rights: "in the case of the human right to welfare it seems to me justified, in these times of concentration of wealth and power in central governments, to place the burden to a large extent on them. And if poor central governments are unable to shoulder the burden, then perhaps the time has come for us to consider whether the burden should not also be placed on a group of rich nations."

The human rights state might also resonate with authors who, like Charles Beitz (2009:128), regard the nation state as a "revisionist appurtenance of a world order of independent, territorial states." The theory of human rights states rises or falls depending on features of at least some of the corresponding nation states. By *features* I mean how well a nation state can allocate obligations that human rights entail. According to Onora O'Neill (2004:247), nation states cannot be "primary agents of justice, which allocate and determine the obligations of other, secondary agents of justice," if they are unjust. They are hardly primary agents of justice if they are "incapable of securing justice for their citizens or members." A human rights state attempts nothing less than making the corresponding nation state an agent of justice. That attempt may be supported by some processes of globalization, those that constrain nation states to "make their borders more porous, thereby weakening state power and allowing powerful agents and agencies of other sorts to become more active within their borders."

With regard to how well a nation state can allocate obligations that human rights entail, I also recognize limits inherent to the nation state form as such, including those identified by Chandran Kukathas (2003:214). The fact that every state has at least some interests independent of its citizenry limits "what a state can do or accomplish in its efforts to shape and control society. We have discovered over this past century that the hope of taking control of a society's economy was a forlorn one: central economic planning was a miserable failure." We have discovered that "central cultural planning may be even more difficult and, so, even less feasible."

How well a nation state can allocate obligations entailed by human rights relates as well to the nation state's corporate capacities. James Nickel (1987:112–113) describes some of the ways the nation state may fail, by "(1) using the criminal law system to suppress opposition to and destroy the enemies of those in power; (2) victimizing unpopular minorities (or even majorities); (3) corruption, favoritism, and ineptitude; (4) using imprisonment, torture, and murder to consolidate political power; and (5) using political power to extend and entrench the favorable position of a dominant group."

My proposal for the human rights state may resonate even with observers such as Thomas Pogge (2002) and Richard Falk (1995). They champion not a global state but a globalist, cosmopolitan agenda in the form of legal cosmopolitanism.

While the idea of a human rights state finds a measure of support in these various authors, it differs from any that proffer a theory of ideal global justice. It contrasts with any that suggest a redemptive politics—for example, in Claude Lefort's (1986:266) sense of a "politics that would stand over the world in which we live and allow it to be struck by the thunderbolts of the Last Judgment." Instead, my proposal for a human rights state addresses the nonideal nation state and proposes a nonideal politics, with the ambitious, not nonideal goal of limiting aspects of state sovereignty and domestic jurisdiction.

Realizing the Potential of the Nation State

The proposal seeks to transform the normative grammar of nation statehood by rendering human rights a feature internal to the state. In doing so, it affirms rather than dispenses with the nation state. It does justice to human rights while preserving the modern sovereign state's indispensable achievements. Those achievements have found recognition in a variety of perspectives. Kant defends statehood on grounds of its indispensability to political and legal autonomy. These forms of autonomy are necessary to establish the processes for participation in public life. They are necessary to further a way of life that resonates with the participants because it is uniquely theirs. Michael Walzer (2004) defends the nation state on nationalist grounds; Richard Rorty (1998), to patriotic ends; David Miller (1995), for communitarian reasons.

The theory of a human rights state focuses diagnostically and prescriptively on the nations state's core traits, toward harvesting their normative and political potential for the human rights project. By *core traits* I point to the fact that the sovereign territorial state remains the primary location at which a person may possess legally backed subjective rights. I stress the experience that only legally backed subjective rights secure legal security and political liberty. And I argue the case that people can fight for rights, acquire rights, and secure rights usually only within an autonomous sovereign state, as a legal community with domestic jurisdiction.

To be sure, these traits can hardly be realized or even approximated under all social, political, cultural, historical, or economic conditions. Only some nation states display them, and those that do are plausible addressees of a human rights state. A plausible addressee is a nation state under the rule of law that provides citizens with actionable rights and legally guaranteed liberty and security and that ensures the stability of citizens' reasonable expectations about current levels of social justice. A plausible addressee preserves its autonomy as a political community. It contributes to preserving a pluralistic world of political communities. It sometimes calms and even solves otherwise ruinous or destabilizing political and social conflicts.

Revising Nation State Sovereignty by Constitutionalizing Human Rights Domestically

To realize its potential in ways urged by the corresponding human rights state, a nation state must revise the idea and practice of its sovereignty to include human rights as an element internal to itself. *Internal* means that, in its legislative, judicial, and executive branches, the nation state is no longer the sole source, foundation, and center of all legitimate domestic power and all domestic law. *Internal* refers to the incorporation of human rights into the national constitution. A nation state thus modified is no longer free of all nondomestic legal constraints on its treatment of its own citizens. This proposal replaces one form of sovereignty—with its apex exclusively in the state—with another: a sovereignty that allows for cosmopolitan rights.

For domestic power to allow for cosmopolitan rights is for domestic power to share the highest instance of legal validity with *all* nation states that have incorporated human rights into their respective constitutions.

Through incorporation, the highest domestic instance becomes the cosmopolitan instance of human rights. This instance is not geographically delimited domestically, nor is it topographically contained within a nation state. Participating states surrender their monopoly on decision making and lawmaking to the extent that they bind themselves to human rights. Yet they do so without surrendering national sovereignty altogether.[1]

I do not propose that nation states should enjoy sovereignty only as long as they observe human rights. I do not make sovereignty an entitlement granted by some supranational or international organization or global power, let alone a world state. Nor do I conceive of human rights as some kind of global administration or policing power. Rather, I include the free embrace of human rights in the nation state's conception of its own autonomy and self-determination as a sovereign political community.

As its core goal, a human rights state seeks a cosmopolitanism situated domestically. It would achieve this goal not by constitutionalizing international law[2] but by constitutionalizing human rights within as many nation states as possible—always and only through voluntary participation. Constitutionalization so understood does not deliver a global polity. Nor does it create a world public legal order providing political and legal autonomy. It is not an inclusive form of postnational statehood, or some variant of global statehood, let alone world government. It does not usher in a complex, differentiated, multilevel cosmopolitan polity. Global-level democratization does not follow from it.[3]

When I propose the domestic constitutionalization of human rights, I seek the benefits of constitutionalism. These include the application of principles of accountability, separation of powers, protection of rights, and legally enforceable constitutional limits to the exercise of lawmaking and regulatory powers. These principles facilitate not only sovereign equality but, I urge, human rights as well.

An Association of Human Rights–Embracing Nation States

I propose constitutionalism at both domestic and supranational levels without denying the sovereign equality of member states. I have in mind a voluntary supranational legal order that arises out of shared commitment, lodged domestically in each of the participating nation states. I imagine multiple autonomous constitutional states, each a site of norm creation and political power, coexisting and cooperating through an overarching commitment to human rights. To the extent that those commitments overlap (always less than completely), they constitute a shared governance of human rights.[4]

By *shared governance* I mean that these various nation states mutually recognize one another in their autonomy and in their human rights commitment. They relate to each other horizontally not vertically, heterarchically not hierarchically. The legal order of each is influenced by the shared commitment to human rights. Yet this constellation of participating nation states is not itself a state, and participating states would remain autonomous vis-à-vis each other.

Members tied to each other through this shared commitment are tied through dialogue and mutual accommodation. These ties hardly preclude differences, competition, or conflict among members. Participating nation states are associated through a shared human rights commitment as an internal feature of each of the participants' domestic orders.

Association of this sort is not statist but a community of political communities. Just as a human rights state exists alongside the corresponding nation state, so nation states transformed by their respective human rights states coexist in a shared cosmopolitan commitment that exceeds the national boundaries of each participant. Together they form a pluralism of nation states each of which observes its own conception of human rights, likely with significant overlap among those conceptions.

By *pluralism* I refer to a world of human rights–observing nation states—to a world of modified legality, modified rights, and modified political autonomy, but also a world of sovereign nation states. Sovereignty so understood might conduce to public autonomy and to collective self-determination, including forms of self-determination other than the liberal-democratic ones favored in the West. Sovereignty so conceived is consistent with far-reaching political pluralism and with many different political and legal institutions. It comports with a rich menu of institutional possibilities, with national self-determination expressed in multiple ways.

Within the federation, sovereignty remains with each participant; the association itself has no sovereignty. A framework of multiple participants does not undermine the integrity of the binding medium—namely, a shared code of human rights. An interrelationship of this design mirrors a form of self-realization by means of communal, "universal," or cosmopolitan, activities as imagined by G. W. F. Hegel (2004). Axel Honneth

(2001:78) extrapolates this trope into a "form of cooperative practice in which every subject can recognize in the activity of the other a contribution to common aims; the subjects achieve freedom by carrying out actions that are intertwined, by 'laws and principles based on thought and hence universal,' to such an extent that their cooperation serves to realize something 'universal.'"[5] To deploy this trope for my vision, for *subject* I read *nation state practicing domestic cosmopolitanism. Universal* then refers to the validity of human rights among participating nation states.

Jurisdictional conflicts are inevitable, of course. If they are to be resolved, then only within the association and always with reference to human rights. There is no third party to adjudicate between or among contesting members of the federation. If resolution is not always possible, if it sometimes fails, the association does not fail (although it may be weakened). As long as resolution is possible some of the time, among at least some of the members, the association perseveres.[6]

Three aspects of this proposal bear emphasis. First, it builds on core political and legal features of the world today: the nation state; the importance of human rights discourse across the world; the proliferation of international covenants; the development of an International Criminal Court; the United Nations that can make resolutions and international courts that attempt to enforce them; the emergence of forms of humanitarian intervention and ideas such as the "duty to protect."[7]

Second, the economic, technological, and military power of nation states does not preclude the possibility of effective international law and organizations. The possibility that participating states may sometimes instrumentalize international organizations for self-serving interests need not destroy the still unrealized promise of international law and organizations. And a world with nation states, some of which have constitutionalized human rights, holds out promise for cooperative international relations. It aligns with the equality of sovereign nation states in the sense of meaningful presence in institutions of international governance, including the United Nations, the International Court of Justice, and the International Criminal Court.[8]

Third, independent yet interdependent nation states in the overarching human rights community require no ultimate locus of authority. *Community* can describe autonomous yet interconnected, domestic constitutional orders bound by their mutual human rights commitment. These overlapping constitutional orders cooperate, but they compete as well; they compete in terms of their respective understandings of human rights to the extent that those understandings differ. (In the Introduction I explain why differences in the interpretation of human rights in meaning and practice do not undermine the possibility of human rights.) Ideally each participating nation state would demonstrate the political will to sustain the community as well as a dedication to common interests and cooperative interaction. Ideally each would work against tendencies that would undermine the community.[9]

Notes

Introduction

1. My translation of Brecht (2000): "Der Paß ist der edelste Teil von einem Menschen. Er kommt auch nicht auf so einfache Weise zustand wie ein Mensch. Ein Mensch kann überall zustandkommen, auf die leichtsinnigste Art, aber ein Paß niemals. Dafür wird er auch anerkannt, wenn er gut ist, während ein Mensch noch so gut sein kann und doch nicht anerkannt wird."

2. See Gregg (2012b), which develops an extended argument in favor of social construction. *The Human Rights State* adopts this 2012 approach but is not concerned with defending it as such. Rather, it deploys the approach with respect to changing contemporary nation states into communities that embrace human rights as an internal feature.

3. And cosmopolitanism requires optimism. Cosmopolitans cultivate moral luck (where luck, of all things, can make a *moral* difference) in the conduct of human affairs over time. For seminal contributions to the development of this concept, see Williams (1981) and Nagel (2012:24–38).

4. To be sure, self-authorship is possible only in political community, as an intersubjective phenomenon. Self-authored human rights are products of social movements, not of individuals themselves. Thus the individual human rights author stands in reciprocal relation with others. Reciprocity is key here; to grant oneself human rights is always also to recognize others in their self-granting activity in a sense captured by George Herbert Mead: the "individual experiences himself . . . from the particular standpoints of other individual members of the same social group, or from the generalized standpoint of the social group as a whole to which he belongs" (Mead 1967:138). For "it is in this form that the social process or community enters as a determining factor into the individual's thinking" (ibid., 155), to some extent giving him "his principles, the acknowledged attitudes of all members of the community toward what are the values of that community" (ibid., 162)—in this case, what I develop as a human rights state.

5. Atheists (and perhaps communities who believe in the wrong god) might have human rights, but they exclude themselves from knowing the true ground of those rights.

6. Compare Marx (1867), part 1, section 4, on the fetishism of commodities.

7. In Chapters 7 and 8 I develop this argument for juridification of human rights.

8. Assembled by René Wolfsteller (2014), on whose examples I base this paragraph.

9. Here I agree with Rorty (1989)—and am pleased that anyone should find my "account of the cultural basis of human rights" to be "much more thoroughly articulated than Rorty's" (Koppelman 2014:383 n. 2).

10. The committee sought agreement "not on the basis of common speculative ideas, but on common practical ideas, not on the affirmation of one and the same conception of the world, of man, and of knowledge, but upon the affirmation of a single body of beliefs for guidance in action" (Glendon 2001:77–78).

11. Conflicts among different normative orders, and conflicts within normative orders, sometimes facilitate democratic will formation, where participants are both authors and addressees of their human rights. Conversely, claims to global agreement on norms are sometimes the systematically distorted communication of authoritarian politics. The argument for disharmony and disagreement finds support in Berman (2007) and Nagel (2005). The argument for anticipating an alternative to the status quo draws on Derrida (1990) to suggest that a human rights state escapes the force of a nation state, in part. It escapes the state precisely where it can anticipate forms of justice not yet imaginable in a nation state, or not imaginable adequately, or not imaginable as realizable. In this way a human rights state constitutes a zone that escapes a nation state in its denial of human rights.

12. See Rawls (1993:144–150).

13. I note the kindred efforts of Simmons (2009).

14. In ways evocative of Kant's (1998:41) "systematic union of different rational beings under common laws," a "kingdom of ends." This regulative moral ideal does not correspond to a particular political community. Kant develops it as the most social of his several formulations of the "categorical imperative." Members treat each other as ends in themselves rather than as means to achieving selfish interests of any one member or group of members. In this "merely possible kingdom," each member is equally author and addressee of universal laws; each has equal share in legislating principles capable, on their intrinsic merits, of free embrace by the community.

15. See Dahbour (2005:214) on some of the difficulties of enforcing norms that restrict the actions of states and corporations globally: "such entities are not easily held accountable," and without "accountability, a community of law will resemble the current regime of international law"; and, of course, the "dangers and uncertainties of entrusting global rule to hegemonic or transnational states or organizations" are legion.

16. See Kant (1795).

Chapter 1. Human Rights as Metaphor

1. The phrase *the peculiarly forceless force of the better argument* alludes to Habermas's (1981) theory of communicative action. In Part II, I explain and deploy discursivity in three different contexts, in each case with an empirical example. In each case,

the chapter title indicates the particular example. Chapter 4 deals with teaching human rights as a cognitive style. Chapter 5 discusses the development of human rights commitment in post-authoritarian societies. And Chapter 6 analyzes digital technology as resource for the human rights project.

2. To be sure, two centuries later, war remains a primary element of international politics. Like Kant's, my proposal bears the burden of providing evidence of its capacity to affect real-world practice.

3. This statement holds regardless of which dimension of the modern nation state one emphasizes—such as self-determination of an ethnic community (Kaiser 1994), or management of territorial power (Giddens 1985 and Agnew and Corbridge 1995), or steward of an economy within a world of competing economies.

4. See Preuss (1994:133).

5. I take the term from Urbinati (2007), whose usage is very different, and who deploys it in a context very different from mine.

6. It is not clear that a human rights state would work for populations governed by formations other than states, such as tribes or militaries. Be that as it may, I focus on nation states.

7. Some persons might be a member of more than one human rights state, for example, someone resident in two or more nation states. As that individual moved from one to the other, he or she would want to be a member of whatever human right state was associated with the current host.

8. Disagreement is generated by disparities in presuppositions, such as how to balance individual and collective interests. Variation follows from competing models, such as citizens' rights given by the state in distinction from human rights declared by nonstate entities such as the United Nations. The question of whether human rights are independent of human design or, alternatively, are socially constructed spawns difference.

9. Collective recognition of the status is not necessarily approval: "Acceptance . . . goes all the way from enthusiastic endorsement to grudging acknowledgment, even the acknowledgment that one is simply helpless to do anything about, or reject, the institutions in which one finds oneself" (Searle 2010:8).

10. For yet a third example of human rights deterritorialized, this time with respect to digital communication and the Internet, see Chapter 6.

11. For critical analysis of MSF, see Redfield (2013), Magone, Neuman, and Weissman (2011), and Debrix (1998).

12. See Benvenisti (2013) and Waters (2007) for critical perspectives.

13. On the idea of human rights claimable only as individual rights enforceable by national and international courts, see Buchanan and Golove (2002); also Gardbaum (2008).

14. On the creation of foundations for such techniques, see Gregg (1999) and (2002).

15. Except if obliged to do so by treaty (which, in some cases, may violate the person's human rights).

16. Who are, after all, members of a self-motivated human rights state.

17. Cohen (2008:579) takes this line of thought even further by arguing that sovereignty and human rights can be codependent.

18. Compare Jessop (2002:210–213).

19. Compare Hirst and Thompson (1999:276).

20. With regard to how this goal of persuasion operates, see Part II, "The Human Rights State Through Persuasion, Not Coercion," which explains and deploys persuasion in three different contexts, each a unique empirical case. Chapter 4 addresses teaching human rights as a cognitive style. Chapter 5 discusses how to develop human rights commitment in postcommunist societies. And Chapter 6 examines digital technology as a resource for the human rights project.

21. See, e.g., the Convention on the Elimination of All Forms of Discrimination Against Women, adopted in 1979 by the UN General Assembly. It defines discrimination against women and proposes an agenda for national action to end such discrimination. Some of its provisions are unenforceable, such as: "Countries that have ratified or acceded to the Convention are legally bound to put its provisions into practice. They are also committed to submit national reports, at least every four years, on measures they have taken to comply with their treaty obligations."

22. See Hathaway (2002).

23. Ibid.

24. For example, see Bacevich (2002) or Ferguson (2004).

25. Declining sovereignty does not lead ineluctably toward global governance, pace Held et al. (1999).

26. See Chapter 8 for analysis.

27. In the Coda I address the problems and prospects not of a community of *human rights states*—a community of advocates—but rather of *nation states* that have constitutionalized human rights domestically. The first kind of community comprises advocates for the creation of the second kind of community, *not yet successful*. The second kind of community incorporates nation states successfully modified through the advocacy of human rights states.

Chapter 2. Human Rights in a Backpack

1. I develop the idea of individuals as authors of human rights at length in Gregg (2012b:87–110).

2. I draw on political geography as Elden (2009), Agnew (2005), and Sidaway (2003) each pursue it.

3. In rejecting theories that would ground human rights either in nature or history, Arendt embraces a kind of political existentialism, according to Jay (1986). In fact, she replaces moral imperative not with existentialism but with political decisionism. She does so where she speaks of "natality," a capacity for politics specifically as

the capability to create political communities whose members recognize each other with an equal right to personality. She intends a capacity for decision making and regards it as foundationless. My reading of Arendt challenges those of Parekh (2008), Ingram (2008), Birmingham (2006), Benhabib (2004), and Isaac (1996). In my reading, human rights are decisionistic because statist as a right "of men to citizenship" (Arendt 1949:37), a right "to belong to some kind of organized community," to "live in a framework where one is judged by one's actions and opinions" (Arendt 1968:296–297). That's but half the story. Human rights are simultaneously a "right of every individual to belong to humanity" (ibid., 298); they emerge historically with a nation state and constitute "national rights" (ibid., 230). Bring the two halves of the story together and one observes human rights as social constructions that aspire to universal embrace. To say that human rights are constructions is to say they are decisions made by groups that construct them. If human rights ever achieve free and global embrace, it is only through the subsequent decisions of other, new participants. People behave decisionistically within institutions (above all a nation state) and not prior to institutions. My argument finds support in Honig (2005:228): institutions "set expectations, generate grammars, and set out norms that are internalized by their members. But individuals then go on to act variously upon those norms and, in their variety, they at some point 'decide.'"

4. To bracket, for now, the more difficult case of noncitizens.

5. I address humanitarian intervention in Chapter 9.

6. To be sure, national politics cross national borders continually. The United States practiced state violence within its borders as constitutionalized slavery between 1787 and 1865 (and after 1865, in the form of Black Codes, white supremacist politics, and the selective enforcement of statues, subjecting some black Americans to involuntary labor). State violence is practiced beyond borders as well when a political community refuses entry to refugees or stateless persons seeking to escape repression at home and with nowhere else to go.

7. As of January 2015; half the prisoners have long been approved for transfer if adequate security conditions can be met in the receiving country.

8. Article 3 of Geneva Convention (III) Relative to the Treatment of Prisoners of War, of 12 August 1949, states in part:

In the case of armed conflict not of an international character occurring in the territory of one of the High Contracting Parties, each Party to the conflict shall be bound to apply, as a minimum, the following provisions. . . . The following acts are and shall remain prohibited at any time and in any place whatsoever with respect to the above-mentioned persons: (a) violence to life and person, in particular murder of all kinds, mutilation, cruel treatment and torture; . . . (c) outrages upon personal dignity, in particular humiliating and degrading treatment; (d) the passing of sentences and the carrying out of executions without previous judgment pronounced by a regularly constituted court, affording all the judicial guarantees which are recognized as indispensable by civilized peoples.

9. In the course of the Trojan War, Achilles inflicts upon Telephus a wound that will not heal. Telephus consults an oracle who makes a typically puzzling pronouncement: "only he that wounded you can also heal you." Achilles deciphers the riddle and scrapes onto Telephus's wound flakes from the spearhead that had pierced Telephus's body, thereby healing him in exchange for Telephus guiding Achilles's army to Troy.

10. I borrow the term "proto-citizenship" from Benhabib (2006:172), who also seeks to describe agonistic political behavior on the part of legally marginalized populations within a nation state.

11. To paraphrase King (1967:43). I use *declarations* in Austin's (1962) sense of performative utterances that not only describe a given social reality but actually change that which they describe.

12. I see two limitations to Rancière's conception. First, the 1789 Déclaration des droits de l'homme et du citoyen provides a right to rebel against one's oppression—but not as some kind of free-floating, nonterritorial right. It provides a right tied to *membership in political community*. The declaration invokes both nature and social construction as the source of human rights: sourced in nature but actionable only in institutions of political community—namely, a nation state—such that the sovereign French republic would be governed by human rights that obtain alongside and in addition to that sovereignty. Second, one can oppose the state in this particular way only because the state makes such opposition possible, possible in the sense of a right to opposition. This particular right to oppose the state can only be exercised within the state. Such a right is not cosmopolitan but parochial: peculiar to the particular state that constitutes the "stage" for the human rights advocates' performance. The revolutionary French state of 1789 was one such theater. In its fragility, it could not survive the terror that began in 1793, nor Napoleon's dictatorship as of 1799. By itself, the mere existence of a theater is not enough to guarantee the success of performances.

13. Participants are continually bound if symbols circulate in self-reinforcing ways, influencing participants' everyday orientation in life as well as their personal ties with each other.

14. But backpackers advocate for recognition of human rights by a nation state—and by other institutions such as NGOs and multinational corporations as well as by such organizations as the United Nations and by religious faiths, family practices, and cultural traditions.

15. In this conception, the list of human rights does not include a right of all residents—citizens and noncitizens alike—to enfranchisement or democracy. It includes a right to live under the rule of law. I discuss the rule of law as a human right in Chapter 8.

16. Note three examples of agonistic persuasion, one each in Chapters 4, 5, and 6.

17. Parekh (2002:42), for example, argues that the modern nation state "represents a homogeneous legal space within which its members move about freely, carrying with them a more or less identical basket of rights and obligations."

18. No country has more slaves than India: between 13.3 and 14.7 million, many through debt bondage or bonded labor but many also as child brides (Walk Free Foundation 2013:43–49). In Norway, by contrast, all identified victims (fewer than seven hundred) are nonnationals (ibid., 82).

19. *Classify* in the sense that some passports convey more "authority" than others with respect to visa requirements. According to an index by Henley & Partners (Upe 2013), passports that allow entrance to 170 or more countries and territories without a visa include the United Kingdom, Finland, Sweden, Denmark, Germany, Luxembourg, the United States, Belgium, Italy, the Netherlands, Canada, France, Ireland, Japan, Norway, Portugal, and Spain. Passports that allow entrance to 160 or more without a visa include New Zealand, Switzerland, Austria, Australia, Greece, Singapore, South Korea, Iceland, Malaysia, and Malta. At the other end of the spectrum are passports issued by Afghanistan (allowing visa-less entry to 28 countries), Iraq (31), Pakistan and Somalia (each 32).

20. Within nation states, human rights carriers constitute a long transnational chain of status functions with deontic power. The chain is independent of its hosts, much as international capital or the headquarters of a multinational corporation can be physically present in this or that geographical location yet always independent of any particular national territory, for unlike people, and unlike rights, capital circulates independently of national borders.

21. The rights themselves are not metaphorical. The individual carries the backpack on the basis not of some metaphysical or theological given but rather as political performance—in Austin's (1962) sense, as a declaration.

22. Only to the extent that collective intentionality can be assumed, of course. Intentionality of this sort is contingent, complex, and often fraught with internal tension if not contradictions. Participants may not understand collective intentionality the same way; to some, it may be rather opaque.

23. Consider status difference in this respect. Someone assigned *strong* rights (think of Marx's factory owner) expects the right to exercise those rights even if he or she chooses not to; someone accorded *weak* rights (think now of Marx's factory worker) regards community more from a supplicant's perspective. The distribution of dignity—the quality of social regard harvested by any given individual—usually tracks the distribution of rights: the bearer of strong rights is more likely treated with dignity than someone with few or no rights.

24. Self-addressing is a political act, one of heightened political self-determination. After all, self-addressees participate in reshaping their individual political subjectivity: they transform themselves cognitively, as political subjects, whether citizens or stateless persons. By granting human rights to themselves, they challenge a human rights–unfriendly environment. They empower themselves, above all if the rights they assign

themselves are then recognized by others, even if initially only by a small, marginal community.

25. In the Coda I discuss some of the failures of international law and international organizations to provide for human rights.

26. Citizenship conceived as nonterritorial and nonnational pluralizes the meaning of citizenship beyond the range of current understandings.

27. One example of her statism: "The disturbing thing about the Dreyfus Affair is that it was not only the mob which had to work along extraparliamentary lines. The entire minority, fighting as it was for Parliament, democracy, and the republic, was likewise constrained to wage its battle outside the Chamber. The only difference between the two elements was that while the one used the streets, the other resorted to the press and to the courts" (Arendt 1968:115).

28. Political emancipation can lead (unintentionally) to a privatization of the political; when it does, it undermines itself. A privatized politics displaces the problem out of the public sphere into the private sphere where a communal problem cannot be addressed and solved: "Man was therefore not freed from religion, he received freedom of religion. He was not freed from property; he received freedom of property. He was not freed from the egoism of trade; he received freedom to trade" (Marx 2000:63). Emancipation here is a species-level phenomenon: "The actual individual man must take the abstract citizen back into himself and, as an individual man in his empirical life, in his individual work and individual relationships become a species-being; man must recognize his own forces as social forces, organize them, and thus no longer separate social forces from himself in the form of political forces. Only when this has been achieved will human emancipation be complete" (ibid., 64).

29. This conclusion is a step Arendt never quite takes; she recognizes that membership in political community is necessary if a person is to enjoy human rights, but she cannot explain how that political community might come to recognize human rights in the first place.

Chapter 3. The Body as Human Rights Boundary

1. In past centuries slavery was widely understood as a form of legal ownership of a person, a form abolished in the eighteenth and nineteenth centuries. But with the movement for abolition, its definition became, and remains, controversial, and today there is no consensually held definition. But no one disputes the contention that other forms of slavery persist today, usually involving economic exploitation, control, and violence. Bales (2005:57) argues that "slavery has three key dimensions: loss of free will, the appropriation of labor power, and the use or threat of violence." Accordingly, "in white slavery, forced labor, debt bondage, child prostitution, forced prostitution, and sexual slavery, all three aspects of our definition are present. Prostitution, forced marriage, and the work demanded of some migrant workers can be manifested as slavery under certain conditions" (ibid.). "Apartheid, incest, organ harvesting, caste,

and abusive treatment of migrant workers have all been defined as slavery-like practices, but should not be defined as slavery, since the theft of labor power in particular does not occur to the same degree as in the practices already identified as consistent with slavery" (ibid., 58). International bodies have widened the definition of slavery—for example, by "designating unfree forms of marriage and child labor as institutions analogous, or similar in certain respects, to slavery," opening a perspective to grasp "phenomena as diverse as prostitution, incest, and the sale of human organs" as forms of slavery (ibid., 48).

2. Estimates vary; this one comes from Lovejoy (1989:368).

3. Bales and Soodalter (2009:xiii) note issues of statistical evidence—namely, the lack of an accurate and reliable system of quantification:

> For years, numbers of victims—both foreign born and domestic—have been put forth by both government and NGOs, only to be withdrawn, recalculated, and resubmitted. One major reason for this less-than-scientific approach is the hidden nature of the crime itself. By its very definition, modern-day slavery lives in the shadows, often making it impossible to locate, let alone count, the victims and their traffickers. Further, there is a temporal restriction built into the crime of modern-day slavery. Whereas other crimes, such as theft, assault, rape and murder, can be viewed as events—incidents that occur within a brief, fixed time frame—slavery, by its very definition, can extend over a period of years, and in some cases decades.

4. Some circumstances that facilitate slavery today are global in extent: poverty, conflict, discrimination, corruption, adverse environmental change.

5. Note key definitions in the Convention to Suppress the Slave Trade and Slavery; the 1957 Supplementary Convention on the Abolition of Slavery, the Slave Trade and Institutions and Practices Similar to Slavery; the International Labour Organization (ILO) Convention Concerning Forced or Compulsory Labour; and the Protocol to Prevent, Suppress and Punish Trafficking in Persons, Especially Women and Children, supplementing the United Nations Convention Against Transnational Organized Crime.

6. See, for example, "Lord's Resistance Army and the Central African Region," 15 May 2013, Office of the Special Representative of the Secretary-General for Children and Armed Conflict, https://childrenandarmedconflict.un.org/countries/lords-resistance-army-and-the-central-african-region/.

7. See, for example, "Slavery in Mauritania," Anti-Slavery International, http://www.antislavery.org/english/slavery_today/descent_based_slavery/slavery_in_mauritania/default.aspx.

8. See, for example, "Sold to the Sea: Human Trafficking in Thailand's Fishing Industry," Environmental Justice Foundation, http://ejfoundation.org/soldtotheseafilm.

9. A *restavek* is a child sent by parents, without adequate resources to support him or her, to work as a domestic servant in a more affluent, usually more urban, household in exchange for room and board and sometimes education. Many *restaveks* live in poverty and are exposed to abuse, including beatings and rape.

10. Ninety-seven countries (49.7 percent of UN members) are party to the 1926 Slavery Convention; 123 countries (63.7 percent) are party to the 1957 Supplementary Slavery Convention; 176 countries (91.1 percent) are party to the Forced Labour Convention; 154 countries (79.7 percent) are party to the UN Trafficking Protocol. Still, China, Japan, and Papua–New Guinea, among other countries, have enacted few antislavery laws (Walk Free Foundation 2013:10 n. 2).

11. See U.S. Department of State, *2013 Trafficking in Persons Report*, p. 46, http://www.state.gov/documents/organization/210737.pdf.

12. Here I focus on a nation state even as other institutions may participate in the human rights project, including nongovernmental organizations, civil society organizations, trade unions, even businesses.

13. *Barcelona Traction* case (Belgium v. Spain), Second Phase, ICJ Reports 1970, p. 3.

14. And note that "none of the more than three hundred laws and agreements written since 1815 to combat first the slave trade and then slavery have been totally effective" (Bales 2005:41).

15. *Vidomegon* refers to the practice of some families who are struggling with extreme poverty and many children (polygamy; no birth control) of giving up some of their children (most often between three and fifteen years old) to traffickers who, traveling from village to village to collect such children, sell them abroad into slavery and sexual abuse.

16. Indeed, even "armed conflicts cannot be understood without reference to such 'root' causes as poverty, political repression, and uneven distribution of resources" (ICISS 2001:22).

17. "While the international community has become increasingly sophisticated in using development assistance to promote conflict prevention, there has in recent years been a marked decline in the overall level of that assistance worldwide" (ibid., 20).

18. A world state, unrealistic in today's world of nation states in any case, is especially unrealistic as a democratic rights–respecting structure. (How would self-government and meaningful participation be possible given the sheer size and geographic dispersion of a global polity?) In the Coda I contrast the cosmopolitanism of a world state with what I propose as the domestic cosmopolitanism of a nation state that embraces human rights as a feature internal to itself.

19. A shared understanding of this universal correspondence of human bodies allows in principle any person to grasp, at a personal level, what bodily and psychological harm is. Slavery certainly takes psychological forms such as escalating debts, intimidation, deception, isolation, and fear.

20. With exceptions such as very young children or the mentally ill, human beings have a resonant understanding of the embodiedness of other human beings.

21. After all, the "body is a complex structure. The functions of its different parts and their relation afford a source of symbols for other complex structures. We cannot possibly interpret rituals concerning excreta, breast milk, saliva and the rest unless we are prepared to see in the body a symbol of society, and to see the powers and dangers credited to social structure reproduced in small on the human body" (Douglas 1966:115).

22. Such rights may include entitlements as well as freedom from various negative possibilities, such as life-threatening work conditions.

23. Compare Brysk and Choi-Fitzpatrick (2012).

24. Geography is, of course, always "external" to human beings, in this case to the rights bearer. The backpack, by contrast, is (metaphorically speaking) "internal" to the rights bearer, in the sense that it accompanies the individual wherever he or she goes.

25. The conventional understanding stresses the historically produced, highly formalized and institutionalized correspondence between state and citizen.

26. Like the nation state, citizenship is prominent in many regions of the world, but hardly all. To reduce the complexity of my analysis, I confine myself to citizenship.

27. Other political principles preclude embodied political agency. Article 1 of the U.S. Constitution of 1787 offers a calculation of the political weight (for white Southerners) of resident slaves as three-fifths of a body: "Representatives and direct Taxes shall be apportioned among the several states which may be included within this Union, according to their respective Numbers, which shall be determined by adding to the whole Number of free Persons . . . three fifths of all other Persons."

28. Compare Plessner (1981:250).

29. In itself, the body unites the objective feature of the human individual who "has" or "possesses" a body with a subjective feature. By *subjective feature* I mean the personal psychological and phenomenological property of being a body. The objective and subjective properties are united in such a way that "having a body" is necessary to "being a body" in the sense that the embodied mind can reflect on its physical embodiment only because it is embodied.

30. Douglas (1970:vii) even argues that "most symbolic behavior must work through the human body."

31. Which can only be particular because each nation state is defined over against other nation states (whereas the world state would not be particular).

32. See Glasius (2006); Bell and Colcaud (2007).

33. I address the relationship between human rights and humanitarian intervention in Chapter 9.

34. I would approach the problem of torture in similar terms.

35. Including 83 million persons in Bihar and 44 million in Uttar Pradesh.

36. By comparison, the endogenization of nonnational agendas or projects is well advanced in the economic sphere, in the form of corporate firms and financial markets. Endogenization of nonnational projects moves from the economic sphere to the sphere of legality, rights, and moral imperatives of how humans are to be treated anywhere, at any time, under any circumstances. The "new concentrations of power and 'legitimacy' that attach to global firms and markets" (Sassen 2006:28) in the economic case offer analogies for new concentrations of moral power and political legitimacy that could attach to a human rights state.

37. "In both Pakistan and India, Kashmiri peoples have experienced long histories of exceptional legal regimes and what they call 'black laws,' which have periodically provided for the legal abrogation of civil and political rights or for the suspension of civil oversight and political review. The concept of *insānī haqūq* [human rights] makes it possible to imagine a political space in which the violation of the body is never legal or legitimate" (Robinson 2013:174–175).

38. The term *human rights politics* is indeterminate, of course. Some militant organizations regard it as legitimating politically directed violence (Robinson 2013:174). One study in Kashmir found that human rights language "could be used to mobilize different political projects and produced no stable progressive or liberatory position against the excesses of state violence. As human rights documentation circulated through different public spaces, it was employed by different publics to legitimate contradictory political movements" (Robinson 2013:177–178). Even to propose human rights politics as humanitarianism is not unproblematic inasmuch as human rights humanitarianism can also be an element in geopolitical competition among elites. Some elites justify their unilateral military interventions as humanitarian (Moyn 2010). I use this term to refer to ordinary individuals, in concert with others, authoring their own human rights.

39. Slavery is not viable for any national economy: "Slave-made products and services are worth about $13 billion a year, exactly what Americans spent on Valentine's Day in 2010. The UN estimates that human traffickers make $32 billion in profits annually—but these sums are tiny drops in the ocean of the world economy. No industry or big corporation, no political party, no state or country or culture is dependent on slavery. No government or business would collapse if slavery ended today" (Bales and Choi-Fitzpatrick 2012:196).

40. Compare Goffman (1963:151–190) on how rituals maintain ties among the members of a group or community.

41. The project for a human rights state contests the "political foundation of an interstate world from which international organizations are built, along with the inside/outside or national/international boundaries this imaginary carries" (Doucet 2001:300). The emerging human rights state begins "within the confines of territorial space and the practice of politics this space entails (i.e., the state as the locus of politics)" (ibid., 294). It deepens and expands the human rights idea by disaggregating rights from territory.

42. The external physical universe (as in topographical boundaries) no longer determines whether one has rights; social construction does. Jurisdiction in this sense determines the political limits and consequences of territory such as who has rights, who has standing to make claims about rights, and on what basis. To be effective, a person's human rights require a *field of recognition*. But this field is not, as in a nation state, physically or territorially specified. It constitutes a "moral territory," a territory of the mind, a belief system, a "social mindscape" (Zerubavel 1997). Hence I construct a human rights state as metaphor.

43. Here we have a model that breaks completely with a territorial basis for the distribution of rights. The model is local but the quality of "localness" is not territorial. Rather, it is local in the sense of human community, as a group of participating believers who *embody* the rights. I find support for this position in the work of Merry (2006).

44. By contrast, Wolff (2002) reads the Thirteenth Amendment in terms of a nation state, as interpreted by American courts in domestic cases.

Chapter 4. Teaching Human Rights as a Cognitive Style

1. By constructing human rights thinking as a cognitive style, I achieve an analytic focus sharper than competing conceptions of human rights. Among those competing conceptions are human rights as a kind of "belief" (a feeling of certainty in the truth of a claim); as a "worldview" (a comprehensive, normative way of regarding social and political life); as an "ideology" (systematically distorted communication); and in all cases, human rights as a "morality" (a system for the normative evaluation of behavior).

2. The Roman emperor Constantine, who reigned from 306 to 337, established the tradition of the Christian monarch that generated a cognitive style combining the theological and the political in subsequent centuries in Western lands. The distinction I draw between theological and political styles finds expression, for example, in the First Amendment to the U.S. Constitution and the doctrine of separation of church and state, a division that characterizes many of the world's political communities today, quite beyond the West.

3. For ease of locution I will speak of *a* human rights style, that is, *in the singular*. This stylistic choice should not obscure a range of human rights styles that differ from each other in some respects even as all of them may be grouped coherently as human rights styles.

4. For example, Darwin concludes *The Origin of Species* (1859:490) by detecting normative and emotional value in biological fact: "Thus, from the war of nature, from famine and death, the most exalted object which we are capable of conceiving, namely, the production of the higher animals, directly follows. There is grandeur in this view of life, with its several powers, having been originally breathed into a few forms or into one; and that, whilst this planet has gone cycling on according to the fixed law of gravity, from so simple a beginning endless forms most beautiful and most wonderful have been, and are being, evolved."

5. Only then do microananalytic issues—"what is meant by 'we,' 'it,' and 'here' and how the implied consensus is accomplished"—pose themselves (Goffman 1974:25).

6. My concern is not the comparative one of analyzing how different disciplines might approach the teaching of human rights. My concern is how college-level instruction *in any discipline* might deploy the notion of a human rights state in teaching about human rights. I would expect a pedagogy of human rights as cognitive style to work out more or less the same regardless of the particular discipline to deploy the pedagogy.

7. Because Chapter 3 treats contemporary slavery at length, analysis in this chapter does not treat those forms of child labor that constitute slavery.

8. My interest here is in long-term processes of cultural, social, political, and economic transformation rather than urgent mobilizations of international resources in human rights emergencies (which I address in Chapter 9; for an additional example of the latter approach, see Risse, Ropp, and Sikkink 1999).

9. But a truly global embrace of complex norms is rare and global validity is best pursued as an aspiration approached asymptotically.

10. Commerce offers an ancient example of potentially broadening interaction, as in cosmopolitan trading centers. But human rights aspire to a very different form of cosmopolitanism, as I show.

11. Global validity of any cognitive style cannot possibly be immediate or a priori unless one assumes a theological or metaphysical perspective (for a critique of such perspectives, see Gregg 2012b, chaps. 1 and 2). From the standpoint of cosmopolitan politics, such perspectives are prohibitively expensive in terms of finding cosmopolitan agreement. To date they have never achieved a global embrace. This is not to say that a cognitive style might one day be embraced universally. But if so, then that embrace can only be achieved contingently, through a politics of human rights, or what I call *the human rights project*.

12. They can span this tension without breaking on it if they resist appeals to universal criteria, which, "because of the multiplication of normative standpoints in our 'disenchanted' modern world, are not (and likely never were) available or plausible to so many of us in contemporary societies. *Disenchantment* implies social fragmentation. Even though normativity equally informs diverse spheres of society—from politics to religious faith, from law to social critique—the multiplication of competing worldviews, together with the rise of empirical science, has fragmented shared worldviews. These phenomena also discourage the creation of shared worldviews where none existed before" (Gregg 2003a:7). The world has always been characterized by "a heterogeneity of normative convictions, commitments, and intuitions. Norms of various worldviews appeal to sources of justification not equally available or plausible to all or even many of the heterogeneous groups that make up the world's various political communities. Under these conditions, no single worldview is likely to resonate with all groups or every individual" in the world (ibid.). A normatively fragmented world compels human rights advocates to distinguish critically among

competing spheres of normative value. And it compels them to distinguish critically among competing spheres of cognitive validity. Toward increasing the local embrace of human rights as widely as possible, "coping with differences in worldview is possible only across heterogeneous groups, and only across normative commitments. It is not possible to cope by reducing one worldview to another. It is possible only by giving full weight to the participants' perspectives as well as to perspectives beyond those of the local participants. It is possible only by speaking to the particular self-understandings of the affected groups and relevant worldviews—as well as to the supraindividual understanding generated by" what I elsewhere develop as "the weakly objectivating approach of enlightened localism" (ibid.).

13. Gendering becomes more complex still: "cocoa bean harvesting is more a male task, whereas plantains are more a female crop," and the "fact that cocoa cash income is more a male income could play a role here [in Côte d'Ivoire] if fathers have a preference for sons over daughters" (Cogneau and Jedwab 2012:528).

14. Workers acquire human capital above all through education and training, and to a lesser extent through health care, migration, and job search.

15. Chapter 8 argues that the possibility of human rights within any given political community does require a specifically democratic form of government.

16. Or not at work: in Brazil, "old-age benefits have the effect of increasing school enrollment of girls co-residing with old-age beneficiaries, particularly girls ages 13–14 . . . with little or no effect for boys. There is also some evidence that increases in benefits have caused reductions in work for pay and work intensity for girls, but only for female benefits. Since male benefits appear to be irrelevant for girls' schooling and labor decisions, the results indicate the existence of differences by gender of receiver and perhaps tensions between male and female adults over girls' use of time" (de Carvalho Filho 2012:431). Precisely a more communitarian organization of the household might defeat sexual bias of this sort.

17. *Employment Division, Department of Human Resources of Oregon v. Smith*, 494 U.S. 872 (1990).

18. Local cognitive styles may display features in tension with the human rights idea, as well as other features that offer themselves as positive resources for the human rights idea. For example, "in almost all countries with substantial communities of Muslims, positive law has replaced *Shari'a* (except with regard to matters of 'personal status,' and more specifically the status of women, where the traditional rules generally continue to be maintained). Similarly, prevailing conceptions and attitudes of everyday life are founded on modern rationality and on doctrines influenced by science and philosophy, rather than on traditional or premodern worldviews" (Filaly-Ansari 1999:23).

19. For a developed theory and practical application of cognitive framing, see Gregg (2012b, chap. 7).

20. For one list that could command agreement across at least some boundaries, political and cultural, see the International Labour Organization's Worst Forms of Child Labour Convention, 1999 (No. 182).

21. That is, I do not argue that poverty is the primary impediment to human rights but rather that poverty, wherever found, always impedes human rights in powerful and enduring ways. Hence the project of advancing human rights must attend to the predicates and perpetuators of poverty. A human rights cognitive style in India, for example, might encourage families that inherit the crushing debt of the previous generation to collectively seek ways to repudiate that debt and its cultural and legal supports. In some cases members of impoverished communities will find resources of political agency within themselves to pursue, in terms of their own human rights state, changes in the status quo. A human rights cognitive style seeks to repudiate inherited debt and its cultural and legal supports. Activists in the human rights state not only could show that education and labor are often at odds with each other for the most economically disenfranchised; they could also configure ways in which child education and child labor might be harmonized in human rights–relevant ways. After all, some forms of child labor are not as such necessarily human rights violative. And some forms may make the child laborer's education possible where it would be otherwise impossible.

22. This is not to say that adults are particularly successful in their efforts, as an example from China shows with respect to negative local consequences of the global economic system: (a) labor legislation is only as good as what is enforced, yet "local government officials, principally motivated to boost their local economies by attracting foreign investment, have molded China's labor regulations to their own ends"; (b) only an independent judiciary can guarantee the implementation of legislation regulating labor, yet in China the judiciary is "effectively controlled by local government officials . . . reluctant to prosecute abusive employers for fear of losing foreign investments"; (c) while trade unions can hardly guarantee a balance of power between capital and labor, without trade unions such a balance is exceedingly unlikely, yet "Chinese workers have no freedom to establish trade unions or to take industrial actions"; and (d) multinational corporations' codes of conduct are often impotent in the face of local conditions, such as the "suppression of rural migrant workers' citizenship rights" and "local governments' noncompliance with central policies and law" in China (Chan and Peng 2011:440).

23. For example, the greater the distance a child must travel to school, the greater the cost of attending school, including a correspondingly smaller amount of time for work.

24. To be sure, there are "distinct differences between the sector composition of child labor in Africa, Asia, and Latin America. In Africa, child labor is considered primarily a rural phenomenon, while in Asia and Latin America, which are more urbanized, child labor is also considered an urban phenomenon" (Canagarajah and Nielsen 2001:72). Child labor in agrarian economies differs from child labor in urban ones. In the rural Brazilian coffee industry, for example, "as child intensive industries decline, child labor falls, suggesting that households do not fully readjust their children's labor supply through endogenous occupational choices," whereas "urban children happen to be much more segregated in specific industries than rural children"

and "child intensive industries account for a small and essentially fixed share of adult employment in urban areas" (Manacorda and Rosati 2011:772).

25. Issues of fertility can complicate women's decisions about school and labor. To reduce complexity, I do not evaluate those issues here.

26. See Bhalotra and Heady (1998).

27. See Nielsen (1998).

28. See Canagarajah and Coulombe (1998); Coulombe (1998).

29. See Canagarajah and Coulombe (1998).

30. See Coulombe (1998).

31. See Bhalotra and Heady (1998).

32. See Coulombe (1998).

33. International treaties often are ineffective as well; see Hathaway (2002).

34. The International Labour Organization's Minimum Age Convention, 1973 (No. 138), was preceded by minimum conventions in industry (1919), at sea (1920), and in agriculture (1921); for trimmers and stokers (1921) and in nonindustrial employment (1932); with respect to minimum age for labor at sea (1936) and in industry (revised, 1937); for fishermen (1959) and for labor underground (1965).

35. ILO Minimum Age Convention, 1973 (No. 138), article 7, paragraph 1. To be sure, a human rights style queries the convention's age specifications and urges locally sensitive answers to such questions as: Why thirteen and above but not twelve and below? Should age limits be independent of some of the various factors explored above, such as the nature of the labor, the question of valuable skill acquisition or other human capital development, the possibility of simultaneous school attendance, and the quality of local schools and road access to them? Where available schooling is of a low quality, would a child be better off by learning by doing, on a farm, for example?

36. As always, caution and humility are warranted. According to Krueger (1996), compulsory school attendance laws often are not enforced in developing countries. The same may be said of trade sanctions targeting child labor. Indeed, "boycotts of products produced by child labor and more generally anti-sweatshop activism" may generate "trade sanctions that reduce average family income," potentially increasing the incidence of child labor (Edmonds and Pavcnik 2005:218). And "preventing children from working in one high-profile job may do nothing more than force children to change employers—perhaps for the worse" (ibid.).

37. A different track would be needed for children engaged in household labor.

38. See Horn (1994).

39. See Psacharopoulos (1997); Akabayashi and Psacharopoulos (1999).

40. For an account of particularism as "enlightened localism" in distinction to "parochial localism," see Gregg (2003a); and for empirical applications, see Gregg et al. (2010).

41. Relevant here is the role of groups in the development of the individual's psychological processes. To participate in "culturally mediated, historically developing,

practical activity involving cultural practices and tools"—activity through which the structure of psychological processes emerges—is to participate in groups (Gutiérrez and Rogoff 2003:21).

Chapter 5. Developing Human Rights Commitment in Post-Authoritarian Societies

1. These particular examples are hardly definitive for deploying the human rights state under all post-authoritarian circumstances, of course, and to that extent the chapter can be read as addressing post-authoritarian regimes and societies more generally.

2. Since the 1960s, about fifty political communities (about one quarter of all states in the world today) have transitioned to more or less democratic orders. About two dozen states have attempted this transition since 2000.

3. On pathways in post-socialist Europe, see Stark (1998). Coffé and van der Lippe (2010:492–493) typify scholarship sensitive to distinctions among Eastern European countries even as they generalize across these countries with respect to the "level of civic mindedness": Polish citizens stress engagement and duty; Hungarians, participation in elections and obeying laws; Slovenians, engagement; and Czechs, who score lowest on citizenship norms. The authors take these four distinct cases together to conclude that the "communist experience and the penetration of communism within society still influences citizens' views on citizenship." Similarly, Letki and Evans (2005:524–525) show comparatively that the "introduction of market democracy in East-Central Europe has been varied in terms of its rate of success, with countries such as the Czech Republic, Hungary and Poland leading in political and economic reforms, and Belarus, Russia and Ukraine struggling to escape the Soviet legacy."

4. See Howard (2003) on the abiding weakness of civil society in Eastern and Central Europe.

5. And requires educators with some understanding and experience of democratic principles, and some idea about how to realize them.

6. In Western civil societies, voluntary associations, pluralism, and relative freedom from state control are realized at best only imperfectly. Such factors should not be idealized even as they offer something of a standard by which to identify and analyze the absence of alternative spaces beyond the grip of authoritarian states.

7. As empirical research indicates, including, e.g., Bache and Taylor (2003), on Kosovo; Uhlin (2010), on Latvia; and Shevel (2011), on Ukraine.

8. This claim assumes a different valence depending on how it is read. From a *cultural* perspective, education in the form of childhood socialization determines the individual to such an extent that the displacement of one set of learned attitudes with another sometimes depends on generational replacement. See Kelly (2005) for a recent example. To be sure, members of a cohort do not experience socialization monolithically; differences in sex, ethnicity, or family position, among other factors, can generate

significant differences within a cohort; see Dalton (1994). From an *institutional* viewpoint, adults always already relearn—as a means of coping with changing social circumstances and regardless of childhood socialization; see, e.g., North (1990). A third approach combines these two perspectives into the idea of lifelong learning; for Russia, e.g., see Mishler and Rose (2007).

9. To frame the world in a particular way is to look for recurring patterns that orient perceptual and intellectual activity and inform a way of doing something. Frames are shared among members of groups and even across groups. Although a shared frame generates shared convictions, it does not require consensus nor does it entail consensus. My notion of cognitive styles draws on cognitive sociology; for an overview of current trends, see Strydom (2007).

10. Systematic distortion characterized the "communist manipulation of concepts such as democracy, justice, progress, and conservatism," constituting a "particularly problematic obstacle for civic education in the early years of post-communist Poland" (Wojcik 2010:397). In the communist period, textbooks "strove to single out relevant words with a positive emotional loading and to steer their meanings so that they could be used as attributes to describe the state of affairs" in Poland and other East bloc countries. The word "democracy," for example, "was applied only to socialist countries; Western countries were called 'pseudo-' or 'bourgeois-democracies'" (Andrzej Janowski, cited in ibid., 398).

11. In many cases but not all, a human rights cognitive style is highly reflected and self-conscious. To that extent it contrasts with Pierre Bourdieu's (1990:74) notion of *habitus* as a "practical sense, which does not burden itself with rules or principles," still less with "calculations or deductions," such that a person can grasp the "meaning of the situation instantly, at a glance, in the heat of the action," and "produce at once the opportune response": an "acquired mastery, functioning with the automatic reliability of an instinct," which responds "instantaneously to all the uncertain and ambiguous situations of practice" (ibid., 103–104). To be sure, *habitus* never becomes entirely unreflective: "Inculcation is never so perfect that a society can entirely dispense with all explicit statement" (ibid., 107). According to Bourdieu, *habitus* derives from the "social structures (the structure of relations between the groups, the sexes or the generations, or between the social classes) of which they are the product and which they tend to reproduce" (ibid., 95). With *habitus*, a human rights cognitive style can become part of a mutually influencing relationship between the individual's social environment and his or her cognitive orientation in the world. Chapter 4 speaks to a human rights cognitive style in the human rights–supportive *habitus* of a liberal democratic political culture and college classrooms in that culture. In this chapter I deploy that cognitive style with respect to a very different *habitus*, that of newly democratizing communities still marked by residua, in their political culture, of an authoritarian past. Bourdieu focuses on how the relationship between *habitus* and mind-set can sustain an oppressive social environment. It does so by reproducing systematically distorted information in the heads of participants. This chapter would show how a

human rights cognitive style might be deployed in a post-authoritarian *habitus* in ways that would motivate participants to examine that environment in terms of human rights standards.

12. A simplistic view of political indoctrination is also "undermined by the peaceful anticommunist revolutions throughout Eastern Europe and the former Soviet Union, dominated by educated people with years of pro-communist indoctrination under their belts" (Glaeser, Ponzetto, and Shleifer 2007:85).

13. Hence I examine only one example (in itself large and very complex): post-authoritarian Eastern European states. This model's methodological localism rejects the idea of addressing all post-authoritarian states as such. Each of the various types needs to be treated separately. They include traditional authoritarian regimes (with personal loyalties, such as Ethiopia under Haile Selassie or Spain under Franco); bureaucratic military authoritarian regimes (less ideological, such as South Korea under Park Chung-hee); post-totalitarian (less ideological, less personalized, with little mass mobilization, such as China after Mao); the corporatist forms of authoritarianism in twentieth-century Latin America; and racist regimes that deny rights to certain racial or ethnic groups (such as South Africa under apartheid). For a compelling deployment of localism in advancing human rights more generally, see Merry (2006).

14. See Gregg (2012b) for examples of human rights pursued in context-sensitive ways.

15. See note 11 on the meaning of *habitus*.

16. See Gregg (2012b) for examples of human rights pursued in context-sensitive ways.

17. A human rights education proceeds on multiple tracks simultaneously. One track is a human rights state; another is the nation state; another, below the level of the state, is concerned with civil society; another, above the level of the nation state, is concerned with nongovernmental organizations such as Amnesty International or the Helsinki Citizens' Assembly. (Chapter 7 extends this multitrack approach by demonstrating possibilities for integrating human rights commitment and national loyalty.)

18. A smaller, more educated citizenry also contributes to an environment facilitative of a human rights cognitive style. "Large population sizes are believed not only to place stress on national resources, but also to increase the incidents of state terrorism by expanding the number of opportunities for coercive acts" (Carlson and Listhaug 2007:472). Indeed, "citizens' perceptions of human rights issues are more negative when the population size is larger" (ibid). Perhaps, as a general pattern, "persons with higher education will have stronger human rights values, which will lead them to be more critical in countries with human rights violations" (ibid., 473).

19. For purposes of a very general orientation, consider a short list of differences (in lieu of a very long one): unlike Aquinas (1886–1887), it does not define human rights as goods or behaviors naturally right because God ordained it so; in distinction to Hobbes (1651), it does not posit them as a natural right to self-preservation; contrary to Kant (1795), it does not ground them as necessary for civil society; unlike

Donnelly (1989), it does not derive them as needed for a life of dignity; by contrast to Gewirth (1985), it does not view them as necessary to protect the basic freedom and well-being necessary for human agency; unlike Galtung (1994), it does not understand them as necessary to provide what is needed for subsistence. Pogge (2002) as well as Talbott (2010) understand human rights primarily as claims on coercive social institutions; I suggest that they are primarily claims against authorities who uphold such institutions. Brock (2009:72) argues that "we must know what our basic needs are before we can sensibly define the entitlement that will be protected by human rights"; I counter that we socially construct our needs no less than our rights, hence that needs and rights are logically coeval, that needs do not ground rights.

20. To view human rights as socially constructed is not to deny that society is prior to any individual's experience and understanding. It is to affirm that "whatever an agent seeks to do will be continuously conditioned by natural constraints, and that effective doing will require the exploitation, not the neglect, of this condition" (Goffman 1974:23).

21. But it remains mindful of contexts where only group rights can deliver some human rights—for example, in the case of some indigenous peoples (see, e.g., Kymlicka 1995).

22. See Kelly (2005) for a recent example; to be sure, members of a cohort do not experience socialization monolithically; differences in sex, ethnicity, or family position, among other factors, can generate significant differences within a cohort (see Dalton 1994).

23. See, e.g., North (1990). A third approach combines these two perspectives into the idea of lifelong learning (e.g., for Russia, see Mishler and Rose 2007).

24. Current economic and social problems, as well as governmental corruption, also generate distrust in contemporary economic and political elites and general disappointment with postcommunist society. No community, regardless of design, can generate trust under severe conditions of significant economic decline, immiseration of the populace, or ethnic strife, let alone civil war or international conflict. Informal networks in the communist era encouraged social trust beyond state control, just as they discouraged trust and engagement in public networks.

25. As sociologists have long recognized, from Émile Durkheim (1984) to Georg Simmel (1908) to Talcott Parsons (1951).

26. Its extirpation requires the "maximum protection for freedom of speech" as well as a "special sensibility to identify censorship or the menace of it as a typical backwards regulation" (Molnár 2009:482).

27. A human rights cognitive style addresses phenomena in post-authoritarian communities that are not themselves residua of that legacy. Uhlin (2006:56ff.), for example, identifies an additional factor: an "NGO-ization" of civil society in postcommunist countries, with few locally available economic resources, where foreign-funded nongovernmental organizations (unintentionally) depress local, indigenous

participation in civil society or provide few incentives for the political mobilization of local residents.

28. In each case I draw on Tibbitts's (2002) conception of epistemic and practical models, although not in ways consistent with her self-understanding. For example, she does not employ a theory of cognitive style. All three models are oriented on long-term processes of cultural, social, political, and economic transformation rather than on urgent mobilizations of international resources in human rights emergencies. For an example of the latter approach, see Risse, Ropp, and Sikkink (1999).

29. Following the explanatory logic, but not the subject matter, of work like that of Coleman (1990).

30. Following the logic but not the content of scholarship in approaches such as Putnam's (1993).

Chapter 6. Digital Technology as Resource for the Human Rights Project

1. I provide here a definition only provisional inasmuch as even core features of the Internet change constantly; rapid technological innovation requires equally rapid redefinitions.

2. See, e.g., McChesney (2000).

3. Of particular concern is the power of Western culture over many of the world's other cultures, especially in developing countries. But concern is warranted within the West as well, for example within the European Union, about cultural homogenization across Europe as well as through American popular culture.

4. As so often in the digital revolution, trends are mixed. On the one hand, the chasm between elites and marginalized groups within any society only increases while the cosmopolitan governing elites residing in the capitals of various developing countries tend to share worldviews and lifestyles with Western elites. On the other hand, diversity of Internet content has increased significantly (along with Internet access) since the 1990s when the Internet was dominated by the United States and other postindustrial countries.

5. Another relevant dimension is generational cohort; in developing countries, for example, younger cohorts tend to be more educated than older ones.

6. Other media also attract relatively distinct clienteles; newspaper readers, for example, tend to be less religious and more inclined to economic liberalism, like cybernauts, yet unlike them, more nationalistic (Norris and Inglehart 2009:282).

7. The phenomenon of disembodiment is not new, nor is it confined to digital communication. The legal sphere in particular has long engaged in disembodiment: the modern corporation, for example, has legal standing analogous to a human subject yet without a human body. And last wills and testaments, as well as assorted codicils and covenants, realize the intentions of a deceased legal subject, that is, a legal subject who no longer has a body. Such legal arrangements create bodiless beings; they endow nonbodied beings with legal content (compare Boltanski 2009). By contrast, digital

disembodiment involves the temporary, online persona of someone very much embodied.

8. Goffman (1961) makes this point with regard to "total institutions" (the Internet is no such institution). Mental patients, for example, are determined in their reactions and coping mechanisms less by their illness than by the psychiatric institution to which they have been committed. Total institutions constitute a kind of "counter world" to everyday mainstream society. But they also model that society in the ways that social extremes can illuminate social "normality" (where "normality" defines itself in part by excluding behavior and beliefs that deviate from the norm).

9. Pace Johnson and Post (1996).

10. For a critique of one liberal ideal of universal citizenship, see Young (1995).

11. See Rummens (2006) on "the co-originality of private and public autonomy" as the possible coexistence of two sources of political authority: in liberalism, the rule of law; in republicanism, the will of the people.

12. For empirical evidence that lends limited support to the claim that political deliberation generally renders participants more thoughtful and considered in their political understanding and analysis of contested issues, see Druckman (2004); Fishkin and Luskin (2005). To be sure, small-scale samples can only model, but not accurately represent, large-scale communities.

13. For empirical examples of legitimation through deliberation, drawn from political institutions, see Steiner et al. (2004); for examples drawn from daily life, see Conover and Searing (2005).

14. See Gregg (2012b) for a theory of human rights as socially constructed.

15. Cf. ibid., chap. 4.

16. My translation of "l'état des citoyens" that provides "tout homme né et domicilié en France, âgé de vingt et un ans accomplis, qui, domicilié en France depuis une année—y vit de son travail—ou acquiert une propriété—ou épouse une Française—ou adopte un enfant—ou nourrit un vieillard; tout étranger enfin, qui sera jugé par le Corps législatif avoir bien mérité de l'humanité—est admis à l'exercice des Droits de citoyen français."

17. Most provisions of modern constitutions are indifferent to the affected person's membership status.

18. See Gregg (2003b) for a theory of "normatively thin" politics as distinguished from "normatively thick" moralities; and Gregg et al. (2012) for a range of empirical applications of that theory.

19. Note that Chapter 8 argues not for democracy as a human right but for the rule of law as such a right.

20. No leadership change in Bahrain or Syria. Rebels overthrew the leadership in Libya, which then descended into civil war.

21. Although liberal democratic polities, because they are liberal democratic, cultivate a limited repertoire of norms and values that concern the protection of individual rights.

22. For an examination of this route with regard to genetic enhancement, see Gregg (2012a).

Chapter 7. Human Rights Patriotism

1. The Preamble appeals to "every individual and every organ of society" to "promote respect" for human rights and to "secure their universal and effective recognition." But the state looms larger than any other political means available within society.

2. One historical precedent: article 4 of the revolutionary constitution of France of 1793 embraces resident foreigners as members, with a right to remain in the community and a right to active citizenship. A European Union offers a precedent of a different sort: the Maastricht Treaty of 1992 imposes reciprocity of voting rights in local elections within the European Union, whereby some states extend the right to EU foreign residents, while others (Sweden, Denmark, Finland, the Netherlands, Belgium, Lithuania, and Slovenia) extend the right to all foreign residents.

3. The change I envision is not a question of democracy or even representation, although it does require the free local embrace of human rights rather than their imposition.

4. Of course, not every nation state may include human rights activists among its residents, and it is these who first construct a particular human rights state.

5. At least by definition of instruments such as the Universal Declaration of Human Rights.

6. My proposal also contrasts with Habermas's (2008:448–449) argument for constitutionalizing international law toward a constitution for a possible world society.

7. Of course, I do not intend *juridification* in the sense ridiculed by Brecht's character quoted in the Introduction, which in fact excludes the person from just treatment by the nation state.

8. Here I describe the social environment necessary for the rule of law; in Chapter 8 I discuss it as a plausible human right.

9. This proposal goes significantly beyond Pogge's (2002:44–48, 64–67) account of the institutional character of human rights.

10. Authors over the centuries have constructed the distinction between perfect and imperfect obligations differently; see Rainbolt (2000) for analysis of the distinctions.

Chapter 8. A Human Right Not to Democracy but to the Rule of Law

1. Some communities are governed not by a state but by a tribal organization, or an army, or a guerrilla movement (and in some cases even by corporations, especially transnational ones), beyond the purview of international law as well as beyond any domestic due diligence standards of treating humans.

2. The stipulation of critical public debate is one technique among others for participants to reassure themselves that the embrace was free and not, say, instrumentalized by propaganda.

3. This is not the epistemology of natural science in which debates find closure through authoritative knowledge. At best, politics is a matter of authoritative opinion; compare Haimes (2012:63).

4. By way of example, I argue for noncoercive human rights advocacy by outside intermediaries together with local participants, translating between local understandings and nonlocal human rights ideas in ways that preserve local authenticity and legitimacy, ways that resonate with local practices and understandings even as they challenge them; see Gregg (2012b, chap. 6).

5. Both Rawls (1971; 1993) and Habermas (1996) develop compelling arguments for testing the survivability of ethical and political claims in robust, unobstructed public debate.

6. And rights in this context do not correlate to one particular duty, and only one, but likely generate "successive waves of duty, some of them duties of omission, some of them duties of commission, some of them too complicated to fit easily under either heading" (Waldron 1993:25).

7. Compare Steiner, Alston, and Goodman (2007).

8. See Broomhall (2003).

9. Smith (1759; 1978) recommends consulting the viewpoints of outsiders to determine the justness or normative reasonableness of an evaluation or course of action (such as commensurate punishment for a crime).

10. For a general theory of enlightened localism, see Gregg (2003a).

11. To be sure, political traditions, values, and culture can change significantly over time, as they certainly have in China over the last century and even in recent decades. No cultural community is static.

12. Authoritarianism and authoritarian regimes are but one of many different examples of nonliberal communities and their political traditions, values, and culture. Confucianism vests rights and obligations in terms of a fixed social hierarchy of social and political relations. It does not regard members lower in the hierarchy as morally capable of performing the roles of members higher in the hierarchy. Hierarchies are registers of inequality. And Islam does not recognize all members of the faith as equally capable of, say, authoritatively interpreting guiding texts, such as the Qur'an, which organize major aspects of social and political life that may be relevant to human rights.

13. *Human rights* in the sense of rights that empower the individual vis-à-vis the state threaten authoritarian regimes, which harbor paranoid fears of domestic popular opposition: "Politicians in democracies rely on public opinion polls with scientifically selected representative samples because they need to know what the average voter is thinking in order to win elections. But politicians in authoritarian countries like China don't worry about losing elections. Their political survival depends instead on being attentive to the people who feel so strongly about something that they might go out on the streets to protest. Individuals willing to risk fulminating on the Internet are the ones likely to take the greater risk of participating in, or even organizing, mass protests" (Shirk 2007:103).

14. Sen (1999a:16) does just that by tying nondemocratic governance to economic catastrophes that may intentionally kill large numbers of people:

> Quite often economic insecurity can relate to the lack of democratic rights and liberties. Indeed, the working of democracy and of political rights can even help to prevent famines and other economic disasters. Authoritarian rulers, who are themselves rarely affected by famines (or other such economic calamities), tend to lack the incentive to take timely preventative measures. Democratic governments, in contrast, have to win elections and face public criticism, and have strong incentives to undertake measures to avert famines and other such catastrophes. It is not surprising that no famine has ever taken place in the history of the world in a functioning democracy—be it economically rich . . . or relatively poor.

Sen develops this position further in Sen (2011b).

15. An authoritarian political community merits reproach from the standpoint of democracy, but no less from a human rights standpoint that does not entail democracy as a human right.

16. This statement is problematic, too, not only because it proffers rights to protect individual autonomy, which inevitably challenge some group memberships, but also because it proffers rights to group preservation that, in some cases, challenge individual preference.

17. Adopted by the General Assembly of the United Nations on 19 December 1966.

18. An earlier formulation includes human rights to freedom of association and to emigration (Rawls 1999a:554).

19. Whereby a decision-making elite consults with all members of the community and takes their viewpoints seriously. Any member may criticize what he or she regards as a violation of his or her basic human rights and demand public discussion and examination. Benhabib (2007:10) is mistaken where she claims that Rawls's conception of human rights provides "no basic human right to self-government"; in principle, nondemocratic self-government could satisfy a putative human right to collective self-determination.

20. By *author* in this context I mean "author via democratic representation in the legislature," for example.

21. Rawls (1999b) makes this argument.

22. Democratic participation is not the only means by which citizens can directly speak on their own behalf. It does not by itself always ensure that a "state speaks on behalf of its citizens" (pace Valentini 2012:589).

23. No political community is monolithic in terms of cultural preference. Thus citizens at the more marginalized or oppressed end of hierarchical nondemocratic communities may not be able to regard this arrangement as just or human rights

compatible. Indeed, the very premise of individual rights is in permanent tension with collective self-determination, regardless of whether self-determination is democratic.

24. For examples with regard to Africa, see Mutua (2002:71–93); for Asia, see Bell (2000:23–105).

25. For an argument advancing a human right of women to be free of genital cutting, see Gregg (2012b:178–182).

26. Renteln (1990) develops this point.

Chapter 9. Human Rights and Humanitarian Intervention

1. Can coercive intervention ever be "humanitarian"? Military coercion as a means to humanitarian ends is defensible only if the ends justify the means—regardless of the interveners' motives. To say "We prefer to talk not of a 'right to intervene' but of a 'responsibility to protect'" is lexical subterfuge seeking to escape a discussion by tweaking vocabulary (ICISS 2001:11).

2. Griffin (2008) offers a view of human rights as morally relativistic that complements my own.

3. States are not the only institutional form taken by abusive power; terror comes in decentralized forms as well, such as Al-Qaeda, the Taliban, and Boko Haram—formations that have no state, hence no sovereignty, even as they control territory. Such formations are beyond the scope of this chapter.

4. Walzer's (2002) analysis of humanitarian intervention is particularly compelling and in this chapter I work out two of its crucial aspects that Walzer himself does not address: moral localism—which I emphasize (Gregg 2003a)—as well as ethicalism (in the sense elaborated by Heinze (2009, chap. 2)), which I embrace (Gregg 2003b).

5. And not only in contexts where the killing is state internal, even as the "overwhelming majority of today's armed conflicts are internal, not inter-state" (ICISS 2001:13).

6. As Hathaway (2002) shows.

7. A state's sovereignty is the coin of the global realm in international relations: recognition, equality, and dignity from other states and self-determination and domestic identities for itself. The United Nations Charter (article 2.1) reinforces this arrangement by declaring all states equally sovereign from the standpoint of international law.

8. Hence talk of the "basic divisions within the international community" (ICISS 2001:2) would more usefully refer to divisions and alliances among the many nation states of the world without invoking a community that does not exist.

9. As I argue at length elsewhere (Gregg 2012b).

10. This is not to say that coercion is always the enemy of justice. On the contrary, the "relationship between members of a political community and their government," the "rules by which a state's coercive force is to be exercised over individuals construed as legal persons, subject to the law," is not a relationship entirely free of coercion (Cohen 2008:590). As a matter of functionality, human rights–respecting behavior

requires the coercion of enforcing corresponding laws, rights, and obligations. A liberal legal order, in its coercion, guarantees freedom. Human rights assume a coercive political function in international relations where a state's human rights record "determines eligibility for development assistance programs"; where human rights conditions are "attached to internationally sponsored financial adjustment measures"; or where "policies of international financial and trade institutions" are evaluated in terms of their effect on the local recognition of human rights (Beitz 2001:269).

11. For example, communities that practice female genital cutting (see Gregg 2012b: 178–181 for extended analysis). Such communities may reject the possible human rights argument that cutting violates an individual's right to bodily integrity. Cutting would not trigger military intervention (even as it might motivate the interventions of aid workers). Given such examples, I confine my analysis to large-scale loss of life such as genocide, massacre, and ethnic cleansing. According to the responsibility-to-protect doctrine, intervention is warranted by "serious and irreparable harm occurring to human beings, or imminently likely to occur," either "large scale loss of life, actual or apprehended, with genocidal intent or not, which is the product either of deliberate state action, or state neglect or inability to act, or a failed state situation," or "large scale 'ethnic cleansing,' actual or apprehended, whether carried out by killing, forced expulsion, acts of terror or rape" (ICISS 2001:xii).

12. Community-level violations undermine a government's sovereignty from the standpoint of the government's putative responsibility to protect—in distinction to a human rights violation outright. According to Badescu (2011, chap. 2), the responsibility-to-protect approach balances sovereignty with human rights by recognizing the central role of the state to the enforcement of human rights.

13. The notion of human rights minimalism is hotly debated, from strong embraces (e.g., Igantieff 2004) to equally strong rejections (e.g., Dinsmore 2007). Neither camp is homogeneous. Some rejecters regard social and economic rights as indispensable to the human rights project (even as who or what is obligated to secure such rights is chronically unclear). Others (e.g., Benhabib 2009:698 n.30) insist that "asking which minimal list of human rights would prevent interventionism" defeats the effort to formulate a conception of human rights adequate to the project for such rights.

14. From what I have said in earlier pages it is clear that I reject the continuation of this sentence: "and which would elicit cooperation by members of the international community for enforcement purposes" (Cohen 2008:582).

15. And such a view is less comprehensive than many major alternatives, including a Western liberal version of a comprehensive moral view based on preventing suffering (see Taylor 2007), a Muslim position counter to Taylor's (see Asad 2003), or a Buddhist version (see Bstan-'dzin-rgya-mtsho 1999).

16. Here I agree with the ICISS: "There must be a reasonable chance of success in halting or averting the suffering which has justified the intervention, with the consequences of action not likely to be worse than the consequences of inaction" (ICISS 2001: xii).

17. This dilemma of intervention looms large: intervention may make a terrible situation even worse (as in Kosovo in 1999) yet inaction helps no one threatened by slaughter (as in Rwanda in 1994).

18. To be sure, nonmembers of the political community have the same human rights of life and liberty as members, and the community is obliged to protect the rights of members and nonmembers equally.

19. Unless of course one argues that human rights require democracy. Rawls (1999b) famously declines to do so, arguing instead that peaceful, decent nonliberal communities that do not threaten international stability are capable of respecting what he describes as "human rights proper."

20. I develop a theory of enlightened localism in Gregg (2003a).

21. As to "whether one country is justified in helping the people of another in a struggle against their government for free institutions," Mill (1867:177) asserts that "there can seldom be anything approaching to assurance that intervention, even if successful, would be for the good of the people themselves. The only test possessing any real value, of a people's having become fit for popular institutions, is that they, or a sufficient portion of them to prevail in the contest, are willing to brave labor and danger for their liberation." The virtues of freemen can indeed be learned in the school of slavery.

22. That list (human rights to life and liberty) cannot possibly justify interveners' imposing a legal system, or a constitution, or even particular laws, on the community invaded. Here I agree with Jean Cohen (2006/2007).

23. To be sure, a government can destroy the possibility of politics without engaging in ethnic cleansing or genocide—for example, by rejecting all political rights. But in that case intervention is not justified on human rights grounds.

24. As the ICISS (2001:22) notes, regional actors are "often not disinterested in the outcomes of deadly conflicts"; but nor are outside actors.

25. In fact, democratic states intervene more often than do nondemocratic ones: between 1960 and 1996 the United States and France intervened more often than did the Soviet Union/Russia, followed by the United Kingdom. In the same period, targets of intervention were mostly nondemocratic: Zaire, Iraq, Egypt, Pakistan, Chad, Israel, and Thailand (Gleditsch, Christiansen, and Hegre 2007).

26. Midsize and small powers are interested in multilateralism because, unlike major powers, they cannot afford not to be.

27. But even authoritarian states are generally reluctant to set an example of intervention, and not only because of a reluctance to draw attention to their own practices.

28. Franck (1992:84) speaks of the "history of unilateral interventionism" that has undermined the "self-denying ordinance" of a requirement "that all states unambiguously renounce the use of unilateral, or even regional, *military* force to compel compliance with the democratic entitlement in the absence of prior Security Council authorization."

29. As Hehir (2008, chap. 6) argues and Walzer (2002) as well.

30. *Breached* in the sense of the UN Charter, chap. 7, article 51; see also articles 2.4 and 53.

31. Atomic bombings present a different situation. Even if most people across the world might believe that the indiscriminate killing of civilians with nuclear weapons is wrong, there is no shared public consensus to that effect. The international prohibition of the use of poison gas and other chemical and biological weapons does not extend to nuclear weapons. The permanent members of the United Nations Security Council oppose the notion of an unconditional ban; they themselves possess nuclear weapons and want to reserve what they regard as their right to use them. A 1996 advisory opinion the International Court of Justice stated that "threat or use of nuclear weapons would generally be contrary to the rules of international law applicable in armed conflict." But it declined to declare the threat or use of nuclear weapons illegal under all conditions, writing that the "Court cannot conclude definitively whether the threat or use of nuclear weapons would be lawful or unlawful in an extreme circumstance of self-defense, in which the very survival of a State would be at stake." One might argue that, because the standing members of the Security Council are all nuclear states, the balance of power within the United Nations itself might be challenged were nuclear weapons banned. While the "threat or use" of nuclear weapons may "generally be contrary to the rules of international law applicable in armed conflict" and is certainly inhumane, it constitutes a perverse foundation of the contemporary world order.

32. Walzer (2002) makes this point cogently.

33. Imperial interests in the sense of Power (2002), for example.

34. As Walzer (2002) notes.

35. Stewart and Knaus (2011), discussing intervention in Afghanistan and in Bosnia, demonstrate how bad intervention can be in practice, in ways that theories of intervention often fail to grasp.

36. Adopted by Resolution 260 (III) A of the UN General Assembly on 9 December 1948; entered into force 12 January 1951. Article 1 specifies: "The Contracting Parties confirm that genocide, whether committed in time of peace or in time of war, is a crime under international law which they undertake to prevent and to punish." The convention defines genocide as "any of the following acts committed with intent to destroy, in whole or in part, a national, ethnical, racial or religious group, as such: (a) Killing members of the group; (b) Causing serious bodily or mental harm to members of the group; (c) Deliberately inflicting on the group conditions of life calculated to bring about its physical destruction in whole or in part; (d) Imposing measures intended to prevent births within the group; (e) Forcibly transferring children of the group to another group."

37. A factor underestimated by Bellamy's (2009) hopeful account of the promise of the responsibility-to-protect doctrine.

38. *Construction* in the sense of Forst (1999) or Gregg (2012b).

Coda

1. Nation states so modified still participate in the creation of some international law and in some decision making at the global level.

2. For a range of supportive arguments, see Cohen (2012), de Wet (2012), and Habermas (2006a).

3. Arguments against a world state are many: it is congenitally susceptible to tyranny; it violates democratic legitimacy; it may resist the rule of law; it has a totalizing character; it eliminates any space not occupied by the state, a space of refuge in cases of tyranny or injustice; it may display imperialist tendencies; it could preclude meaningful political participation, hence self-government; it possesses martial tendencies in light of the great power and coercive apparatus it yields; it may be inclined against diversity.

4. This conception differs from the Habermasian one of global governance without government. Guided by a belief in the primacy of global law, it pursues democracy beyond the nation state in the form of postnational democratization without postnational statehood. Compare, critically, Schmalz-Bruns (2007).

5. Honneth cites Hegel (2004), §258.

6. For a skeptical view of legal pluralism, see Fischer-Lescano and Teubner (2004).

7. To be sure, none of these items ensures progress on the human rights front; in particular, Chapter 9 rejects the notion of an a priori responsibility to protect. And the danger remains that powerful nation states and regional alliances may deploy institutions and discourses toward new hegemonic powers and global hierarchies that retard the advance of human rights.

8. Compare Chayes and Chayes (1995), who provide hopeful evidence for current widespread compliance with the norms, rules, and practices of multilateral regimes.

9. This book examines the dangers and potential of the currently existing nation state for the human rights project, and this Coda ends with that examination. A future work, the next step in advancing the human rights project, will explore the cosmopolitan order, developing the idea of a human rights state at a global level. That book will address the challenging questions generated by the Coda's vision of domestic cosmopolitanism. First, how could such an association ever be constructed? Where are the actors? How would it achieve a level of political integration sufficient to generate the requisite solidarity and trust, making it possible to resolve conflicts among member states without hierarchical means? Is heterarchy even possible, given the contentious nature of political life, even among polities that share a common commitment to human rights? Further, can the heterogeneity of the membership mesh adequately with integrative solidarity? Second, would the association have shared functions? If so, circumscribed by what? Third, absent some overarching legal order, some ultimate constitutional authority, some final authoritative instance, what ensures coequal respect for the autonomy of the association's component units? What about legal differences, disagreements, conflicts between or among members? Are they resolvable

without some third instance? How do horizontally related entities resolve differences? What happens when valid claims of one member clash with equally valid claims of another member? Could different members with equally legitimate arguments arm themselves for political battle and conflict? Would such conflict generate irresolvable conflicts and undermine the association's core normative functions? Fourth, to negotiate disagreements, would participants need to draw on political virtues quite beyond legal forms and obligations? Here I refer to nonlegal, political *relationships* in distinction to political *institutions*. Such relationships might follow from demands that legal actors internalize, say, a Weberian ethic of responsibility, as well as political virtues such as moderation. What are the political and social preconditions of such demands on individual personality structure? What are the preconditions for committing to such political virtues?

References

Ackerman, Bruce. 1980. *Social Justice in the Liberal State*. New Haven, CT: Yale University Press.

Agnew, John. 2005. "Sovereignty Regimes: Territoriality and State Authority in World Politics." *Annals of the Association of American Geographers* 95:437–461.

Agnew, John, and Stuart Corbridge. 1995. *Mastering Space: Hegemony, Territory and International Political Economy*. London: Routledge.

Akabayashi, Hideo, and George Psacharopolous. 1999. "The Trade-off Between Child Labor and Human Capital Formation: A Tanzanian Case Study." *Journal of Development Studies* 35:120–140.

Ake, Claude. 1987. "The African Context of Human Rights." *Africa Today* 32:5–12.

Anderson, Benedict. 1983. *Imagined Communities*. London: Verso.

An-Na'im, Abdullahi Ahmed. 1992. "Toward a Cross-Cultural Approach to Defining International Standards of Human Rights: The Meaning of Cruel, Inhuman, or Degrading Treatment or Punishment." In *Human Rights in Cross-Cultural Perspectives: A Quest for Consensus*, ed. Abdullahi Ahmed An-Na'im. Philadelphia: University of Pennsylvania Press: 19–43.

Aquinas, Thomas. 1886–1887 [1265–1274]. *Summa Theologica*. Rome: Ex Typographia Senatus.

Arendt, Hannah. 1949. "'The Rights of Man': What Are They?" *Modern Review* 3:24–37.

Arendt, Hannah. 1968 [1951]. *The Origins of Totalitarianism*. New York: Harcourt.

Arendt, Hannah. 1990 [1963]. *On Revolution*. London: Penguin.

Asad, Talal. 2003. *Foundations of the Secular: Christianity, Islam, Modernity*. Stanford, CA: Stanford University Press.

Austin, J. L. 1962. *How to Do Things with Words*. Oxford: Oxford University Press.

Axtmann, Roland. 2004. "The State of the State: The Model of the Modern State and Its Contemporary Transformation." *International Political Science Review / Revue internationale de science politique* 25:259–279.

Bacevich, Andrew. 2002. *American Empire: The Realities and Consequences of U.S. Diplomacy*. Cambridge, MA: Harvard University Press.

Bache, Ian, and Andrew Taylor. 2003. "The Politics of Policy Resistance: Reconstructing Higher Education in Kosovo." *Journal of Public Policy* 23:279–300.

Badescu, Cristina. 2011. *Humanitarian Intervention and the Responsibility to Protect: Security and Human Rights*. New York: Routledge.

Bales, Kevin. 2005. *Understanding Global Slavery*. Berkeley: University of California Press.

Bales, Kevin, and Austin Choi-Fitzpatrick. 2012. "The Anti-Slavery Movement: Making Rights Reality." In *From Human Trafficking to Human Rights: Reframing Contemporary Slavery*, ed. Alison Brysk and Austin Choi-Fitzpatrick. Philadelphia: University of Pennsylvania Press: 195–216.

Bales, Kevin, and Ron Soodalter. 2009. *The Slave Next Door: Human Trafficking and Slavery in America Today*. Berkeley: University of California Press.

Barber, Benjamin. 2002. "Constitutional Faith." In Martha C. Nussbaum, *For Love of Country?* ed. Joshua Cohen. Boston: Beacon Press: 30–37.

Bass, Gary. 2008. *Freedom's Battle: The Origins of Humanitarian Intervention*. New York: Alfred Knopf.

Beegle, Kathleen, Rajeev Dehejia, and Roberta Gatti. 2004. "Why Should We Care About Child Labor? The Returns to Schooling vs. the Returns to Experience in Vietnam." NBER Working Paper No. 10980. National Bureau of Economic Research, Cambridge, MA.

Beitz, Charles. 2001. "Human Rights as a Common Concern." *American Political Science Review* 95:269–282.

Beitz, Charles. 2009. *The Idea of Human Rights*. New York: Oxford University Press.

Beitz, Charles. 2013. "From Practice to Theory." *Constellations* 20:27–37.

Bell, Daniel. 2000. *East Meets West: Human Rights and Democracy in East Asia*. Princeton, NJ: Princeton University Press.

Bell, Daniel, and Jean-Marc Colcaud, eds. 2007. *Ethics in Action: The Ethical Challenges of International Human Rights Nongovernmental Organizations*. New York: Cambridge University Press.

Bellamy, Alex. 2009. *Responsibility to Protect*. Cambridge, UK: Polity.

Benhabib, Seyla. 2004. *The Rights of Others: Aliens, Residents and Citizens*. New York: Cambridge University Press.

Benhabib, Seyla. 2006. *Another Cosmopolitanism*. With commentaries by Jeremy Waldron, Bonnie Honig, and Will Kymlicka; ed. and introd. Robert Post. Oxford: Oxford University Press.

Benhabib, Seyla. 2007. "Another Universalism: On the Unity and Diversity of Human Rights." *Proceedings and Addresses of the American Philosophical Association* 81:7–32.

Benhabib, Seyla. 2009. "Claiming Rights Across Borders: International Human Rights and Democratic Sovereignty." *American Political Science Review* 103:691–704.

Benhabib, Seyla. 2013a. "Moving Beyond False Binarisms: On Samuel Moyn's *The Last Utopia*." *Qui Parle* 22:81–93.

Benhabib, Seyla. 2013b. "Reason-giving and Rights-bearing: Constructing the Subject of Rights." *Constellations* 20:38–51.

Benvenisti, Eyal. 2013. "Sovereigns as Trustees of Humanity: On the Accountability of States to Foreign Stakeholders." *American Journal of International Law* 107:295–333.

Berman, Paul. 2007. "Global Legal Pluralism." *Southern California Law Review* 80:1155–1237.

Bhalotra, Sonia, and Christopher Heady. 1998. "Child Labor in Rural Pakistan and Ghana: Myths and Data." Working Paper, Department of Economics, University of Bristol, UK.

Bianchi, Gabriel. 1997. "Training in Skills for Coping with Democracy." *Annals of the American Academy of Political and Social Science* 552:114–124.

Birmingham, Peg. 2006. *Hannah Arendt and Human Rights: The Predicament of Common Responsibility*. Bloomington: Indiana University Press.

Bok, Sissela. 2002. "From Part to Whole." In Martha C. Nussbaum, *For Love of Country?* ed. Joshua Cohen. Boston: Beacon Press: 38–44.

Boltanski, Luc. 2009. *De la critique*. Paris: Editions Gallimard.

Bourdieu, Pierre. 1990 [1980]. *The Logic of Practice*. Trans. R. Nice. Stanford, CA: Stanford University Press.

Brock, Gillian. 2009. *Global Justice*. Oxford: Oxford University Press.

Broomhall, Bruce. 2003. *International Justice and the International Criminal Court: Between Sovereignty and the Rule of Law*. Oxford: Oxford University Press.

Brecht, Bertolt. 2000. *Flüchlingsgespräche*. Frankfurt am Main: Suhrkamp Verlag.

Brubaker, Rogers, and Frederick Cooper. 2000. "Beyond 'Identity.'" *Theory and Society* 29:1–47.

Brysk, Alison, and Austin Choi-Fitzpatrick. 2012. "Introduction." In *From Human Trafficking to Human Rights: Reframing Contemporary Slavery*, ed. Alison Brysk and Austin Choi-Fitzpatrick. Philadelphia: University of Pennsylvania Press: 1–10.

Bstan-'dzin-rgya-mtsho, Dalai Lama XIV. 1999. *Ethics for the New Millennium*. New York: Riverhead Books.

Buchanan, Allen, and David Golove. 2002. "Philosophy of International Law." In *The Oxford Handbook of Jurisprudence and Philosophy of Law*, ed. Jules Coleman and Scott Shapiro. Oxford: Oxford University Press: 868–934.

Buk-Berge, Elisabeth. 2006. "Missed Opportunities: The IEA's Study of Civic Education and Civic Education in Post-Communist Countries." *Comparative Education* 42:533–548.

Burtt, Shelley. 1994. "Religious Parents, Secular Schools: A Liberal Defense of an Illiberal Education." *Review of Politics* 56:51–70.

Canagarajah, Sudharshan, and Harold Coulombe. 1998. "Child Labor and Schooling in Ghana." Policy Research Working Paper No. 1844. World Bank, Washington, DC.

Canagarajah, Sudharshan, and Helena Nielsen. 2001. "Child Labor in Africa: A Comparative Study." *Annals of the American Academy of Political and Social Science* 575:71–91.

Canovan, Margaret. 2000. "Patriotism Is Not Enough." *British Journal of Political Science* 30:413–432.

Carlson, Matthew, and Ola Listhaug. 2007. "Citizens' Perceptions of Human Rights Practices: An Analysis of 55 Countries." *Journal of Peace Research* 44:465–483.

Chan, Chak Kwan, and Zhaiwen Peng. 2011. "From Iron Rice Bowl to the World's Biggest Sweatshop: Globalization, Institutional Constraints, and the Rights of Chinese Workers." *Social Service Review* 85:421–445.

Chayes, Abram, and Antonia Handler Chayes. 1995. *The New Sovereignty: Compliance with International Regulatory Agreements*. Cambridge, MA: Harvard University Press.

Coffé, Hilde, and Tanje van der Lippe. 2010. "Citizenship Norms in Eastern Europe." *Social Indicators Research* 96:479–496.

Cogneau, Denis, and Rémi Jedwab. 2012. "Commodity Price Shocks and Child Outcomes: The 1990 Cocoa Crisis in Côte d'Ivoire." *Economic Development and Cultural Change* 60:507–534.

Cohen, Jean. 2006/2007. "The Role of International Law in Post-Conflict Constitution-Making: Toward a *Jus Post Bellum* for 'Interim Occupations.'" *New York Law Journal* 51:498–532.

Cohen, Jean. 2008. "Rethinking Human Rights, Democracy, and Sovereignty in the Age of Globalization." *Political Theory* 36:578–606.

Cohen, Jean. 2012. *Globalization and Sovereignty: Rethinking Legality, Legitimacy, and Constitutionalism*. Cambridge: Cambridge University Press.

Cohen, Joshua. 2006. "Is There a Human Right to Democracy?" In *The Egalitarian Conscience: Essays in Honour of G. A. Cohen*, ed. Christine Sypnowich. Oxford: Oxford University Press: 226–248.

Coleman, James. 1990. *Foundations of Social Theory*. Cambridge, MA: Harvard University Press.

Collins, Randall. *Interaction Ritual Chains*. 2004. Princeton, NJ: Princeton University Press.

Conover, Pamela, and Donald Searing. 2005. "Studying 'Everyday Talk' in the Deliberative System." *Acta Politica* 40:269–283.

Coulombe, Harold. 1998. "Child Labor and Education in Côte d'Ivoire." Background Paper. World Bank, Washington, DC.

Dahbour, Omar. 2005. "Three Models of Global Community." *Journal of Ethics* 9:201–224.

Dalton, Russell. 1994. "Communists and Semocrats: Semocratic Attitudes in the Two Germanies." *British Journal of Political Science* 24:469–493.

Darwin, Charles. 1859. *On the Origin of the Species by Means of Natural Selection; or, The Preservation of Favoured Races in the Struggle for Life*. London: John Murray.

Debrix, François. 1998. "Deterritorialised Territories, Borderless Borders: The New Geography of International Medical Assistance." *Third World Quarterly* 19:827–846.

de Carvalho Filho, Irineu Evangelista. 2012. "Household Income as a Determinant of Child Labor and School Enrollment in Brazil: Evidence from a Social Security Reform." *Economic Development and Cultural Change* 60:339–435.

Derrida, Jacques. 1990. "The Force of Law: The 'Mystical Foundation of Authority.'" *Cardozo Law Review* 11:920–1046.

de Wet, Erika. 2012. "The Constitutionalization of Public International Law." In *The Oxford Handbook of Comparative Constitutional Law*, ed. Michel Rosenfeld and András Sajó. Oxford: Oxford University Press: 1209–1230.

Dewey, John. 1966 [1916]. *Democracy and Education.* New York: Free Press.

Dingwerth, Klaus, and Philipp Pattbert. 2006. "Global Governance as a Perspective on World Politics." *Global Governance* 12:185–203.

Dinsmore, Greg. 2007. "When Less Really Is Less—What's Wrong with Minimalist Approaches to Human Rights." *Journal of Political Philosophy* 15:473–483.

Donnelly, Jack. 1989. *Universal Human Rights in Theory and Practice.* Ithaca, NY: Cornell University Press.

Doucet, Marc. 2001. "The Possibility of Deterritorializing Democracy: Agonistic Democratic Politics and the APEC NGO Forums." *Alternatives: Global, Local, Political* 26:283–316.

Douglas, Mary. 1966. *Purity and Danger: An Analysis of Concepts of Pollution and Taboo.* New York: Praeger.

Douglas, Mary. 1970. *Natural Symbols: Explorations in Cosmology.* New York: Pantheon Books.

Druckman, James. 2004. "Political Preference Formation." *American Political Science Review* 98:671–686.

Dumas, Christelle. 2012. "Does Work Impede Child Learning? The Case of Senegal." *Economic Development and Cultural Change* 60:773–793.

Durkheim, Émile. 1965 [1912]. *Elementary Forms of Religious Life.* Trans. J. Swain. New York: Free Press.

Durkheim, Émile. 1984 [1893]. *The Division of Labor in Society.* Trans. W. Halls. New York: Free Press.

Edmonds, Eric, and Nina Pavcnik. 2005. "Child Labor in the Global Economy." *Journal of Economic Perspectives* 19:199–220.

Elden, Stuart. 2009. *Terror and Territory: The Spatial Extent of Sovereignty.* Minneapolis: University of Minnesota Press.

Emerson, Patrick, and André Portela Souza. 2011. "Is Child Labor Harmful? The Impact of Working Earlier in Life on Adult Earnings." *Economic Development and Cultural Change* 54:345–385.

Etchichury, Horacio Javier. 2006. "Argentina: Social Rights, Thorny Country; Judicial Review of Economic Policies Sponsored by the IFIs." *American University International Law Review* 22:101–125.

Etzioni, Amitai. 2010. "The Normativity of Human Rights Is Self-Evident." *Human Rights Quarterly* 32:187–197.

Evans, Geoffrey. 2006. "The Social Bases of Political Divisions in Post-Communist Eastern Europe." *Annual Review of Sociology* 32:245–270.

Falk, Richard. 1995. *On Humane Governance: Towards a New Global Politics.* Cambridge, UK: Polity.

Falk, Richard. 2002. "Revisioning Cosmopolitanism." In Martha C. Nussbaum, *For Love of Country?* ed. Joshua Cohen. Boston: Beacon Press: 53–60.

Falk, Richard. 2009. *Achieving Human Rights.* New York: Routledge.

Ferguson, Niall. 2004. *Colossus: The Price of America's Empire.* New York: Penguin Press.

Filaly-Ansari, Abdou. 1999. "Muslims and Democracy." *Journal of Democracy* 10:18–32.

Filipova, Lyudmila, Sergey Patrushev, and Elena Kondratieva. 2012. "Political Engagement in Non-Political Institutional Orders: The Case of Russia." Paper presented at 22nd World Congress of Political Science, 8–12 July, Madrid, Spain.

Finkel, Steven. 2002. "Civic Education and the Mobilization of Political Participation in Developing Democracies." *Journal of Politics* 64:994–1020.

Fischer-Lescano, Andreas, and Gunther Teubner. 2004. "Regime-Collisions: The Vain Search for Legal Unity in the Fragmentation of Global Law." *Michigan Journal of International Law* 25:999–1046.

Fishkin, James, and Robert Luskin. 2005. "Experimenting with a Democratic Ideal: Deliberative Polling and Public Opinion." *Acta Politica* 40:284–298.

Forst, Rainer. 1999. "The Basic Right to Justification: Toward a Constructivist Conception of Human Rights." *Constellations* 6:327–346.

Forsythe, David, ed. 2009. *Encylopedia of Human Rights.* Vol. 1. Oxford: Oxford University Press.

Franck, Thomas. 1992. "The Emerging Right to Democratic Governance." *American Journal of International Law* 86:46–91.

Franck, Thomas. 1997. "Is Personal Freedom a Western Value?" *American Journal of International Law* 91:593–627.

Galtung, Johan. 1994. *Human Rights in Another Key.* Oxford: Polity.

Gardbaum, Stephen. 2008. "Human Rights as International Constitutional Rights." *European Journal of International Law* 19:749–768.

Gewirth, Alan. 1985. "Why There Are Human Rights." *Social Theory and Practice* 11:235–248.

Giddens, Anthony. 1985. *The Nation-State and Violence.* Berkeley: University of California Press.

Ginsberg, Tom, and Tamir Moustafa, eds. 2008. *Rule by Law: The Politics of Courts in Autocratic Regimes.* New York: Cambridge University Press.

Glaeser, Edward, Giacomo A. M. Ponzetto, and Andrei Shleifer. 2007. "Why Does Democracy Need Education?" *Journal of Economic Growth* 12:77–99.

Glasius, Marlies. 2006. *The International Criminal Court: A Global Civil Society Achievement.* London: Routledge.

Glazer, Nathan. 2002. "Limits of Loyalty." In Martha C. Nussbaum, *For Love of Country?* ed. Joshua Cohen. Boston: Beacon Press: 61–65.

Gleditsch, Nils, Lene Christiansen, and Håvard Hegre. 2007. "Democratic Jihad? Military Intervention and Democracy." http://elibrary.worldbank.org/doi/pdf/ 10.1596/1813–9450–4242. Creative Commons Attribution CC BY 3.0.

Glendon, Mary Ann. 2001. *A World Made New: Eleanor Roosevelt and the Universal Declaration of Human Rights.* New York: Random House.

Goffman, Erving. 1961. *Asylums: Essays on the Social Situation of Mental Patients and Other Inmates.* Garden City, NY: Anchor Books.

Goffman, Erving. 1963. *Behavior in Public Places: Notes on the Social Organization of Gatherings.* New York: Free Press.

Goffman, Erving. 1974. *Frame Analysis: An Essay on the Organization of Experience.* Cambridge, MA: Harvard University Press.

Gould, Carol. 2004. *Globalizing Democracy and Human Rights.* New York: Cambridge University Press.

Gregg, Benjamin. 1999. "Using Legal Rules in an Indeterminate World: Overcoming the Limitations of Jurisprudence." *Political Theory* 27:389–410.

Gregg, Benjamin. 2002. "The Law and Courts of Enlightened Localism." *Polity* 35:283–309.

Gregg, Benjamin. 2003a. *Coping in Politics with Indeterminate Norms: A Theory of Enlightened Localism.* Albany: State University of New York Press.

Gregg, Benjamin. 2003b. *Thick Moralities, Thins Politics: Social Integration Across Communities of Belief.* Durham, NC: Duke University Press.

Gregg, Benjamin. 2012a. "Genetic Enhancement: A New Dialectic of Enlightenment?" In *Perspektiven der Aufklärung: Zwischen Mythos und Realität*, ed. Dietmar Wetzel. Paderborn, Germany: Verlag Wilhelm Fink: 133–146.

Gregg, Benjamin. 2012b. *Human Rights as Social Construction.* New York: Cambridge University Press.

Gregg, Benjamin, Patti Tamara Lenard, Kristen Johnson, William O'Neill, Aaron Stuvland, Pete Mohanty, and Harry Dahms. 2012. "Comparative Perspectives on Social Integration in Pluralistic Societies: Thick Norms Versus Thin." *Comparative Sociology* 11:629–781.

Gregg, Benjamin, Lea Ypi, Jonathan White, Junmin Wang, Ko Hasegawa, and Manu Ahedo Santisteban. 2010. "Enlightened Localism in Comparative Perspective." *Comparative Sociology* 9:594–710.

Griffin, James. 2008. *On Human Rights.* Oxford: Oxford University Press.

Gutiérrez, Kris, and Barbara Rogoff. 2003. "Cultural Ways of Learning: Individual or Repertoires of Practice." *Educational Researcher* 32:19–25.

Habermas, Jürgen. 1981. *Theorie des kommunikativen Handelns.* Frankfurt am Main: Suhrkamp.

Habermas, Jürgen. 1996. *Between Facts and Norms: Contributions to a Discourse Theory of Law and Democracy.* Trans. W. Regh. Cambridge, MA: MIT Press.

Habermas, Jürgen. 2006a. *The Divided West.* Cambridge, UK: Polity.

Habermas, Jürgen. 2006b. "Political Communication in Media Society: Does Democracy Still Enjoy an Epistemic Dimension? The Impact of Normative Theory on Empirical Research." *Communication Theory* 16:411–426.

Habermas, Jürgen. 2008. "The Constitutionalization of International Law and the Legitimacy Problems of a Constitution for a World Society." *Constellations* 15:444–455.

Haimes, Erica. 2012. "The Contributions of Social Constructionism to the Study of the Ethical, Social and Political Aspects of the Life Sciences." In *Genomics and Democracy*, ed. Peter Derkx and Harry Kunneman. Amsterdam: Rodopi B.V.: 61–79.

Hart, H. L. A. 1984 [1955]. "Are There Any Natural Rights?" In *Theories of Rights*, ed. Jeremy Waldron. New York: Oxford University Press.

Hathaway, Oona. 2002. "Do Human Rights Treaties Make a Difference?" *Yale Law Journal* 111:1935–2042.

Hegel, G. W. F. 2004 [1820]. *Elements of the Philosophy of Right.* Ed. A. Wood, trans. H. B. Nisbet. New York: Cambridge University Press.

Hehir, Aidan. 2008. *Humanitarian Intervention After Kosovo: Iraq, Darfur and the Record of Global Civil Society.* New York: Palgrave Macmillan.

Heinze, Eric. 2009. *Waging Humanitarian War: The Ethics, Law, and Politics of Humanitarian Intervention.* Albany: State University of New York Press.

Held, David. 1998. "Democracy and Globalization." In *Re-Imagining Political Community: Studies in Cosmopolitan Democracy*, ed. Daniele Archibugi, David Held, and Martin Köhler. Stanford, CA: Stanford University Press: 11–27.

Held, David. 2004. *Global Covenant: The Social Democratic Alternative to the Washington Consensus.* Cambridge, UK: Polity.

Held, David, and Anthony McGrew, David Goldblatt, and Jonathan Perraton. 1999. *Global Transformations: Politics, Economics and Culture.* Stanford, CA: Stanford University Press.

Himmelfarb, Gertrude. 2002. "The Illusions of Cosmopolitanism." In Martha C. Nussbaum, *For Love of Country?* ed. Joshua Cohen. Boston: Beacon Press: 72–77.

Hirschl, Ran. 2004. *Towards Juristocracy: The Origins and Consequences of the New Constitutionalism.* Cambridge, MA: Harvard University Press.

Hirst, Paul, and Graham Thompson. 1999. *Globalization in Question: The International Economy and the Possibilities of Governance.* Cambridge, UK: Polity.

Hobbes, Thomas. 1651. *Leviathan.* London: Andrew Crooke.

Honig, Bonnie. 2005. "Bound by Law? Alien Rights, Administrative Discretion, and the Politics of Technicality: Lessons from Louis Post and the First Red Scare." In *The Limits of Law*, ed. Austin Sarat, Lawrence Douglas, and Martha Merrill Umphrey. Stanford, CA: Stanford University Press: 209–245.

Honneth, Axel. 2001. *The Pathologies of Individual Freedom: Hegel's Social Theory.* Princeton, NJ: Princeton University Press.

Horn, Pamela. 1994. *Children's Work and Welfare, 1780–1890*. Cambridge: Cambridge University Press.

Hoskins, Bryony, Jan Germen Janmaat, and Ernesto Villalba. 2012. "Learning Citizenship Through Social Participation Outside and Inside School: An International, Multilevel Study of Young People's Learning of Citizenship." *British Educational Research Journal* 38:419–446.

Howard, Marc. 2003. *The Weakness of Civil Society in Post-Communist Europe*. Cambridge: Cambridge University Press.

ICISS (International Commission on Intervention and State Sovereignty). 2001. *The Responsibility to Protect*. Ottawa: International Development Research Centre.

Igantieff, Michael. 2004. *Human Rights as Politics and Idolatry*. Princeton, NJ: Princeton University Press.

Illner, Michal. 1996. "Post-Communist Transformation Revisited." *Czech Sociological Review* 4:157–169.

Ingram, James. 2008. "What Is a 'Right to Have Rights'? Three Images of the Politics of Human Rights." *American Political Science Review* 102:401–416.

Isaac, Jeffrey. 1996. "A New Guarantee on Earth: Hannah Arendt on Human Dignity and the Politics of Human Rights." *American Political Science Review* 90:61–73.

Jay, Martin. 1986. "Hannah Arendt's Political Existentialism." In *Permanent Exiles: Essays on the Intellectual Migration from Germany to America*. New York: Columbia University Press: 237–257.

Janmaat, Jan, and Nelli Piattoeva. 2007. "Citizenship Education in Ukraine and Russia: Reconciling Nation-Building and Active Citizenship." *Comparative Education* 43:527–552.

Jessop, Bob. 2002. *The Future of the Capitalist State*. Cambridge, UK: Polity.

Johnson, David, and David Post. 1996. "Law and Borders—The Rise of Law in Cyberspace." *Stanford Law Review* 48:1367–1402.

Kaiser, Robert. 1994. *The Geography of Nationalism in Russia and the USSR*. Princeton, NJ: Princeton University Press.

Kant, Immanuel. 1795. *Zum ewigen Frieden*. Königsberg: Friedrich Nicolovius.

Kant, Immanuel. 1956 [1788]. *Critique of Practical Reason*. Trans. L. Beck. Indianapolis: Bobbs-Merrill.

Kant, Immanuel. 1998 [1785]. *Groundwork of the Metaphysics of Morals*. Trans. M. Gregor. Cambridge, UK: Cambridge University Press.

Keller, Simon. 2005. "Patriotism as Bad Faith." *Ethics* 115:563–592.

Kelly, Catriona. 2005. *Comrade Pavlik: The Rise and Fall of a Soviet Boy Hero*. London: Granta.

King, Martin Luther. 1967. *Where Do We Go from Here: Chaos or Community?* New York: Harper and Row.

Kleingeld, Pauline. 2000. "Kantian Patriotism." *Philosophy & Public Affairs* 29:313–341.

Koppelman, Andrew. 2014. "Critical Exchange on *Human Rights as Social Construction.*" *Contemporary Political Theory* 13:380–386.

Kozakiewicz, Mikolaj. 1992. "Educational Transformation Initiated by the Polish Perestroika." *Comparative Education Review* 36:91–100.

Krapf, Peter, Rolf Gollob, and Wiltrud Weidinger, eds. 2010. *Taking Part in Democracy: Lesson Plans for Upper Secondary Level on Democratic Citizenship and Human Rights Education.* Strasbourg: Council of Europe Publishing.

Krueger, Alan. 1996. "Observations on International Labor Standards and Trade." NBER Working Paper No. 5632, National Bureau of Economic Research, Cambridge, MA.

Kukathas, Chandran. 2003. *The Liberal Archipelago: A Theory of Diversity and Freedom.* New York: Oxford University Press.

Kymlicka, Will. 1995. *Multicultural Citizenship: A Liberal Theory of Minority Rights.* Oxford: Clarendon Press.

Lefort, Claude. 1986. *The Political Forms of Modern Society: Bureaucracy, Democracy, Totalitarianism.* Cambridge, MA: MIT Press.

Lefort, Claude. 1988. *Democracy and Political Theory.* Trans. D. Macey. Cambridge, UK: Polity.

Letki, Natalia, and Geoffrey Evans. 2005. "Endogenizing Social Trust: Democratization in East-Central Europe." *British Journal of Political Science* 35:515–529.

Liebman, Benjamin. 2007. "China's Courts: Restricted Reform." *China Quarterly* 191:620–638.

Lovejoy, Paul. 1989 "The Impact of the Atlantic Slave Trade on Africa." *Journal of African History* 30:365–394.

Luhmann, Niklas. 1995. *Social Systems.* Stanford, CA: Stanford University Press.

Luhmann, Niklas. 1998. *Die Gesellschaft der Gesellschaft.* Frankfurt am Main: Suhrkamp.

Lyotard, Jean-François. 1993. "The Other's Rights." In *On Human Rights: The Oxford Amnesty Lectures 1993*, ed. Stephen Shute and Susan Hurley. New York: Basic Books: 135–148.

Magone, Claire, Michael Neuman, and Fabrice Weissman, eds. 2011. *Humanitarian Negotiations Revealed: The MSF Experience.* New York: Columbia University Press.

Manacorda, Marco, and Furio Camillo Rosati. 2011. "Industrial Structure and Child Labor Evidence from the Brazilian Population Census." *Economic Development and Cultural Change* 59:753–776.

Marasinghe, Lakshman. 1984. "Traditional Conceptions of Human Rights in Africa." In *Human Rights and Development in Africa*, ed. Claude E. Welch, Jr., and Ronald I. Meltzer. Albany: State University of New York Press.

Maritain, Jacques. 1949. "Introduction." In UNESCO, *Human Rights: Comments and Interpretations.* London: Allan Wingate.

Marx, Karl. 1867. *Das Kapital: Kritik der politischen Ökonomie.* Erster Band. Hamburg: O. Meissner; New York: L. W. Schmidt.

Marx, Karl. 2000 [1844]. "On the Jewish Question." In *Karl Marx: Selected Writings*, ed. David McLellan, 2nd ed. Oxford: Oxford University Press: 46–70.

McChesney, Robert. 2000. *Rich Media, Poor Democracy: Communication Politics in Dubious Times*. New York: New Press.

McConnell, Michael. 2002. "Don't Neglect the Little Platoons." In Martha C. Nussbaum, *For Love of Country?* ed. Joshua Cohen. Boston: Beacon Press: 78–84.

Mead, George Herbert. 1967 [1934]. *Mind, Self and Society from the Standpoint of a Social Behaviorist*. Chicago: University of Chicago Press.

Merry, Sally Engle. 2006. *Human Rights and Gender Violence: Translating International Law into Local Justice*. Chicago: University of Chicago Press.

Meyer, John, Patricia Bromley, and Francisco Ramirez. 2010. "Human Rights in Social Science Textbooks: Cross-national Analyses, 1970–2008." *Sociology of Education* 83:111–134.

Mill, John Stuart. 1867. "A Few Words on Non-Intervention." In *Dissertations and Discussions: Political, Philosophical and Historical*, vol. 4. Boston: William Spencer: 157–182.

Miller, David. 1995. *On Nationality*. Oxford: Oxford University Press.

Mills, C. Wright. 1963. "Mass Media and Public Opinion." In *Power, Politics and People: The Collected Essays of C. Wright Mills*. New York: Oxford University Press: 577–598.

Mishler, William, and Richard Rose. 2007. "Generation, Age, and Time: The Dynamics of Political Learning During Russia's Transformation." *American Journal of Political Science* 51:822–834.

Molnár, Péter. 2009. "Laws and Policies—Enabling or Withholding the Development of the Culture of Constitutional Democracy." *International Journal of Politics, Culture, and Society* 22:465–484.

Monroe, Kristen. 2003. "How Identity and Perspective Constrain Moral Choice." *International Political Science Review* 24:405–425.

Monshipouri, Mahmood. 2003. "Human Rights and Child Labor in South Asia." In *Human Rights and Diversity*, ed. David Forsythe and Patrice McMahon. Lincoln: University of Nebraska Press: 182–228.

Morgenthau, Hans. 1948. *Politics Among Nations: The Struggle for Power and Peace*. New York: Knopf.

Moustafa, Tamir. 2009. *The Struggle for Constitutional Power: Law, Politics, and Economic Development in Egypt*. Cambridge: Cambridge University Press.

Moyn, Samuel. 2010. *The Last Utopia: Human Rights in History*. Cambridge, MA: Harvard University Press.

Mutua, Makau. 2002. *Human Rights: A Political and Cultural Critique*. Philadelphia: University of Pennsylvania Press.

Nagel, Thomas. 2012. *Mortal Questions*. Cambridge: Cambridge University Press.

Nagel, Thomas. 2005. "The Problem of Global Justice." *Philosophy & Public Affairs* 33:113–147.

Nickel, James. 1987. *Making Sense of Human Rights*. Berkeley: University of California Press.

Nielsen, Helena. 1998. "Child Labor and School Attendance in Zambia: Two Joint Decisions." Working Paper No. 98–15. Centre for Labour Market and Social Research, Aarhus, Denmark.

Norris, Pippa, and Ronald Inglehart. 2009. *Cosmopolitan Communications: Cultural Diversity in a Globalized World*. New York: Cambridge University Press.

North, Douglass. 1990. *Institutions, Institutional Change and Economic Performance*. New York: Cambridge University Press.

O'Neill, Onora. 2004. "Global Justice: Whose Obligations?" In *The Ethics of Assistance: Morality and the Distant Needy*, ed. Deen K. Chatterjee. Cambridge: Cambridge University Press: 242–259.

OSCE/ODIHR (Organization for Security and Co-operation in Europe; Office for Democratic Institutions and Human Rights). 2012. *Guidelines on Human Rights Education for Secondary School Systems*. Warsaw: OSCE/ODIHR.

Parekh, Bhikhu. 2002. "Reconstituting the Modern State." In *Transnational Democracy: Political Spaces and Border Crossings*, ed. James Anderson. London: Routledge: 39–55.

Parekh, Serena. 2008. *Hannah Arendt and the Challenge of Modernity: A Phenomenology of Human Rights*. New York: Routledge.

Parker, Stephen. 2014. *Bertolt Brecht: A Literary Life*. London: Bloomsbury.

Parsons, Talcott. 1951. *The Social System*. Glencoe, IL: Free Press.

Pastuović, Nikola. 1992. "Problems of Reforming Educational Systems in Post-Communist Countries." *International Review of Education* 39:405–418.

Perry, Michael. 2007. *Toward a Theory of Human Rights: Religion, Law, Courts*. Cambridge: Cambridge University Press.

Plessner, Helmuth. 1981 [1928]. *Die Stufen des Organischen und der Mensch: Einleitung in die philosophische Anthropologie*. In *Gesammelte Schriften*, Band 4. Frankfurt am Main: Suhrkamp.

Pogge, Thomas. 2002. *World Poverty and Human Rights*. Cambridge, UK: Polity.

Power, Samantha. 2002. *"A Problem from Hell": America and the Age of Genocide*. New York: Basic Books.

Preuss, Ulrich. 1994. *Revolution, Fortschritt und Verfassung: Zu einem neuen Verfassungsverstandnis*. Frankfurt am Main: Fischer Taschenbuch.

Psacharopolous, George. 1997. "Child Labor Versus Educational Attainment: Some Evidence from Latin America." *Journal of Population Economics* 10:377–386.

Putnam, Hilary. 2002. "Must We Choose Between Patriotism and Universal Reason?" In Martha C. Nussbaum. *For Love of Country?* ed. Joshua Cohen. Boston: Beacon Press: 91–97.

Putnam, Robert. 1993. *Making Democracy Work: Civic Traditions in Modern Italy*. Princeton, NJ: Princeton University Press.

Quint, Peter. 1999. "The Constitutional Guarantees of Social Welfare in the Process of German Unification." *American Journal of Comparative Law* 47:303–326.

Rainbolt, George. 2000. "Perfect and Imperfect Obligations." *Philosophical Studies* 98:233–256.

Rancière, Jacques. 2004. "Who Is the Subject of the Rights of Man?" *South Atlantic Quarterly* 103:297–310.

Rancière, Jacques. 2010. *Dissensus: On Politics and Aesthetics*. Ed. and trans. Steven Corcoran. London: Continuum.

Rawls, John. 1971. *A Theory of Justice*. Cambridge, MA: Harvard University Press.

Rawls, John. 1993. *Political Liberalism*. New York: Columbia University Press.

Rawls, John. 1999a. "The Law of Peoples." In *Collected Papers*, ed. Samuel Freeman. Cambridge, MA: Harvard University Press: 529–564.

Rawls, John. 1999b. *The Law of Peoples*. Cambridge, MA: Harvard University Press.

Raz, Joseph. 2010. "Human Rights Without Foundations." In *The Philosophy of International Law*, ed. Samantha Besson and John Tasioulas. Oxford: Oxford University Press: 321–337.

Redfield, Peter. 2013. *Life in Crisis: The Ethical Journey of Doctors Without Borders*. Berkeley: University of California Press.

Renteln, Alison. 1990. *International Human Rights: Universalism Versus Relativism*. Newbury Park, CA: Sage.

Risse, Mathias. 2012. *On Global Justice*. Princeton, NJ: Princeton University Press.

Risse, Thomas, Stephen Ropp, and Kathryn Sikkink, eds. 1999. *The Power of Human Rights: International Norms and Domestic Change*. Cambridge: Cambridge University Press.

Robinson, Cabeiri deBergh. 2013. *Body of Victim, Body of Warrior: Refugee Families and the Making of Kashmiri Jihadists*. Berkeley: University of California Press.

Rorty, Richard. 1989. *Contingency, Irony, and Solidarity*. Cambridge: Cambridge University Press.

Rorty, Richard. 1998. *Achieving Our Country*. Cambridge, MA: Harvard University Press.

Rosenau, James. 1995. "Governance in the Twenty-first Century." *Global Governance* 1:13–43.

Rubenstein, Kim, and Daniel Adler. 2000. "International Citizenship: The Future of Nationality in a Globalized World." *Indiana Journal of Global Legal Studies* 7:519–548.

Rummens, Stefan. 2006. "Debate: The Co-Originality of Private and Public Autonomy in Deliberative Democracy." *Journal of Political Philosophy* 14:469–481.

Saco, Diana. 2002. *Cybering Democracy: Public Space and the Internet*. Minneapolis: University of Minnesota Press.

Sassen, Saskia. 2002. "The Repositioning of Citizenship: Emergent Subjects and Spaces for Politics." *Berkeley Journal of Sociology* 46:4–26.

Sassen, Saskia. 2006. *Territory, Authority, Rights: From Medieval to Global Assemblages.* Princeton, NJ: Princeton University Press.

Scarry, Elaine. 2002. "The Difficulty of Imagining Other People." In Martha C. Nussbaum, *For Love of Country?* ed. Joshua Cohen. Boston: Beacon Press: 98–110.

Schmalz-Bruns, Rainer. 2007. "An den Grenzen der Entstaatlichung: Bemerkungen zu Jürgen Habermas' Modell einer 'Weltinnenpolitik ohne Weltregierung.'" In *Anarchie der kommunikativen Freiheit: Jürgen Habermas und die Theorie der internationalen Politik,* ed. Peter Niesen and Benjamin Herborth. Frankfurt am Main: Suhrkamp: 269–293.

Searle, John. 2010. *Making the Social World: The Structure of Human Civilization.* Oxford: Oxford University Press.

Sen, Amartya. 1999a. *Development as Freedom.* New York: Knopf.

Sen, Amartya. 1999b. "Human Rights and Economic Achievement." In *The East Asian Challenge for Human Rights,* ed. Joanne Bauer and Daniel Bell. Cambridge: Cambridge University Press: 88–99.

Sen, Amartya. 2002. "Humanity and Citizenship." In Martha C. Nussbaum, *For Love of Country?* ed. Joshua Cohen. Boston: Beacon Press: 111–118.

Sen, Amartya. 2011a. "The Global Status of Human Rights." *Proceedings of the Annual Meeting* (American Society of International Law) 105:3–12.

Sen, Amartya. 2011b. *The Idea of Justice.* Cambridge, MA: Harvard University Press.

Schutz, Alfred. 1962. *Collected Papers.* Vol. 1. The Hague: Martinus Nijhoff.

Seppala, Nina. 2009. "Business and the International Human Rights Regime: A Comparison of UN Initiatives." *Journal of Business Ethics* 87:401–417.

Shevel, Oxana. 2011. "A Comparison of Post-Franco Spain and Post-Soviet Ukraine." *Slavic Review* 70:137–164.

Shirk, Susan. 2007. *China: Fragile Superpower.* New York: Oxford University Press.

Sidaway, James. 2003. "Sovereign Excess: Portraying Postcolonial Sovereigntyscapes." *Political Geography* 22:157–178.

Simmel, Georg. 1908. "Die Kreuzung sozialer Kreise." In *Soziologie: Untersuchungen über die Formen der Vergesellschaftung.* Leipzig: Duncker & Humblot: 403–453.

Simmons, Beth. 2009. *Mobilizing Human Rights: International Law in Domestic Politics.* New York: Cambridge University Press.

Slomczynski, Kazimierz, and Goldie Shabad. 1998. "Can Support for Democracy and the Market Be Learned in School? A Natural Experiment in Post-Communist Poland." *Political Psychology* 19:749–779.

Smith, Adam. 1759. *The Theory of Moral Sentiments.* London: A. Millar.

Smith, Adam. 1978. [1762–1763]. *Lectures on Jurisprudence.* Ed. R. L. Meek, D. D. Raphael, and P. G. Stein. Oxford: Clarendon Press.

Smith, Michael. 2009. "The Inequality of Participation: Re-examining the Role of Social Stratification and Post-Communism on Political Participation in Europe." *Sociologick. Časopis / Czech Sociological Review* 45:487–517.

Stark, David. 1998. *Postsocialist Pathways: Transforming Politics and Property in East Central Europe.* New York: Cambridge University Press.

Steiner, Henry, Philip Alston and Ryan Goodman. 2007. *International Human Rights in Context.* Oxford: Oxford University Press.

Steiner, Jürg, André Bächtiger, Markus Spörndli, and Marco Steenbergen. 2004. *Deliberative Politics in Action.* Cambridge: Cambridge University Press.

Sternberger, Dolf. 1990. *Verfassungspatriotismus.* Frankfurt am Main: Insel Verlag.

Stewart, Rory, and Gerald Knaus. 2011. *Can Intervention Work?* New York: W. W. Norton.

Strydom, Piet. 2007. "A Cartography of Contemporary Cognitive Social Theory." *European Journal of Social Theory* 10:339–356.

Suárez, David. 2008. "Rewriting Citizenship? Civic Education in Costa Rica and Argentina." *Comparative Education* 44:485–503.

Sunstein, Cass. 2007. *Republic.com 2.0.* Princeton, NJ: Princeton University Press.

Talbott, William. 2010. *Human Rights and Human Well-Being.* Oxford: Oxford University Press.

Taylor, Charles. 2002. "Why Democracy Needs Patriotism." In Martha C. Nussbaum, *For Love of Country?* ed. Joshua Cohen. Boston: Beacon Press:119–121.

Taylor, Charles. 2007. *A Secular Age.* Cambridge, MA: Harvard University Press.

Tibbitts, Felisa. 1994. "Human Rights Education in Schools in the Post-Communist Context." *European Journal of Education* 29:363–376.

Tibbitts, Felisa. 2002. "Understanding What We Do: Emerging Models for Human Rights Education. *International Review of Education / Internationale Zeitschrift für Erziehungswissenschaft / Revue Internationale de l'Education* 48:159–171.

Trim, D. J. B. 2011. "Conclusion: Humanitarian Intervention in Historical Perspective." In *Humanitarian Intervention: A History,* ed. Brendan Simms and D. J. B. Trim. Cambridge: Cambridge University Press: 381–401.

Uhlin, Anders. 2006. *Post-Soviet Civil Society: Democratization in Russia and the Baltic States.* London: Routledge.

Uhlin, Anders. 2010. "The Structure and Culture of Post-Communist Civil Society in Latvia." *Europe-Asia Studies* 62:829–852.

Upe, Robert. 2013. "What's the Best Passport in the World for Travellers?" *Sydney Morning Herald.* 9 October.

Urbinati, Nadia. 2007. "Politics as Deferred Presence." *Constellations* 14:266–272.

Valentini, Laura. 2012. "Human Rights, Freedom, and Political Authority." *Political Theory* 40:573–601.

Waldron, Jeremy. 1993. *Liberal Rights: Collected Papers, 1981–1991.* Cambridge: Cambridge University Press.

Walk Free Foundation. 2013. *Global Slavery Index 2013.* Available at http://www.globalslaveryindex.org.

Walzer, Michael. 1977. *Just and Unjust Wars: A Moral Argument with Historical Illustrations.* New York: Basic Books.

Walzer, Michael. 1980. "The Moral Standing of States." *Philosophy & Public Affairs* 9:209–229.

Walzer, Michael. 2002. "The Argument About Humanitarian Intervention." *Dissent* 41:29–37.

Walzer, Michael. 2004. *Arguing About War*. New Haven, CT: Yale University Press.

Wang Jisi. 2012. "Understanding Strategic Distrust: The Chinese Side." In Kenneth Lieberthal and Wang Jisi, *Addressing U.S.-China Strategic Distrust*. Washington, DC: Brookings: 7–19

Waters, Melissa. 2007. "Creeping Monism: The Judicial Trend Toward Interpretive Incorporation of Human Rights Treaties." *Columbia Law Review* 107:628–705.

Williams, Bernard. 1981. *Moral Luck*. Cambridge: Cambridge University Press.

Wojcik, Teresa. 2010. "The Role of School-Based Civic Education in Poland's Transformation." *Polish Review* 55:387–403.

Wolff, Tobias. 2002. "The Thirteenth Amendment and Slavery in the Global Economy." *Columbia Law Review* 102:973–1050.

Wolfsteller, René. 2014. "Review of *Human Rights as Social Construction*." *Human Rights Quarterly* 36:492–496.

Young, Iris Marion. 1995. "Polity and Group Difference: A Critique of the Ideal of Universal Citizenship." In *Theorizing Citizenship*, ed. Ronald Beiner. Albany: State University of New York Press.

Young-Bruehl, Elisabeth. 1982. *Hannah Arendt: For Love of the World*. New Haven, CT: Yale University Press.

Zerubavel, Eviatar. 1997. *Social Mindscapes: An Invitation to Cognitive Sociology*. Cambridge, MA: Harvard University Press.

Zwart, Tom. 2012. "Using Local Culture to Further the Implementation of International Human Rights: The Receptor Approach." *Human Rights Quarterly* 34:546–569.

Index

Acknowledgments

Good teaching finds inspiration in Kant's slight article of 1784, "What Is Enlightenment?" The famous answer: the individual's emergence out of his or her self-induced intellectual immaturity. The goal of local enlightenment in the classroom facilitates the student's capacity for growth in thinking, autonomy in judgment, and wonder at the general connection between how we think and how we act. Guidance is found only in those answers the student clearly understands and finds persuasive. Instruction advances that end by leading the student finally to teach him- or herself. The best teaching makes itself ultimately dispensable as students realize the learning process as a lifelong project far beyond institutionalized arrangements. It fosters critical, independent thought and sound judgment, not privately but within a community, a little republic of letters of which each participant is a full-fledged citizen.

As for one's disciplinary colleagues, Hobbes fits better than Kant: "Such is the nature of men, that howsoever they may acknowledge many others to be more witty, or more eloquent, or more learned; yet they will hardly believe there be many so wise as themselves." And yet sometimes the community of critical interlocutors is the profession's most salutary feature: a community of critics as one's permanent education, mutual learning and reciprocal edification—without which, nothing.

I have known such communities at the annual meetings of the American Political Science Association, the American Sociological Association, and the Midwestern Political Science Association; in the Netherlands at the Annual Conference of the Association for Social and Political Philosophy, University of Amsterdam, 2015; in the United Kingdom at the Glasgow Human Rights Network, University of Glasgow, at which I delivered the keynote address; at the Centre for Contemporary Aristotelian Studies in Ethics and Politics, London Metropolitan University, as well as at the University of the West of Scotland, both 2015; at the University of Missouri at

Columbia, 2015; at the European Consortium for Political Research General Conference, Standing Group on Political Theory, Université de Montréal, Canada, 2015; at the International Political Science Association World Congress, Montréal, Québec, 2014; in Japan at the International Sociological Association World Congress, Tokyo, 2014; at Critical Sociology Conferences in San Francisco, 2014, and New York, 2013; and at the National Research University, St. Petersburg, Russian Federation, 2013; at the Student World Assembly in Norwalk, Connecticut, 2013; at the Rapoport Center for Human Rights and Justice, University of Texas at Austin Law School, 2012; at the Southern Sociological Society, New Orleans, 2012; at the Dritter gemeinsamer Kongress für Soziologie der Deutschen Gesellschaft für Soziologie, der Österreichischen Gesellschaft für Soziologie und der Schweizerischen Gesellschaft für Soziologie, Innsbruck, Austria, 2011; at the Political Studies Association, London, 2011; at the University of Nebraska, 2011; and at the Société suisse de sociologie, Bern, Switzerland, 2010.

I am particularly grateful for the discerning feedback of a master class hosted by the postgraduate cluster of the Glasgow Human Rights Network at the University of Glasgow in May 2015 on a draft form of this book's manuscript several months before its publication: René Wolfsteller, Carole Baillie, Anita Horn, Claire Cassidy, Richard Georgi, Johannes Fahner, Ulisses Terto Neto, Bethia Pearson, Matthew Waites, Zuleykha Mailzada, Yingru Li, Gayatri Patel, Basak Baglayan, Auriane Botte, Jeanette Rowley, Helena Burgrova, Patrick Butchard, Louis Karaolis, Jeanrique Fahner, and Karin Kuhlemann.

For critical commentary on various parts of this project I am also indebted in particular to Andrew Koppelman, Martin Woessner, Rachel Wahl, Jonathan Allen, Kristen Johnson, Adam Seagrave, John Dale, Sonia Cardenas, Lisa Disch, Michael Goodhart, Micheline Ishay, Alison Brysk, Alex Tuckness, Patti Lenard, William O'Neill, Aaron Stuvland, Pete Mohanty, Harry Dahms, Lea Ypi, Jonathan White, Junmin Wang, Ko Hasegawa, David Prindle, Ross Zucker, David Emory, and Alexander Sungurov. I am grateful to the editorial guidance of Peter Agree of the University of Pennsylvania Press. For perspicacious criticism I am indebted to the anonymous reviewers he commissioned.

Chapter 4 was first published, in a different version, as "Teaching Human Rights in the College Classroom as a Cognitive Style," in *Social Justice and the University*, ed. Jon Shefner, Harry Dahms, Robert Emmet

Jones, and Asafa Jalata (Basingstoke, UK: Palgrave Macmillan, 2014), 253–279, © 2014 by Palgrave. Used by kind permission of Palgrave. Chapter 5 initially appeared, in a discrepant form, as "Advancing Human Rights in Post-Authoritarian Communities Through Education," *Journal of Human Rights Practice* 7, no. 2, pp. 199–222, © 2015 by Oxford University Press. Displayed by cordial permission of Oxford University Press. Chapter 6 originally came out, in another rendition, as "Politics Disembodied and Deterritorialized: The Internet as Human Rights Resource," in *Theorizing Modern Society as a Dynamic Process*, Current Perspectives in Social Theory, vol. 30, ed. Harry Dahms and Lawrence Hazelrigg (Bingley, UK: Emerald, 2012), 209–233, © 2012 by Emerald. Here by friendly permission of Emerald.